AF189812

liberated
COMPANIES

How to Create Vibrant Organizations
In The **DIGITAL AGE**

FRANK THUN

Let's make the workplace better than ever before.

Bibliographical Information of the German National Library ("Deutsche Na-
tionalbibliothek"): The German National Library records this publication in
the German National Library ("Deutsche Nationalbibliografie"). Detailed bibliographical data can be found under **http://dnb.dnb.de**

© Management Digital GmbH, 2019
Production and Publisher:
BoD – Books on Demand, Norderstedt, Germany

ISBN 978-3-7504-6681-4

This book is dedicated to all those who want to make a difference.

■ Table of Contents

Part III: Company Configurations

Part IV: A Compass for the Digital Age

Part V: How to Configure Companies

■ Foreword

Around the age of fourteen, I started to think that I was born too early. The new digital technology—in the form of a Commodore 64 personal computer—captivated me, as it did so many others. I imagined all the wonderful changes that would be created in the emerging digital age, but when I compared these visions to the technological reality of the 1980s, I recognized that I was born 100 years too early.

However, I have changed my mind in recent years. Now I am happy to be alive at this potent time in our history as the world gears up to fight the ultimate battle between human technological mastery and biological survival: the extinction crisis.

It's not that I used to be a fundamentalist about anything. On the contrary, I made my career serving more or less conventional companies in their quest to utilize digital technology. Like everyone else I met during that time, I had a utilitarian outlook on technology: Technology is merely a tool to be used. How wrong we were. My job as a technophile economist has always been bridging organizational, technological, and human needs. The more I learned about my trade, the more I realized that bridging those three elements is all about connection—connection between people and technology, connections between technology and organizations, and connections between organizations and people. It was the quality of these connections, their depth and their strength, that determined the outcome of the projects I have been responsible for as a manager.

The more I advanced in my career, the more it dawned on me that the current organizational hierarchy is just not built to allow strong connections between any of these three elements: people, technology, and organizations. With so much arbitrary power in the hands of superiors over subordinates, negative political behavior and exploitation are bound to run rampant. Like so many others in the digital technology field, my eyes have been opened by the contemporary movements that highlight the need for more connected ways of working—Agile, Lean Startup, New Work, DevOps. During the three years that I have spent researching and writing this book, it dawned on me that stronger connections between people and organizations not only change the internal dynamics and performance of organizations for the better; they make organizations and people more connected to the outer world. They make organizations more caring about society and the environment than the naturally exploitative organizational hierarchy we have become accustomed to.

Alas, this book is not primarily about self-managed, fully democratic workplaces. It is rather about finding intelligent, resilient organizational designs that go beyond a simple dichotomy of hierarchical and self-managed organizations. This book is about building great workplaces that let organizations, technology, people, and the environment flourish together.

■ Introduction: Today's Inept Businesses

We need to reinvent the technology of human accomplishment.
– Gary Hamel

Human society has come a long way at what seems like breathtaking speed. It has taken humanity just a couple of generations to progress from largely agrarian communities to the industrial age to the dawning of the digital age. It is a great time to be alive, with nearly all indicators of human well-being improving in recent decades.[1] Yet there are challenges, even existential threats, inherent to this new way of life. Never have so many people enjoyed such material wealth as today, but never before has material wealth been so decoupled from physical means.

Let's start with the most obvious example: digitalization. From a company perspective, the complexities of the ever-more-rapidly changing digital land-scape are creating huge social upheavals. Some have gone so far as to say that software is "eating the world."[2] In a world where smartphones have become an extension of people—lenses through which people perceive the world—digital platforms rule. It is the immaterial, the elusive software, the algorithms that structure the way we interact with our surroundings and make decisions that increasingly matter. We continue to run companies and organizations, however, on a foundation that was built for the industrial age with its coal mines, steel mills, and manufacturing plants. The results are costing us dearly. Whole sectors and industries are being uprooted by digital disruptors, while most businesses remain stagnant and incapable of change.

In the digital age, companies need three things. First, they need to learn to produce or at least utilize software better. It is not that every company will

---

1   (Rosling, 2018)
2   (Andresen, 2011)

become a software company, but every company that finds innovative ways to utilize software will surely be better off than those that do not. Second, companies need to continuously reconfigure themselves to the rapidly chang-ing technological environment. Third, such a degree of organizational learning and readiness to change can only be achieved if people at all levels in com-panies are willing (and able) to learn and change. As we will examine in the chapters to come, the way most companies are organized today suppresses learning and prevents change.

The second challenge is even more urgent: it is the "extinction crisis" cur-rently facing life on this planet. Our victory over nature, wherein we have harnessed the natural environment to suit humanity's needs, may turn out to be our downfall. The climate catastrophe, the mass extinction of other forms of life on earth, and the poisoning of our soils and oceans with microplastics are all signs that our ecosystem is hurtling towards the edge of a cliff. Much of our inability to find common ground on those measures needed to keep our planet hospitable, however, is rooted in the discontent created by income and wealth inequality. So long as people have to struggle for their material existence, everything other than short-term concerns over how to provide for themselves and their families seems irrelevant.

Companies need to measure up to the extinction crisis—whether they like it or not. First, they must put an end to the exploitation of the natural environ-ment. As natural disasters take their toll, customers are likely to favor compa-nies that have more sustainable and regenerative practices, and governments must regulate these businesses accordingly. Anticipating this trend is bound to be both wise and profitable. Second, and more difficult to understand, is that companies need to become more distributive by design. The current deal between the employer and the employed is "money for submission," with the lion's share of profits going to the employer. We find this natural—it's just the way things are. Yet, if we continue to ask people for submission in a system of exploitation, we do not create the systems of learning that we actually need. Even more fatally, by doing so we have built exploitation as a central value into the inner workings of companies.

Organizations are cultural engines of modern societies,[3] and every organizational system comes with its own values attached. By continuing to choose the organizational hierarchy, we are choosing submission and exploitation— by design. People spend 50% of their waking hours working for companies, and spending this time in a system built upon submission and exploitation is bound to be detrimental not only to their outlook on the world, but to the very fabric of society itself. Yet, there are alternatives. There are novel organizational systems that get people to take a more wholesome, interconnected, and purposeful outlook on life. These systems are distributive by design because they do not monopolize economic outcomes as strongly. They are more egalitarian, more liberating.

There have been attempts at the team level to conjure liberating work environments in otherwise conventional companies: such as the Lean, Agile, and New Work movements, to name a few. However, these initiatives do not make an impact beyond the team level because they fail to address the three most important factors that systematically influence human behavior in the workplace: power, power, and power. The uneven distribution of power in companies is the elephant in the room. No amount of entrepreneurial risk-taking, innovation, leanness, or agility will be effective if the workplace is not seen as a safe place where people can speak up.

Power as the main villain in companies is hardly a new idea. Out of the struggle of competing ideas such as communism, anarchism, and unbridled capitalism, a form of regulated economic activity has emerged such that, since 1990, the social market economy has reigned supreme not only in the West but globally. The social market economy limits the exploitative nature of companies caused by the asymmetrical distribution of power between employer and employee. The 40-hour workweek, workers' rights and benefits, trade unions and worker representation, and a host of other government regulations have by and large succeeded in curbing the worst excesses of asymmetrical power exercised by employers.

---

3   (Zucker, 1983)

Today, however, there is a new and different reason to focus on power. The subordination of employees to the will of their superiors is impeding their ability to engage and their willingness to speak up, try new things, fail, learn, change, and innovate, resulting in a systematic bias against agile, engaging, learning, and innovative companies. Curbing the use of hierarchical power by the employer—the capitalist, the manager—will result in a more powerful company that can achieve better results.

Companies have served society well by harnessing people and coordinating their actions to provide us with ever better goods and services. Companies in their turn shape us because they are also the place where most of us spend the majority of our waking hours. From time to time we complain about the idiosyncrasies of the workplace or overbearing superiors; we struggle against incompetence, lack of purpose, stress, or boredom. Now, however, is the time to allow people more individual self-expression and give companies more of a bias to do good. It is time to liberate ourselves, and the planet, from the exploitative system upon which the companies of the previous era were built. It is time to create more Liberated Companies.

What This Book is About

The increasing complexity of the digital age requires a system of organization that is also more complex. This book seeks to provide a map and a compass that business leaders can use to navigate the digital age. The map illustrates the often-overlooked multitude of ways that work can be done by people working together. It is an open-ended, structured collection of classical and modern work designs with which companies can be configured to handle short- and long-term challenges. The compass is a set of guidelines on how to blend new and innovative methods with traditional forms of work. There are eleven principles encompassing a combination of old truths that are truer today than ever before, and the emergent truths of the new digital age.

This book is a travel companion for companies journeying in the digital age. But there is no final, ultimate destination, and no single best way to run a company. The diversity of good organizational solutions, even for companies in the same sector, has value in itself. A company that is different is more likely to be perceived as *being* different. In a world where a customer's attention is the scarcest resource of all, this is no small advantage. Nobel Prize winner Ronald Coase famously wrote: "In a market economy we find islands of conscious power in this ocean of unconscious cooperation like lumps of butter coagulating in a pail of buttermilk."[4] Well, it looks like we need more butter.

The Structure of this Book

This book begins by describing the dominant force in today's economy and society—technology—from an unusual angle. What does technology want? We will see that companies must recognize and adopt the inert needs of technology in their business structures if they truly want to master the digital age.

Part II describes the main features of the organizational terrain that defines the outlines of the map: power. Stark power differences between people determine the main regions on the map—the basic types of organizations. While the digital age is not likely to see forms of organization disappear, it will discourage excessive hierarchies and encourage more liberated, self-managed forms of organization.

In Part III, we focus on the map's various locations—the work designs that companies use to get things done. Around 200 different work designs in nine categories are considered in an exploration of the myriad ways of running and managing organizations—without losing the big picture. Most managers have lost the ability to imagine the many different ways in which things could be done if we made different choices. Part III concludes by describing the work design configurations of four very different companies.

In Part IV, we provide a compass for navigating a company or team in the digital age. Rather than showing a single true north, however, this compass points in eleven different directions. The Eleven Principles of Liberated Companies are vectors determining the trajectory of a company.

---

4   (Coase, 1937).

Part V lists a number of practical guidelines for the configuration of companies, including where to start and how to sustain the journey.

If the reader ends by feeling that the workplace can be so much more than it is today, and that the systematic bias of companies towards exploiting everything they touch can be changed into a bias for the betterment of people, societies, and the planet, then this book will have served its purpose.

Some Notes on Style

You won't find many stories of what different companies have done here. There are many good books that explore those stories in depth. Instead of providing case studies, this book will explore the structure behind the more progressive organizational efforts in our age. With all that has been written on digitalization, management, and leadership, the role of this book is to provide orientation—a map and a compass—rather than motivation. For further reading and lots of good stories, see the list of great books at the end of each part and in the Appendix.

Additionally, you will find a box called "Dark Arts" at the end of each chapter that summarizes its contents. I call them "Dark Arts" because these lessons are all too often heresy against the church of conventional management.

PART I:
TECHNOLOGY AND POWER

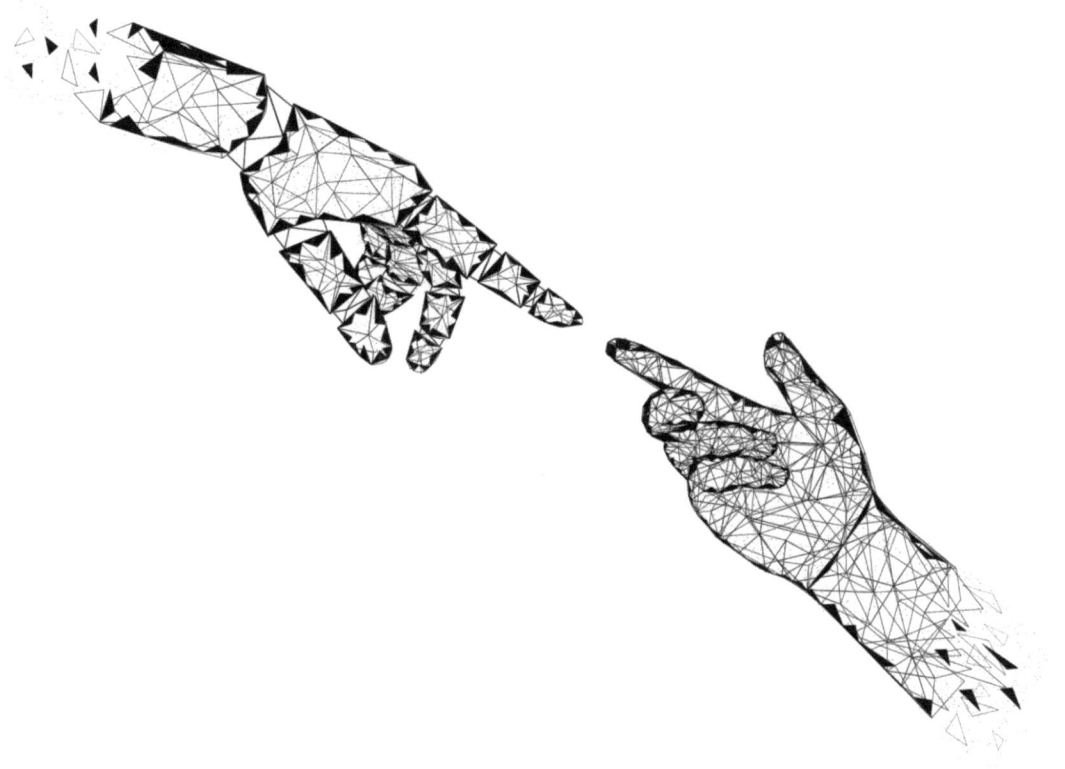

■ Chapter 1:
The Trajectory of Technology

So, you tell me that you are taking your company digital?
I want to hear your idea of technology, not that you introduced this or that app...
– Paraphrased from Friedrich Nietzsche, *Thus Spoke Zarathustra* (1891)[5]

To devise an organizational design that works well in a world increasingly dominated by technology, one has to understand two things. First, we must grasp the essence of technological progress, the direction in which it is leading us—in short, we must understand the "wants" of technology. Second, as technology and humans become ever more closely intertwined, we must ask: how do humans and technology flourish together? Let's save the first question for later and answer the second question first.

The three ways of understanding technology

Old truth: technology is just a tool

A hammer, a coffee machine, or a smartphone app is a tool, a technology that we are using. Humans use these tools to manipulate the world around them, to get results. Natural problem-solvers that we are, we look around for the best tool to assist our efforts. If the tool is available, we simply need the skill to use it, and our lives will be easier. The basic thinking of many people in business is similar: tools help to solve problems. All we need to do is to make a tool available to workers and train them how to use it.

But is this really true? Of course not. For as long as technology has existed, the relationship between tools and people has never been a one-way street. Humans invented and used tools, and their use shaped human culture. No

---

5   (Nietzche, 1974)

technology was ever inconsequential to human mindsets, values, social systems, even the rise and fall of empires. Anthropologists even divide cultures according to their tools: Stone Age, Bronze Age, Iron Age, Age of the Sail, and Information Age, to name a few. The impact of tools doesn't have to be as dramatic as gunpowder or printing; even the inconspicuous coffee machine intervenes in the way we structure our day, determines where and when we gather, takes up a prominent place in our homes, changes our biological mode of operation by drugging us slightly, and sends many of us into fits of rage when dysfunctional.

Tools have shaped us into what we are today. There is every reason to believe that with ever more technology available, the more and more we are shaped by it. As Marshall McLuhan is often attributed to have said, "We shape our tools and thereafter tools shape us."

Even more true: technology as a maker of decisions

People in companies have already lost control over many things they used to do. In the information age, companies have delegated many tasks to complex systems, be it in production, distribution, accounting, or sales. These systems are so complex that no single person knows what the systems are really doing. Even teams of experts often struggle to make sense of the sheer complexity of modern systems—a fact that is clearly visible in the high failure rates of modern software projects. Humans have set up these systems, but are they fully in control? Are they making the decisions? Our control is limited by design because we want the machines to take over our work, to automate much of what is happening. The algorithms humans have set up mesh with other algorithms to produce the outcomes that we want, and we tend to understand less and less of their inner workings and true complexity. Still, we choose to rely on them out of necessity.

How much will we be in control tomorrow? Certainly less, as artificial intelligence becomes more pervasive in the workplace. The more we utilize technology, the more that technology will make decisions for us: today, just simple deterministic decisions, those that can be easily automated;

tomorrow, more complex decisions, those requiring judgment. Without experts to act as translators between business and technology—be they engineers or highly specialized functional experts in logistics and accounting, for instance—modern businesses could not exist today. Yet even experts are limited in their ability to control, as it takes five things to be in control of complex systems.[6]

1. The correct information.
2. A group of knowledgeable people (a single individual's cognitive abilities are usually too narrow and biased).
3. The right group process to analyze and weigh hard (measurable) and soft (intuitive) data.
4. The discipline to keep to a proven process of synthesis every single time, avoiding shortcuts.
5. The discipline to evolve the process itself.

This is a five-point recipe for making solid decisions about complex matters. The better an organization is able to apply this recipe, the more it will prosper. The trouble is that hierarchical companies find it hard to apply this recipe effectively, for the following reasons:

1. "Correct" information is hard to get. If the workplace is not a safe place to speak up, people will suppress some information. People subjected to powerful bosses will react in a politically correct manner so as not to upset anyone with power over them.
2. The people making decisions are the ones furthest removed from the problem: the managers.
3. The process for analyzing data in hierarchies is often skewed towards everything that can be measured. It is further limited by the fact that it is usually quite unsafe for people to speak up about their intuition or express divergent views.
4. The discipline to keep to a process can easily be undermined by an arbitrary personal decision of the highest-paid person in the room

---

6   Adapted from (Silver, 2012). Silver describes what a good forecast is built upon. I think that this list is applicable to the management of any complex system.

(HIPPO). It takes tremendous listening skills for superiors to refrain from dominating decision processes.

5. The discipline to evolve the process itself is likewise undermined. Evolution and betterment might not be the target of a hierarchy at all. A hierarchy inherently favors stability, not change.

Major power differentials between people are systematically detrimental to making sense of complex systems, and this defect has grave consequences. As technology becomes increasingly complex and important for the survival of companies, conventional hierarchical companies will be less and less able to benefit from technology.

New truth: technology as a co-worker

As Kevin Kelly mentions in his book, *What Technology Wants*, "technology is an independent force in itself. Nobody is in control now and humanity will be less in control tomorrow. The technium is already whispering to itself."[7]

Today, most companies are already so complex that decisions are made by a mixture of humans and machines. In companies like Amazon, Google, Netflix, and Facebook, most day-to-day business decisions are made by algorithms in real-time. Have you ever tried to talk to their "customer service people"? Overwhelmingly, the product itself, in the form of some specialized algorithm, is in charge of customer interactions—and those algorithms are doing their job extremely well. Much better than the customer service peoples of cable or telecom companies usually do.

People inside technologically advanced companies tend to work more on maintaining and experimenting with algorithms. The algorithm becomes a co-worker—one that is extremely skilled in specific functions. Humans specialize in those things that they are more adept at, such as the holistic perception of contexts and setting purposeful directions. AI researchers have concluded that humans in the digital age will be an asset to any company, as they supply a cer-

---

7 (Kelly, 2011)

tain form of specialized intelligence.[8] Supplemented by all the multiple forms of intelligence that AI has to offer, the human-algorithm team can achieve much more than either can alone. Take chess, for example. There is no human on earth today who is able to beat modern chess programs. However, in tournaments where humans are allowed to play assisted by AI, the combination of human and machine tends to beat AI that is not supported by humans. There may, of course, come a point in the future when human interference in chess AI will no longer increase but may actually impair performance, but business is much more complex than chess—its rules are much more fluid, and its streams of information are much more ambiguous. In the context of businesses, human intelligence and machine intelligence are likely to have a productive relationship for a longer period. If humans and machines are more and more equal co-workers, the companies that benefit will be those that manage to create a work environment that fosters this cooperation.

Today, we work and live with companies that are a reaction to the challenges of the industrial age, and the work-environment design that best suited industrial technologies was bureaucracy. Bureaucracy replaced charismatic domination with legal domination, replaced haphazard arrangements with standardized processes and a clear hierarchical way of making decisions that was focused on analytics, efficiency, consistent outputs, and reduction of waste.[9] At the time of its invention, bureaucracy was considered an antidote to bad management. Max Weber, a German sociologist credited with "inventing" bureaucracy, wrote in 1922 that "organizations are shaped by the relentless march of technological and managerial reality."[10]

Today we face the relentless march of the algorithm. There is so much benefit inherent in algorithms that we adapt our beliefs, behaviors, values, and social norms to them, personally, socially, and in companies. According to Max Weber, technology puts us in an "iron cage": we are defined by technology and will be redefined every time technology changes. In the industrial revolution, the "iron cage" trapped individuals in systems of efficiency, rational analysis,

---

8   (Kelly, 2011)
9   (Birkinshaw, 2012)
10   (Weber, 2019)

top-down control, and digressional power. Now, with the rise of dematerialized digital technologies and artificial intelligence, we feel the need to adapt our ways once again in order to catch up with technology.

If technology is rapidly evolving and technologies are quickly becoming obsolete, today's challenge for humanity is not to align itself to any single new technology, but rather to find a method to keep evolving its cooperation with technology continuously and forever. Companies need a work design that is so sensitive and adaptable that technological and social innovation at the workplace occurs naturally and permanently. It is not enough to understand individual technologies: the internet of things, social media, 3D printing, virtual reality, block-chain, self-driving cars, big data, cloud systems, or AI, to name a few emergent technologies of the last decade alone. To overcome the challenge of building a design for human, social, and technological cooperation that is able to flourish in ever more technologically driven times, we need to understand what technology wants and how a company can serve these needs best.

The trajectory of technology

Company leaders often ask: What does our company want from technology? How can technology help our company to be more competitive? To answer these questions, companies engage in all kinds of futuristic ideation workshops, creative sessions, company visits, and pilgrimages to Silicon Valley or coastal China. They declare success if they have identified or implemented or invested in this technology or that start-up. This is naïve.

The really important question to ask is: What does technology *want* from companies? This is an unusual question. Can technology "want" something? There are some thinkers, like Ray Kurzweil, who predict that a "singularity" will occur around 2045[11]—a point where machines become sentient to such an extent that they will be able to self-construct. A point where the power of the kingdom of technology outstrips the power of the kingdom of biology, to which we humans belong. That point will be a point of no return for the human race—a singularity.

---

11 (Kurzweil, 2006)

The chances are high that technology will become more independent in the future. Machines are becoming sentient in unexpected ways—it may not be that machines will trump the general versatility of biological human intelligence in the coming years, but machines are already coming up with alien forms of intelligence that make them superior for many specific applications. Recommendation engines determine what we buy, filter algorithms determine how we perceive reality, navigation apps shape the way we experience geography. The sheer numbers of proliferating specialized forms of intelligences are replacing more and more areas where our generalist human intelligence once reigned. Over time, the area where we use our human intelligence will become increasingly focused. This process has already begun.

What I am getting at here is something else. We know from systems theory that complex systems develop emergent properties, which are behaviors that are revealed on an aggregate level but cannot be observed in any single component of the system. The system of biology, as an example, always moves towards greater specialization of species in a process of evolution determined by its inherent characteristics. The biochemical algorithms surrounding DNA shape the trajectory of biology, pointing toward what biology wants.

The system of technology can be visualized in the same way. Instead of biochemical realities, technology is based on the physical and mathematical realities that the world is made of. The laws of physics and mathematics are the algorithms that technology uses to progress. At first, that may sound outlandish. After all, if my computer bothers me, I can cut its power supply. But I can't unplug the whole system of technology, everything that surrounds us and that is manmade. No one can unplug the internet. And the more the internet of things becomes a reality, the less it will be possible to disconnect physical reality from virtual reality.

More shocking and significant is that we do not *want* to unplug technology because we are already a part of it. The American author Kevin Kelly, who is known as the philosopher of Silicon Valley, has devoted most of his adult life to thinking and writing about technology. Kelly uses his own definition of technology, the Technium, which he defines as "the accumulation of stuff, lore, practices, traditions, and of choices that allow an individual human to generate and participate in a greater number of ideas."[12]

The Technium is made up of technology and humans. Our current culture still holds onto a human-centric view of the universe—a view that puts the rational human mind in control of technology. But in academia it is generally accepted today that no human, no institution, absolutely no one is in control of technology.[13] Technology is an independent force that worms its way forward as a result of technical, social, political, psychological and commercial forces. It is a system that has inert wants, just as biological evolution has. The wants of technology have been making themselves felt for decades and can only become more prominent over time, especially after artificial intelligence becomes sentient.

Today, many companies are lumbering slowly along the technological highway, only to be smashed by Amazon, smashed by Airbnb, smashed by Netflix, smashed by online pure-plays with their data and algorithms. It can be argued that these major successful companies today do not stand in the way of technology but are simply traveling on the same trajectory as technology. What if we could find a way of organizing a company where the use of technology proliferates naturally? Where the technological, social, and commercial spheres establish self-reinforcing feedback loops and evolve together? That company would be on the same trajectory *as* technology—and it would be a very powerful design for a company indeed.

To sketch a work design of the future, more is needed than just looking at today's technologies; sn understanding of the inner workings of technology as a whole is required. So, what does technology want? Kevin Kelly has discerned a number of directions that technology works towards that together make up what he terms the "trajectory of technology" (Table 1). Let's go through this list and consider its implications for the work design of a company.[14]

---

12 (Kelly, 2011)
13 (Harari, 2016)
14 (Kelly, 2011)

Technology wants to increase...	Effect
Efficiency	More efficient technologies will replace less efficient ones
Opportunity	Technology offers more and more options how to solve problems
Diversity & Specialization	Every single technology, or tool, will ever be more adapted to a specific situation, and ever less viable in others
Complexity	New technologies do encompass old ones. Thus, they are more complex.
Emergence & Sentience	Technology becomes ever more able to organize itself, thereby producing ever more forms of intelligence
Ubiquity & Freedom	Technologies spread inexorably, increasing the number of options
Mutualism & Structure	Technologies progress by building upon other, reliable technologies
Evolvability & Beauty	Technology favors those technologies that are able to evolve faster

Table 1 The trajectory of technology

Technology wants efficiency

Technology loves efficiency. The more efficient a technology gets, the more it begets other technologies. Take electric cars, for example, which only became a mass-market option with more efficient batteries. Or virtual reality, which was invented in 1989 but became viable only when high-resolution smartphone screens became cheaply available in the 2010s.

Humans are in love with efficiency, too. Efficiency has been our faithful companion since the industrial revolution, and it won't leave us now that we have passed into the digital age. Efficiency is clarity; it is rational and comforting in a world of uncertainty. Efficiency gives us a problem to solve. Dealing with the brother of efficiency—effectiveness—is much more tedious. Effectiveness, which is about choosing *what* to do rather than *how* to do it, comes with too many options and is less rationally computable for us than efficiency. It is not only humans' laziness that lets us seek efficiency; it is technology itself that seeks efficiency. The quest for ever more efficient solutions is one we share with technology. Companies will continue to seek efficiency today and tomorrow. The change is that there will be much more potential to find efficiencies as technology has more and more to offer over time. Therefore, the way work is done in companies—their "work design," a term we will use extensively throughout this book—needs to adapt more and more often. Organizing must become more of a process of evolution and less of an incremental exercise.

Technology wants opportunity

Over time, technologies offer more and more opportunities to do things differently. The Amazon bookstore begot the Amazon marketplace, which begot Amazon Prime, Kindle Unlimited, and Amazon Dash, which begot Amazon Web Services, and so on. The peer-to-peer file-sharing technology underpinning Napster begot the streaming mediums of Youtube, Netflix, and Spotify, which begot advanced artificial intelligence used for recommendations, which begot social collaboration on videos and music with friends. Youtube, Netflix, and Spotify in turn became possible because of cloud technologies such as those offered by Amazon Web Services, Google Cloud, and similar cloud services that offered server capacity on demand.

As options for technologies to progress increases, so too does the number of options companies have for solving problems. This is increasingly true not only for the design of products but also for the way companies do their internal work. In the 1990s, companies grew a nervous system for the processing of information, called enterprise resource planning (ERP) systems, in the form of packages like SAP or Oracle. These core systems contributed a great deal to a company's ability to go global and outsource work. Today, web technology has joined ERP systems as the backbone of internal and external collaboration, enabling real-time business and new forms of combining humans and algorithms into new creative solutions.

As we discussed earlier, humans are problem-solvers. Companies are always desperate for better solutions, and technology provides them. An organizational design that is to stand the test of the technological tsunami must ensure that people are aware of the solutions technology has to offer. The need for more opportunity is the same for technology, for companies, and for people: they all want more opportunities. It is up to the work design of a company to transform opportunity into benefits. If people feel encouraged to be on the lookout for new opportunities, can conduct experiments without fear of failure, and have the autonomy to decide on their own to include this or that technology in their daily work, the needs of technology and companies will be aligned.

Technology wants diversity and specialization

One technology begets another, but no technology will ever go away. They stick with us as part of the Technium, forever offering an option of how to do things. Even once-obsolete technologies may be rediscovered and suddenly become attractive again if they are combined with new technologies. The Technium never forgets.

More than that, technologies come in multiple variants. For example, they change form according to their area of application. Google's search algorithms are both similar and different for searching pictures, videos, geographies, or medical scans.[15] They are similar to and different from filter algorithms used by Facebook, Tinder, or Amazon. Every technology is adapted to the specifics of a situation and becomes ever more specialized, thereby increasing diversity.

The more diverse and specialized the technologies on offer are, the more decentralized and varied a company must become to make good use of the richness of the technological environment—more varied than can be supported by company hierarchies, which are designed to suppress variance, as we shall see in Chapter 2: The Corrosive Impact of Power Differentials.

Technology wants complexity

Technology is one of the main reasons why doing business is becoming more and more complex. Companies must organize themselves in such a way as to handle this complexity, but ever-increasing complexity cannot be controlled; it can only be worked with. Failures will be unavoidable, but research has shown that competent people who are in close proximity with technology, and who are authorized to make decisions, can prevent failures from becoming disasters.[16] Two proven methods to increase a company's ability to handle

---

15   To get an impression, skim through the AI Services offered by Amazon Web Services today. All these world-class algorithms are available today, for everyone. https://aws.amazon.com/machine-learning/

16   (Spears, 2010).

complexity are to let the people who are closest to the problem make the decisions, and to ensure that they are competent. Give them competence and freedom, then trust them to act.

Technology wants emergence and sentience

Handling the increasing complexity caused by technology is difficult—so we use technology to stay on top of it. Intelligent agents that keep technologies in check are already at work in every smartphone, every computer center, in cloud systems, in medical systems, or in routing algorithms at call centers. Companies specialized in this field are mostly hidden from public view but are worth billions of dollars. Take ServiceNow, a company that came from nothing in 2014 and is now valued at US$50 billion in 2019. Their business model is to provide companies with the capability to stay on top of their sprawling IT operations, no matter whether the workers are humans or machines.

Technology will increasingly be running itself in the coming years. Indeed, it has already taken on a life of its own, and determining where sentience starts is an open-ended debate. Some think it starts with intelligent, self-organizing behavior that apparently works but that we are unable to fully understand. We will be using more and more algorithms and intelligent assistants over time. Kelly and others predict that the benefits we are able to give to our organizations will crucially depend upon our ability to collaborate with machines. A work design for the digital age must provide an environment where people can get acquainted with their new technological companions and quickly adapt to the fast pace of change.

Technology wants ubiquity and freedom

Technologies, even dangerous ones, spread no matter what we do. There is no way to control the very real problem of nuclear proliferation, for instance, but there are less dramatic examples. The so-called "washing nuts"—the fruits of the *Sapindus saponaria*—have been used by local communities in India for thousands of years, but they recently became popular in Western households seeking more sustainable ways of cleaning fabric. Demand for them caused prices to rise so much that Indian communities were forced to switch to "modern" washing powder. Any technology, old or new, spreads.

Companies align themselves with technologies' desire for ubiquity by making it easy for technologies to both enter and flow forth from the company: they pull in technology by making it easy for people or units to observe and adapt whatever technology other people, units, or companies are using, and they also let technologies travel from the inside to the outside. Why should a company share its technologies with the outside? The more technologies change, the less a single technology represents a competitive advantage for any prolonged period. Technologies become stale if they are cut off from contact with the outside world; if outside observers cannot scrutinize a technology, if insiders cannot freely discuss its merits and opportunities, its full potential benefits will fail to develop. There will still be a case for secrecy in areas where technological progress is not fast—such as preserving the recipe for a vintage drink like Coca Cola—but in most other cases, openness and the freedom for technology to spread in all directions is a better choice. More and more options become available to an organization that is open to the spread of technology. Freedom begets options begets progress.

It takes an open organization to let technology proliferate. The primary mechanism for this is to make it easy for people at all levels to take a break from their close colleagues and explore other technologies "out there," then come back and synthesize their findings at home.[17]

Technology wants mutualism and structure

Technologies build (and rely) upon each other. A car's navigation, parking, and voice control systems rely on its electrical systems, which in turn rely on the car's mechanical systems. Technologies are mutually dependent, and the more advanced the technology, the more dependent it is.

---

17 (Pentland, 2014)

However, there are two traits that a successful technology—one that spreads—must show. First, it must be reliable. Those technologies prone to breakage are unlikely to spawn new technologies or combine with other technologies to form more complex solutions. Second, its structure must be easy for those interacting with it to understand. Today's phone apps, for example, are only so ubiquitous because they are built on very stable operating systems (ioS, Android) and developers can access the published library of Application Programmable Interfaces (APIs) released by Apple or Google. Another, more low-tech example is the way that a light bulb interacts with the electrical grid. It can only do its job because it can rely on a stable grid with well-described properties and because its socket conforms to mechanical norms.

In the digital age, work designs need to be geared towards creating combinations of human and technological activity. Therefore, they must cater to experimentation, playfulness, and local variation while still providing a high level of reliability.

Technology wants evolvability and beauty

The result of all of the above is that technology will necessarily evolve. Becoming both ever more efficient and increasingly complex, it will create more opportunities, greater diversity, and more specialized uses. It will show more forms of sentient behavior, will increase freedom, and will rely on and be relied upon by other stable, structured technologies.

Kelly argues that technological evolution and biological evolution are very similar. The specialization of species, the striving of all life forms to become ubiquitous, and the ever-increasing complexity of biological systems is not unlike the process of technological evolution that we have been exploring. The biggest difference between these two types of evolution is that biological evolution is much, much slower. Biological evolution is bound by the realm of biochemistry and scarce resources. Technological evolution is not bound by any material constraints; it is only limited by the laws of physics and mathematics. Technological evolution happens in a realm of abundance; biological evolution happens in a realm of scarcity.

The implications are quite shocking. There is no way that technological evolution will not outpace biological evolution. That means that humans will need to cut loose from their biological origins and humanity will need to come to grips with artificial forms of intelligence that will become ever-more superior. Humans and technology are players on the same team, however. It's likely that they will become closer and closer entwined.[18] In humanity's fight to gain dominance over nature and biology, technology has always been our greatest ally.

Of course, with the limits of our planet so clearly visible, the time has come for us to stop fighting with biology. After all, we are biological creatures, and continuing to fight against biology is likely to get us all killed. It is time to change our ways through a better understanding of holistic ecosystems.[19] Technology can be our ally if we stop using it to overpower biological systems.

Technology wants to increase...	Effect	A company in sync with technology needs to emphasize...
Efficiency	More efficient technologies will incessantly replace less efficient ones	Learning
Opportunity	Technology offers more and more options how to solve problems	Exploration
Diversity & Specialization	Every single technology, or tool, will ever be more adapted to a specific situation, and ever less viable in others	Networks
Complexity	New technologies do encompass old ones. Thus, they get ever more complex	Networks, freedom & decentralized decision making
Emergence & Sentience	Technology becomes ever more able to organize itself, thereby producing ever more forms of intelligence	Engaging with technology
Ubiquity & Freedom	Technologies spread inexorably, increasing the number of options	Transparency
Mutualism & Structure	Technologies progress by building upon other, reliable technologies	Discipline, community, ecosystems
Evolvability & Beauty	Technology favors those technologies that are able to evolve faster	Evolutionary purpose

Table 2 How to position a company on the trajectory of technology

Positioning companies on the trajectory of technology

How can a company align itself with a trajectory of technology that calls for continual evolution? The answer is simple: it needs to evolve, too. However, evolution is something totally different than the typical corporate transformation programs of today. A traditional change program follows a number

---

18 Historian Yuval Harari believes the emergence of "super humans" is likely—that is, humans augmented with technology in ways that make them significantly less human. (Harari, 2016)
19 (Raworth, 2017)

of steps: (1) decide on a vision for the company; (2) assess the status quo; (3) determine the delta between vision and status quo; (4) create an implementation plan; and (5) execute this plan, which usually requires people to be trained, processes and systems to be established, and accountabilities restructured. Five years on, however, the company usually ends up with an outdated vision, implementation that has become bogged down, and a general sense of disillusionment. The classic change program, though rational and controllable, is a relic of the industrial age. It has four fundamental flaws that render it obsolete in the digital age:

1. *Reliance on prediction.* It assumes that the future can be predicted.
2. *Assumption of no important unknowns.* It assumes that this vision can be broken down through a rational process into an implementation plan.
3. *Assumption of rational agents.* It assumes that people at the top have the objective ability to sense what's needed for both vision and implementation.
4. *Assumption of relative stability.* It assumes a period of stability after the change has been made so that all implementation costs can be recouped.

An evolutionary work design is quite different. It rests on the following four assumptions: [20]

1. *Reliance on mental models:* Multiple predictions are great for building mental models that prepare for the possibilities that the future holds.
2. *Assumption of fundamental learnings.* There are very important things to learn that we are not even aware of. A high-level yet meaningful organizational mission is enough to give direction to the evolution of a company. Visions become more like forecasts, repeated along the way, and less like directions.
3. *Assumption of collective intelligence.* Individual actors are even better if they support themselves. A company's work design must be open and transparent so everyone can sense technological, market, or customer needs.

---

20 The list is inspired by (Sanford, 2017).

4. *Assumption of fluidity.* The future consists both of stability and change of any magnitude. We don't know how long stability will last, nor do we know how fundamental a change will be. But we do know that we need to be prepared.

Biological evolution brings to life highly complex things that humans often call beautiful: zebras and giraffes on the savannah, a flock of geese in flight, meadows filled with flowers. In the same sense, technological evolution brings about beautiful things through its evolutionary drive: virtual worlds, beautiful tableware, sleek cars. The chances are that organizational evolution will bring about companies that we experience as beautiful, too. Places where people are free to invent, to heed their inner calling, to look after others, to contribute to the world with less fear of oppression.

As a very earth-bound North German, I need to add a caveat here. Evolution brings about many highly specialized things that we do not classify as beautiful: cockroaches, bed bugs, intestinal worms. There will also be ugly, exploitative organizations. However, organizational evolution will make sure that the safari will be much more colorful than ever before.

A bonanza of possibilities

More and more technologies are invented every day. In fact, the rate of technological progress outpaces the rate at which, for example, the number of academic research papers grows.[21] Technology doesn't care whether academics make sense of it or connect it to the foundations of human knowledge—it progresses anyway. There is an exponentially widening gap between the possibilities of technology and the rate at which science is able to keep up with those possibilities (see Gap 1 in Figure 1).

---

21 (Kelly, 2011)

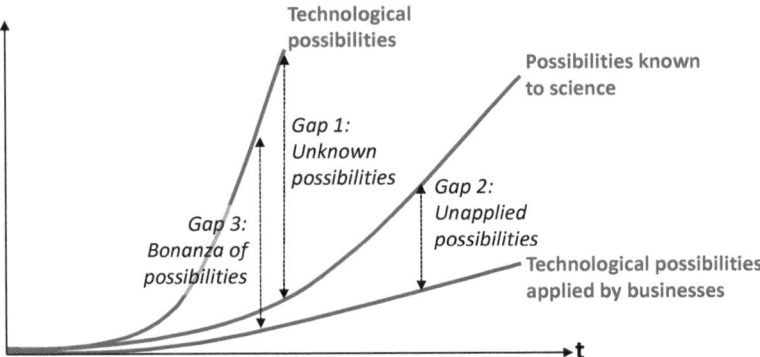

Figure 1 A bonanza of possibilities

Companies have always been slow to apply scientific knowledge (Gap 2). There is good reason to expect that this gap will increase as the concentration of power in the hands of global companies, especially the monopolists of digital platform companies, continues to suppress competition.

For companies, this opens up a bonanza of possibilities (Gap 3). If technology offers more possibilities than science (as we know it can process), there is an even greater bonanza of possibilities out there than can be utilized by companies. More and more, the race in business becomes not just about scaling new technologies discovered by science, but about businesses finding new possibilities for themselves.

Investing in start-ups is a great way to tap into these possibilities, but it doesn't work very well in a world that is less and less predictable. To evolve a company that is already fully immersed in its market may become a more effective and efficient strategy than to make big, incremental, multi-million bets on unproven companies again and again. Evolution trumps prediction, a theme to which we will return again and again throughout the remainder of this book.

Running companies in the digital age means revitalizing the way they work. It entails coming up with an organizational model that puts a company on the trajectory of technology, and increasing the rate at which companies are able to change. This kind of organization is more than just an agile one.

An agile organization is able to adapt fast to market needs; this is a very useful trait but ultimately a reactive one. More useful would be a company that senses technological possibilities, explores them, and applies what's best. The company of the future is one that puts itself on the trajectory of technology and is dedicated to growing the options available to it and its customers.

How can a company structure itself to benefit from the ever-expanding possibilities that technology offers? To do that will require humans to immerse themselves in technology. Not just nerds and software engineers, but ordinary people—i.e., the "users." We need people who never stop learning how to work with the best multi-purpose tool that humanity has: technology. Unfortunately, the way we currently run companies through hierarchies is not geared for this kind of on-going learning.

Dark Arts

- We think of technology as something we use, but it uses us, too— maybe in greater ways than we imagine.
- Hierarchy systematically degrades the ability of any group of experts to make sense of complex systems.
- Today, technological reality has changed, while managerial reality has not.
- Ultimately, technology wants to evolve on a trajectory towards ever greater efficiency, complexity, opportunity, sentience, number of choices, and structure.
- A modern work design for companies needs to put companies on the same trajectory as technology.
- When designing companies, evolution trumps prediction.
- A liberated company puts itself on the trajectory of technology that is evolving and grows the options available to it over time.
- Your challenge: make your idea of technology explicit.

Further reading

- Ray Kurzweil (2006), *The Singularity is Near* (Penguin)
- Kevin Kelly (2011), *What Technology Wants* (Penguin)
- Salim Ismael (2014), *Exponential Organizations* (Diversion Publishing)
- Andrew McAfee and Erik Brynjolfson (2014), *The Second Machine Age* (Norton & Company)
- Yuval Harari (2016), *Homo Deus: A Brief History of Tomorrow* (Vintage)

■ Chapter 2: The Corrosive Impact of Power Differentials

Do you call yourself free? I want to hear your ruling idea,
and not that you have escaped from the yoke.
– Friedrich Nietzsche, Thus Spoke Zarathustra[22]

The terrain that any book on organizational development needs to map is made up of many features—people, teams, companies, technology—all with their own unique traits and inherent complexity. Some features of the terrain are easy to traverse, others not. Of all those features, one element defines whole regions, just as mountains, rivers, or shorelines would. That element is power.

Companies are, in essence, nothing more than a human construct to distribute power between people. We wouldn't need companies if it were efficient and effective for individuals to cooperate as independent actors without the overall framework of an organization. With too much independence, people tend to argue endlessly about tasks and remuneration, and they lose interest in caring for the common good. To get anything major done in business, people huddle up in companies, accepting centralized control over their actions to achieve something together, which no group of individual actors could achieve otherwise. In 1937, Nobel Prize laureate Ronald Coase described in his seminal paper "Theory of the Firm" that centralized control and submission to authority is much more efficient than leaving coordination to the egalitarian alternative of individual actors—i.e., the anonymous market.[23] The crucial point of Coase's work focuses on how efficiency shapes the distribution and organization of power in companies or markets. Competition between companies will ensure that inefficient organizational arrangements—those with higher transaction costs—will exit the market over time.

---

22 (Nietzche, 1974)
23 (Coase, 1937)

Since the industrial revolution, we have been accustomed to thinking about companies in terms of their hierarchical organization. There are, however, indications that it is no longer a good idea to run modern and increasingly digitalized companies in the same way we ran steel mills and coal mines. The distribution of power within a company can be achieved in a multitude of ways—more ways than we are used to imagining. Our collective lack of organizational imagination is quite striking. We seem to have sleepwalked our way out of the industrial and into the digital revolution, only to awaken with incredulous doubt that there are alternatives to the usual hierarchical system of wide-ranging subordination. In this chapter, we look at two ways of distributing power in companies: the classic hierarchical model, and the empowered model. The next chapter looks at a third alternative: the self-managed organization.

The hierarchy: A tale of sclerosis, over-simplification and corrosion

Organizational hierarchy is a great human invention, and it has been around since long before the industrial revolution. Roman legions, for example, made excessive use of hierarchies. The military system of command, with ranks from optios to centurions and tribunes to legates, was one of the keys to the Romans' enduring success against contemporary opponents who were less well-structured.[24] Some even say it is the natural state of human societies to order things into a hierarchy of superior and subordinate positions, not unlike other groups of animals that form pecking orders.

A company hierarchy is based on a simple idea: all power is concentrated in one central node, the CEO. Everyone else is connected to the hierarchy through a superior. This way, it is clear who makes decisions and who is to follow, and orders cascade down the chain of command. The surprising fact is that this form of organization is a very extreme form of network.

Every network is made up of two elements: nodes and links. In an organizational network ,the nodes are individual people, teams, companies, or any

24 (Goldsworthy, 2000)

other organizational entities that are capable of acting independently. Links between nodes signify a relationship.

There are two things that make a hierarchy a very extreme and specialized kind of network. First, every node has exactly one link to a higher-level node, so that everyone in it has exactly one superior. Consequently, every person is connected to another only through the highest-level node, the CEO. Second, every link is a superior–subordinate relationship. Other less formal types of links, like communication, acquaintance, and influence, are removed from the hierarchy, making it a formal chain of command with the highest degree of centrality possible. This has four major advantages:

1. *Control.* The CEO controls the whole organization through the nodes linked to him/her—i.e., the senior leadership team—who in turn control the nodes linked to them, and so on. The will of the superior to get something done is absolute and its only limitation is the law.
2. *Robustness.* Each node of a hierarchy is replaceable; it only takes the recruitment of a sufficiently qualified candidate to fill a vacant node.
3. *Clarity.* Hierarchies are easy to understand for everyone—you just have to look at the organization chart to get to know the formal power structures.
4. *Rationality.* The hierarchy can be built from a rational analysis of the challenges that a company faces. It can be constructed like a machine.

These immense advantages have made hierarchical organizations the second-most successful social innovation of all time, behind only the family. Yet despite its successes, it has three major weaknesses: the need for stability, the need for low complexity, and the existence of corrupting power differentials between people. All three make a hierarchy an inadequate answer to the digital age.

Hierarchy needs stability

One of the great things about a hierarchy is that it can be built by rational reflection about the challenges ahead. It can be designed to best fit a specific anticipated future in which a business is operating. That strength turns into a weakness whenever the rules of the market shift; in these instances of rapid change, the rationale upon which the organization chart is built quickly becomes outdated. People have been assigned to positions, departments, processes, and systems that may suddenly be redundant or inefficient. Reporting and rewards have all been set up to support the hierarchy, but its foundation is now outdated.

This wouldn't be a problem if hierarchies could quickly pivot, but most hierarchies find it hard to adapt to changes. Re-distributing power is laden with difficulties and runs into opposition from those who face their power being questioned or diminished. Re-organizations tend to drag on endlessly, often resulting in half-hearted compromises or superficial changes (or failing to happen at all). Hierarchical companies, especially in the digital revolution, often appear to be on a path of slow, agonizing decline even though they often have the resources, the talent, and the market position to succeed.[25]

Changing the intricate set of organizational, physical, logical, and power structures is a huge challenge, but the digital revolution leaves companies with no choice but to reconfigure themselves and evolve, again and again. The increasing frequency of reorganization can be observed today—along with the difficulties of doing so. The trouble with reorganization in rapidly changing, ambiguous, and complex market environments is that even the best rational analysis fails to provide a company a long enough period of stability to recoup the costs of reorganization. Even if one could predict the future wants of customers and the market, devise a suitable business model, and build an optimal design of the organizational hierarchy upon it, the speed of the change will often be too fast. During the time it takes for hierarchies to react to changes, they are likely to be outcompeted by nimbler start-ups or face completely new challenges. The result is that many companies are facing a near-permanent state of reorganization and agonizing decline, often both at the same time. This lengthy period of change ultimately achieves nothing; it only increases entropy.

---

25 There are many theories on "natural" organizational life cycles. A useful modern version based on constant rejuvenation can be found in (Hurst, 2012).

In fast-changing and unpredictable times, the hierarchy's lack of agility is simply inefficient. It is hard to overstate the importance of this point. The chronic, ever-increasing uncertainty and unpredictability of the market alone is a death knell for the dominance of the hierarchy in today's companies. Still, hierarchies refuse to die. Not every company or market is faced with an environment that values agility more highly than the four things in which the hierarchy excels (control, robustness, clarity, and rationality), but the chances are that the high tide of hierarchy is already slowly receding as the increasing instability of the marketplace gives rise to alternative forms of organizations.

Hierarchy needs low complexity

Instability is a major problem that undermines the performance of the hierarchy, and another is the need for low complexity. While instability refers to the frequency of change, complexity refers to the unpredictability of change. The capability to rationally design a hierarchy is worthless if no one can predict what to rationalize for.

Prediction is of utmost importance to the art of managing in general. Edwards Deming, one of the great management thinkers of all time, famously said that "management is prediction."[26] Prediction is especially important for hierarchies, as (i) changes to its structures are costly, and (ii) the quality of its central nodes is of utmost importance to the performance of the whole company. A hierarchy needs competent managers, or it will be dysfunctional. Only the "best" are to lead the organization. Most companies try, more or less successfully, to devise a system where the most competent are hired or promoted. This type of organization, where people progress in their career by virtue of their competence alone, is called a meritocracy. The key to a functioning meritocracy in a hierarchy is to be able to predict the performance of a person in a particular position.

Of all predictions that a manager ever needs to make, the prediction of individual job performance is routinely described as the most important. In his 2016 book *Work Rules!*, Lazlo Bock, HR Director at Google, gives a glimpse

26 (Deming W. E., 2012)

of the lengths to which Google, one of the most elitist organizations in the world, goes to get that prediction right by deploying big data, algorithms, a multitude of personality and performance tests, a structured interviewing process, panel-based evaluation and selection committees, ranking of interviewers based on the success of their previous recruits, making interviewing a privilege that can be earned by merit, and much more.[27] Predicting personal performance is crucial for hierarchies, especially at the management level. Get the prediction wrong and everyone, especially direct or indirect subordinates, will suffer. The whole branch of the hierarchy will wither.

Yet, in every company, including Google, there are several fundamental problems that severely impair the chance of getting the prediction of individual performance right:

- *Job descriptions are subjective and arbitrary.* We assume we know what competencies and personality it takes to deliver high performance in a certain position, but this assumption is often totally subjective. It is built on the perception of those creating the job profile, and as such, there are usually no objective checks on these perceptions.
- *It is hard to measure humans and social systems.* Performance and personality tests help, but they are limited in their prediction value.[28]
- *People change once they are in a new position.* Prior success is a weak predictor of success in the future. The so-called Peter Principle states that "everyone rising through the ranks to higher and higher positions is promoted until a level where one is incompetent."[29] The result is that all hierarchical organizations tend to end up with incompetent managers.
- *The more complex the work environment, the harder the prediction.* Recruiting for high-level jobs has always been more of an art than a science. In recent years, recruitment for lower-level jobs has also become more difficult as the workplace has grown in complexity along

---

27 (Bock, 2016)

28 (Bock, 2016), based on a 1998 study by Schmidt and Hunter.

29 "The Peter Principle is a logical concept and cannot be proven or invalidated scientifically: The measurement of 'success' in managerial posts is way too complex." (Peter & Hull, 1969)

with globalization, the ever-increasing amount of technology used, and the rate of change in the market.

- *All prediction is biased by and towards the hierarchy.* When considering a candidate for a management position, there is a need to extrapolate a candidate's performance from the past. The past success of candidates, especially at higher levels of the corporate ladder, has been in no small measure a result of their ability to work inside the hierarchical system. Therefore, candidates who know how to work the hierarchical system tend to be selected. As will be argued later in more detail, those who successfully make their way in a hierarchy are more likely to be fawning courtiers than enterprising, innovative individuals. Fawning courtiers tend not to change the system but to sustain it. The matching algorithm is systematically corrupted so that a hierarchy becomes self-sustaining.
- *A hierarchy tends to create more complexity than is actually needed.* Managers at all levels of the hierarchy are eager to leave their mark on the organization, prove their worth, and start their own signature projects. This systematically creates an initiative overload, overstretching resources and creating a more complex environment.[30] Yet, more complex environments are harder to predict. In this way, a hierarchy is self-defeating.

The quest to come up with the ultimate matching algorithm between job profile and candidate has always been very hard. Today, with the digital revolution, every "fit" of the candidate–job matching algorithm is doomed to be quickly outdated, yet jobs in a hierarchy are assigned on a near-permanent basis. Very few people are ever demoted.

With increasing complexity there comes a point at which predictions cease to be useful at all. Yet hierarchies have no choice but to use prediction as a proxy for merit. In perfect meritocracies, everyone would begin on a level playing field in positions of equal privilege and would advance, remain in place, or be demoted solely by merit. People acting as a central node—"managers"—would

---

30 (Hollister & Watkins, 2018)

face scrutiny from all sides, not just from their superiors, and their positions wouldn't be permanent. In hierarchies, however, people are given near-permanent jobs because of a prediction of which the accuracy cannot reliably be measured. The result? Not a very meritocratic system.

So what's the alternative to predicting a person's performance? Surely companies need to assess people to sort out good apples from bad? That is certainly the case, but getting the prediction right is of outsized importance in a hierarchy compared to all other forms of organization. As we mentioned earlier, hierarchy is an extreme form of network as it relies on the highest degree of centrality possible: there is one central node (the CEO) and a number of other central nodes (managers at all levels) through which all information, decision-making, and authority flow. In this type of network configuration, it is incredibly important to get the central nodes working well, or the lower nodes (employees), and indeed the whole branch below the defunct node, will not perform. Once a prediction has been made and a candidate selected for a management position, it may take years to even identify their incompetence, much less do anything to resolve the problem. Sometimes, incompetent managers are even promoted just to get them out of the real work to a place where they can do less damage.[31]

We pretend as if we can predict the performance of managers to any satisfying degree, but people and social systems are complicated (even more so in digital times). In complex systems, prediction doesn't work well. If we are to keep companies working well, we will need other mechanisms—ones that do not rely so heavily on prediction. We need mechanisms that decrease the "blast radius" of bad predictions, make errors in prediction less permanent, and rely more on dynamic adaptation. Self-managed companies, which we shall explore later, are based on these three forward-thinking mechanisms.

Of all networks, the hierarchy is the form that is most reliant on good managers, whose ability to lead can only be guessed but who are assigned to their posts on a near-permanent basis. In the digital age, with its ever-increasing

---

31 An even more radical version of the Peter Principle, commonly known as the Dilbert Principle.

rate of change and complexity, this sounds like a recipe for disaster. But there is more bad news.

The corrosive work of power differentials

Every system of organization has its own inert set of behaviors that are encouraged or discouraged by its very structure. The most striking feature of the hierarchy is that it makes for a very odd form of network: the formal concentration of all authority on the superior node, the manager, and the relative powerlessness of the subordinate node, the employee. This gives rise to all kinds of exploitative behaviors.

There is no organization and no network structure in the universe that concentrates more power in managers, the central nodes of the system, than a hierarchy. The company hierarchy, which is so pervasive today, is an extremist system. If an alien landed on Earth, conquered it, and set out to consciously design a system where power and control are most concentrated, they would come up with the hierarchy. Granted, alien technologies for mind control would make the hierarchy much more efficient or even superfluous, but the fact remains that the system we humans chose as our dominant way of organizing work is an inherently extremist one. The extreme concentration of power in a manager has been somewhat moderated over the last 130 years by laws, but these regulatory actions only served to curb the worst abuses of power. The systematic imbalance of power between people remains, as do its dysfunctional results. These are neither good for company performance nor for the humans working in such a system.

Managers hold extreme power over subordinates. They make decisions about promotion, reward, the tasks people do, the office space, people's work environment, and their mental health. They can fire people or make work unbearable if they choose to do so. Empirically, managers are by far the most important reason why people quit their jobs or choose to actively engage or disengage in their work.[32] The result of this huge power discrepancy between manager and employee is fear. People are naturally anxious about the behaviors

---

32 (Gallner, Harrington, & Grant, 2018)

of their superior, which are all but decisive for their own mental and financial well-being. Faced with such a hazardous power differential, the best insurance for a bearable work life, a good job, and material success (through reward and promotion) is to please one's superior. To please your superior, your clan chief, your Caesar, your king in any way you can has always been a necessity for both survival and prosperity. The famous French diplomat of the Napoleonic age, Talleyrand (1754–1838), summed this dictum up masterfully: "In autocracy every statesman must be a courtier, in democracy a demagogue."

In a hierarchy, the act of control and the act of pleasing are inseparable, and pleasing is a core skill in every employee's arsenal. Things that never fail to please the superior include: delivering the results the boss really wants; putting in the extra hours; demonstrating engagement as visibly as possible; reliability; adhering to the norms of the workplace, including its dress code; and appealing to the superior's own values. Pleasing, at its core, is about delivering whatever the superior wants. If she seeks affirmation, affirm her. If she seeks activity, demonstrate activity. If she seeks formality, deliver formality. If rules are important to her, stick to the rules. If she wants to be entertained, entertain her. Some forms of pleasing are frowned upon today, such as bribes or sexual favors, but these are few. Co-workers may dislike the dishonest, fawning courtier, but that does not really matter much. What is of overriding importance is what the superior and the superior's superior think of you. Good relationships with co-workers are a bonus, but they are nowhere near as essential as good relations with the manager.

There are two major snags to this system of servitude. First, people seek to please individuals, not abstract entities, i.e. "the company." Results would be optimal if a manager was driven by analytical calculus that only included all objective and emotional factors that are important for the well-being of the company. Alas, managers are not all-knowing algorithms, they are real people with biases, idiosyncrasies, and constructed worldviews. There is no such thing as an impartial, objective manager. Therefore, the fundamental need to please bosses results in actions that are primarily aligned with the needs of the superior and only sometimes aligned with the needs of the company.

Second, people that are so focused on pleasing lose a lot of their self-esteem and motivation. Being overwhelmingly focused on managing a superior's impression leads over time to self-disenfranchisement: my own happiness becomes much less relevant than my superior's, and I begin to value the same things as my superior and take on their definition of happiness.[33] People become less able to contribute their inert talents and views, more like their bosses, or at least more compatible with their bosses and the prevailing culture of the organization. Edwards Deming said that "management that denies their employees dignity and self-esteem will smother intrinsic motivations."[34] Even well-meaning managers in a hierarchy will smother intrinsic motivations, as people recalibrate and change their inner selves to fit into the system.

The concentration of power in any manager is high, but it rises exponentially the higher one moves up the corporate ladder. The power to distribute rewards and punishments become greater, and the checks on power become smaller. A modern CEO holds a position of power similar to that of an ancient clan chief: not over life and death, but certainly over the financial and emotional well-being of many people. The enormous and unavoidable power differential in the hierarchy creates hubris, narcissistic behavior, and feelings of entitlement amongst those on the upper levels of the corporate ladder.[35] Even if a manager is able to rein in their hubris, when forced most managers will prioritize control over performance. Control is what a hierarchy is all about, and control is what you get. As John Dahlberg Acton said in 1887: "Power corrupts; absolute power corrupts absolutely."

Employees naturally guard themselves against those who hold discretionary power over them. First of all, they watch their superior closely to detect or anticipate their intentions. Second, they align their behavior so as not to run afoul of the perceived intentions. Third, they seek ways to influence their boss's intentions. To please the boss is a prime tactic, but intrigue and undermining others are common tactics, too. Faced with an immense power differential, there is an incentive for people to engage in asymmetric warfare and become guerilla fighters.

---

33 (Shorris, 1983)
34 (Deming W. E., 2012).
35 (Pfeffer, 2015))

Hierarchies are by nature very political organizations. While political behavior may be unwelcome in companies, the more intense the power differential, the higher the incentive to engage in political tinkering, and the more essential it becomes for people to get good at politics just to survive within the organization. There is nothing bad about organizational politics per se, as any group of humans needs to find a means of making decisions. It is simply that politics turn ugly if the power differential inside a group is too large.

Power differentials are corrosive to human relations, to human health, and to the performance of organizations. The symptoms of this appear in numerous ways:[36]

- If you want to avoid disappointing your boss, do not take risks.
- Predictability is valued higher than results. With the pressing need to deliver what has been promised, people set lower targets and avoid experimentation.
- Entrepreneurship is a form of insubordination. Entrepreneurs break rules; they take risks and go for results, not predictability.
- Information is both an asset and a weapon. People hold it back and use it covertly or strategically to further their aims when the time is ripe.
- The fawning courtier wins over the enterprising individual every time.
- Innovation is lacking. People will neither speak up nor experiment.
- The status quo is cemented.

The hierarchical system comes at a cost: it drives companies away from the intended outcomes and centers it on new outcomes, directing it away from its core goal of providing goods and services and towards personal enrichment and power. On a personal level, it systematically disenfranchises people, making them ever-more dependent upon their bosses' definition of happiness rather than their own, changing society and curbing human potential. This is a bad idea in any era, but even more so in digital, complex, and knowledge-based times.

---

36 This list is based on, but not limited to "Inside Bureaucracy", a paper written by Anthony Downs, a professor of economics. This paper focuses on the most common form of hierarchy in any organization, the bureaucracy. (Downs, 1964)

None of this is news. Asymmetric power will be misused. The dynamics behind this are very well researched in economics in the form of the principal-agent or moral hazard problems, or in psychology under the topics of fear, vulnerability, and shame.[37] So far, businesses have swallowed these costs as unavoidable. No serious alternative to the hierarchy has been put forth.

Rethinking power might be worth a try

Getting a hierarchy to function has always been a tough job. Now, with the ever-increasing pace of the digital revolution, the sclerosis of the hierarchy, the need to make impossible predictions, and the asymmetrical power distribution (which poisons relations between people and curbs the contributions they are willing to make), building a truly functional hierarchy seems like pure folly.

The basis for the relationship between an individual and a company has not changed since antiquity: money for submission—easy, fair, and simple. However, this deal might be too simplistic for the digital age. The more we face complexity, the more we need engaged people to master it. We can no longer rely on submission. Instead, people need to be trusted to do the right thing. In the digital age, when hierarchy is an increasingly mediocre tool for running businesses, the basic deal between companies and people needs to shift from "money for submission" to "money for engagement." According to Gallup, only 15 percent of employees worldwide declare themselves "actively engaged" in their jobs.[38] Can this be fixed?

Empowerment – "Hierarchy light": A tale of good intentions

Questions about the fitness of the hierarchical model to run modern companies have resulted in a call for organizations that are much more responsive to change. A popular way of making organizations more agile is to update the hierarchical model with an infusion of practices intended to increase the ability to adapt while leaving the core of the hierarchy intact. This tactic can be

---

37 (Brown, 2016); (Edmondson & Schein, Teaming, 2014)
38 (Gallup, 2019)

described as "empowerment." Here the basic assumption is that there is nothing fundamentally wrong with hierarchy itself so long as the people working in it take on a more entrepreneurial mindset. These "intrapreneurs" will not care so much about organizational silos, rules, and politics; they will take the initiative and act in response to whatever the situation demands.

The term empowerment refers to "measures designed to increase the degree of autonomy and self-determination in people ... in order to enable them to represent their interests in a responsible and self-determined way, acting on their own authority".[39] Empowerment calls on managers to become aware of their power and use it sensitively. Empowered management practices seek to patch up the negative impacts of the hierarchy, requiring managers to establish structural checks and balances to curb the excesses of power differentials and to inject a bit more flexibility and engagement into the tired old structures. A measure of empowerment is that employees display less defensive, risk-averse, negative political behavior and instead become more willing to speak up, engage, and grow in stature. Most of today's mainstream management practices can be categorized under the term "empowerment," for example:[40]

- Management by objectives or results
- Participative decision-making
- Managerial feedback
- Managerial delegation
- Flatter hierarchies
- Cross-functional teams
- Matrix organizations
- Open and appreciative team cultures
- Quality circles
- 360-degree evaluations
- Personality type assessments (e.g., Meyer–Briggs)
- Lists of corporate values

---

39 Definition according to Wikipedia, **https://en.wikipedia.org/wiki/Empowerment** accessed 4th of June, 2019.

40 More on those and on empowered practices specifically can be found in Part II of this book.

About 99 percent of the management and leadership training industry caters to the mantra of empowerment. The central theme is to squeeze out productivity (and a bit of innovation) from the pre-existing organizational hierarchies. The advice given by consultants and trainers is occasionally sound, but more often it is just management fashion.[41]

A short history of empowerment

At the beginning of the last century, with the industrial revolution still in full swing, Frederick Winslow Taylor came up with a theory of what he called "scientific management."[42] This early and most influential theory of management called for three things: an educated manager; the detailed analysis of every work step to find out the one best way to do things; and the strict control of the worker. In this model, there was no way a worker could acquire any authority; in fact, jobs were systematically de-skilled so that they could be filled by cheap, uneducated workers. The logical, analytical, top-down way of arranging work didn't leave much leeway for lower-level workers to choose how to do their work, and authority within the organization was strictly centralized.

While this model achieved miracles in the first half of the twentieth century, with its countless factories and massive workforces of unskilled labor, the system resulted in the sclerosis of companies once workers became more skilled and work more complex. This became visible in the 1980s in the United States. The American automobile industry, and later many other manufacturing industries, were incapable of competing with Japanese companies that gave their shop-floor work teams a mandate to speak up more freely. This is symbolized by the Andon Cord, which can be pulled by any worker to stop the flow of a manufacturing line in order to draw attention to a problem. Under what was later termed "lean management," workers had more influence over the way they were doing things—unthinkable in the realms of the "scientific management" that had dominated most of the 20th century. Eventually, after horrendous losses in market share, American companies such as General Motors and Ford were forced to adopt "lean" too.

41 (Rosenzweig, The Halo Effect, 2007)
42 (Taylor, 1911)

At first, the changes were thought to be at shop-floor level only, but over time a greater delegation of authority to lower-level employees became a part of what is nowadays seen as "good" management. Two influential books facilitated this: 1982's *In Search of Excellence*, by Tom Peters and Robert Waterman, and *From Good to Great* by Jim Collins in 2001.[43] *From Good to Great* has practically defined current public perception of what "good management" is all about. A third book of this genre, *What Really Works*, published in 2003, was even more impressive, with dozens of professors involved and thousands of companies researched.[44] These books were based on intensive field studies to find out what makes a company successful. They were best sellers for many years and are to this day often found on the desks or bookshelves of managers. They called for more authority to be distributed, for more autonomy and entrepreneurship, for people to be given more space to engage more fully, and for things like "level 5 leadership," wherein the leader takes a supportive instead of a dominating role in order to maximize a team's potential. Empowerment caught on, and to this day most managers embrace it, at least on a superficial level.

Today, the delegation of work or authority is a central part of the canon of good management. Listening to employees, delegating tasks, developing people, and better utilizing individual skills are all seen as productive and clever uses of a manager's time. Managers use delegation all the time; the assignment of a person to a task or a job, even the creation of a job description itself and the design of business processes, can be seen as acts of delegation. Delegation is the act of providing to subordinates the freedom to act within certain boundaries, transferring a part of the manager's given authority to employees. Good delegation—the right task, for the right person, with the right boundaries in place—is a basic management skill and is universally encouraged in today's management literature. While this represents a great improvement on the industrial age's command-and-control style of management, there are significant problems with the concept. The first problem is that good delegation cannot be measured and is therefore totally subjective. What is a right task? Who is the right person? What are the right boundaries? To answer

---

43   (Peters & Waterman, 1982); (Collins, 2001)
44   (Nohira & Joyce, 2003)

these questions, a manager needs enormous insight into the tasks, intimate knowledge of a person, and a deep understanding of the work environment. There is as much objectivity in this process as a manager can muster at a certain point of time, yet what makes good delegation is a very subjective thing.

This leads to the second problem: delegation tends to paternalize and therefore undermine the individual initiative of workers. If the only way to get good at delegation is by being very involved with each person and with the work itself, people's freedom to act is automatically limited by the presence of a meddling, micro-managing manager. Delegation requires a manager to think for the subordinate and anticipate what would be good for both the success of the task and the person doing the task. Employees do not volunteer for the task themselves; they are being assigned to it. This is an inherently paternalistic approach that treats employees as children rather than adults.

What is the dividing line between command and delegation, anyway? Every command needs a clear definition of the task, a capable person to execute it, and a set of boundary conditions such as a schedule and resources. A command becomes delegation if the task is bigger—i.e., requires a higher number of work steps and the worker has some say in how it will be done—but ultimately the boundary between order and delegation is fluid. Managers may choose to negotiate the terms of a delegated task with an employee, or even ask for their acceptance of the task, but subordinates know better than to negotiate too hard or reject a task. The aforementioned power differential makes it hard to upset the boss.

A less paternalistic way of delegating is to delegate decisions instead of tasks: letting subordinates decide how to set up a process, what software package to buy, how to solve an issue, whether to launch a project, how to run an important meeting, which consultant to hire, or which supplier to choose. Delegating decision-making transfers real power to subordinates; however, this approach is frowned upon in most organizations. A manager delegating decisions is often seen as indecisive, not in control, unknowing, weak. Nobody wants a weak manager. Delegating decisions is often not even in the best interests of the manager themselves, as every delegated decision-makes the manager a bit more irrelevant. After all, a managerial position is a managerial position because it has been endowed with decision-making power. Strip away this power piece-by-piece by delegating, and people might ask the existential question: Why have a manager at all if most decisions are made by co-workers?

Patching up the hierarchy is hard. Hierarchy tends to re-assert itself in the form of disenfranchising parent-child relations; the power differential works to systematically undermine any effort towards empowerment. Let's have a deeper look at three ways some companies have been experimenting with empowerment on a larger scale: the matrix organization, dual mindsets, and the self-managed team.

Empowerment by matrix

A matrix is a configuration of a network where nodes have multiple superiors (rather than just one) to improve communication, cooperation, and agility across business units and functions. In a matrix, managers need to coordinate with other managers and subordinates need to learn to prioritize the needs of multiple bosses. This blurring of reporting lines is intended to increase alignment between independent parts of the organization and to focus more on a holistic picture, instead of just the needs of single departments. In the 1970s, it became a popular idea for revitalizing the hierarchy, but the results have been mixed.

Nowadays the matrix is an established feature at large companies where two-dimensional matrices of functions and products are more or less the norm. Some even add a third dimension, such as geography. However, most matrix organizations clearly identify a "strong line," or the dominant dimension of the matrix, and one or multiple "dotted lines" that signify a dependency of sorts. Most companies today just sprinkle in some elements of the matrix at higher levels of management or staff functions but remain strongly hierarchical. Follow the strong line, and the hierarchy is clearly visible. Experience has shown that a true matrix organization (where leadership is genuinely shared) is very difficult to sustain, as it is often a confusing and conflict-rich environment in which to work. People tend to crave the clarity that the hierarchy brings.

Nevertheless, research has shown that matrix organizations work so long as they are supported by management practices that foster the informal coordination of people. These practices include shared common purpose, supportive and collaborative leadership, a mindset that values team effort, efficient meeting practices where everyone feels obliged to state their views, and practices that evaluate and reward people based on their efforts and are more tolerant of diverse outcomes.[45] The lesson that can be learned from matrix organization is this: once you move away from a hierarchy, informal methods of coordination need to replace formal ones or companies will become dysfunctional.

Empowerment by mindset

Another way to empower people is to leave the hierarchy as it is but get managers to use their power more wisely. This way, the power differential is still there but it is not felt by co-workers. John Kotter, a business professor and prolific writer, encourages managers to hold two separate belief systems about how work should be done.[46] The first represents the belief of the classical hierarchy, while the second is the belief in a flat, self-managed, networked organization without bosses. If managers could achieve this latter feat, they would be open to working with new management practices; they could hold the space that empowered teams need to succeed, and they could more easily collaborate with people at all levels of the networked organization.

Kotter explains how this feat of managerial schizophrenia can be pulled off. First, managers should be educated on the need for less hierarchical approaches to management. The success of the digital giants of our times, which went from garage start-up to world dominance, is a popular metaphor that is used to implant the desire to learn a "second operating system." Second, managers need to practice the second operating system by allowing communities

---

45 (Martin, 2015); (Galbraith, 2008)
46 (Kotter, 2014)

of interest to spread—e.g., groups where people join and engage of their own volition. Such groups are free to pick targets and organize in any way they want. Communities of interest are self-managed teams that exist in parallel to the hierarchy at any level. Kotter argues that communities of interest invariably surface if managers hold an open space for engaged, driven, missionary, entrepreneurial people. Managers must signal that it is OK to support those free-wheeling groups working alongside the hierarchy; they must let their employees know that they see the value of running things in parallel, ambiguous, overlapping, and sometimes inefficient ways in order to achieve greater diversity, engagement, and innovation.

Kotter's call for two mental models is easy to criticize. It is just an appeal to managers, it is hard to measure, it is a tightrope walk to weigh the needs of the hierarchy against the needs of the social dynamics of self-managed teams, and so on. The appeal to have a "second operating system" is as much a mental reframing exercise as it is an exercise in self-restraint. I have at times been a vocal critic of Kotter's dual "mental operating systems," but in recent years I have come to see that the mental transformation of leaders is a prerequisite for many major changes in companies—even more so for such a crucial move as relinquishing control. Mental reframing is as important for change as is cool, analytical thinking.

In order to empower self-managed teams, companies need supportive leaders who have already mastered this reframing. The capacity to hold dual mental operating systems not only bridges the way with more agile approaches, it is a permanent necessity for any leader in the digital age. Even in the digital tsunami, periods of stability and low complexity will still be found, and the hierarchy can do a good job there. The need to learn two operating systems, to understand both hierarchy and self-management, is here to stay.

Empowerment by bolting on self-managed teams

Why not use the hierarchy where it works—i.e., in stable and less complex work environments—and just supplement it with a number of self-managed teams where dynamism, creative problem-solving, and knowledge work is important?

As explained in the previous chapter, despite its ubiquity the hierarchy is actually a very radical way of laying out a network. In other less-centralized network configurations, central nodes don't have such a huge impact. If information, decision-making, and authority are more distributed, single nodes won't matter so much. The network will find a way to get things done even if single nodes are defunct—much in the same way that the internet works, having no central servers that can bring it down. By choosing the hierarchy as our way of organizing companies, we are confronted by the need for perfect central nodes. Some organizational researchers and liberated companies have already solved this problem by not relying on central nodes as much and instead distributing information processing and decision-making throughout the network.

After the first experiments with flat organizations in the 1950s at the Tavistock Institute, [47] the success of empowered work teams at Toyota in the 1980s,[48] and the "agile" movement that emerged in 2001, it has become clearer with each successive decade that self-managed teams—i.e., network structures with fewer central nodes—deliver vastly superior results compared to hierarchical teams. Many companies have introduced or experimented with self-managed teams, and lean manufacturing, agile software engineering, and lean start-up work designs are more or less business standards today.

However, working with more self-managed teams has proved difficult for hierarchical companies. Hierarchies have a tendency to meddle in self-managed teams, and overreach by superiors, HR, IT, or purchasing departments is the norm. There are many practitioners who complain bitterly about the corruption of the lean or agile movements by the hierarchy. Often, those methods become just another exploitative tool in the arsenal of overbearing and paternalistic managers. Practices like daily stand-ups, Kanban boards, or meta-plan walls with a lot of post-it notes is taken to be the essence of a lean or agile way of working, but is really just a symbolic "cargo cult"—showing a lack of deeper understanding of self-managed teams. Self-managed teams are being bolted onto hierarchies all over business today, but it is often no more than a façade.

---

47 (Emery & Trist, 1969)
48 (Deming W. E., 2012); (Ohno, 1988)

Why has empowerment failed to materialize more widely?

Empowerment, the "participative enterprise" which started in the 1960s, has had more than 50 years to change the business world. By now, it is safe to say that it has failed to make a significant impact. There are few indications that companies are any less authoritarian today than in the 1960s. Yes, suits and ties are often no longer mandatory, and bosses learn in training that empowerment helps everyone, but empowerment has been nothing but a drop in the managerial ocean and has failed to significantly mitigate any of the systematic weaknesses of hierarchies. There are a number of reasons for this: [49]

- *Managers often are not system thinkers*—i.e., they may not take the complexity of social systems seriously. In a hierarchical system, they are primarily power brokers and skill influencers. Managers rise more due to their ability to deal with factions than through technical or managerial skill. Even if they are system thinkers, it is the system of the hierarchy that any manager needs to understand much more urgently than any other system, such as entrepreneurship, self-management, or the business itself.
- Managers do not seek to divest themselves of power; *rather they seek to expand their powers.* Even well-meaning leaders push towards more power in order to "do more good." As Earl Shorris, an American author, notes, "The flaw lies not in leaders, but in the failure of men to recognize their own totalitarian traits."[50]
- *Participation is inherently difficult.* Participation means that people will be speaking up, raising dissent and conflict. The apathy of the hierarchy and the harmony of a closed group are closely related. It's much easier to achieve apparent unity by autocratic means than by more liberated, democratic means.[51] To coordinate a company by hierarchy and order is much easier and more direct than it is to create systems of liberation—i.e., more egalitarian environments that facilitate cooperation.

49 See also (Marquet D. L., 2015), **https://hbr.org/2015/05/6-myths-about-empowering-employees**
50 (Shorris, 1983)
51 (Arendt, 1951)

- *You can't vacillate between empowerment and un-empowerment.* Voice, authority, and information should always be with the people you seek to empower. Empowerment that is taken away arbitrarily at times doesn't make people feel empowered at all.
- *The route to empowerment is not a program.* You can't implement a bottom-up concept in a top-down fashion; in other words, you can't order people to change their mindsets.
- *What you think empowerment is might not be what others think it is.* If you prescribe what empowerment means instead of letting people explore and find their own authority, no one will feel empowered.
- *Exploitation can buy immense rewards.* Skimming the system can generate profits—at least in the short term. Participation is not very helpful if you are looking out for your own interests first.
- *Empowerment is just an appeal to managers.* A call to allow more participation because it's better for performance is usually not enough to convince people to change their ways.
- *Arbitrary power will be used arbitrarily.* A key strength of the hierarchy is that it provides managers with open-ended authority—i.e., authority that can be used flexibly, according to the demands of the situation.[52] It is impossible to specify in advance all the contingencies that might require an alteration of the initial understanding of what a worker must do. Efficient employment contracts are therefore necessarily incomplete, and managers' authority is open-ended. Some disenfranchising overreach is unavoidable collateral damage.

According to David Marquet, a former US submarine officer and writer on progressive organizations, successful empowerment needs three things: (i) organizational clarity and consistency; (ii) competence at work level; and (iii) a purpose.[53] However, telling managers to empower people and limit their arbitrary of power is not enough to create organizational clarity and consistency. The development of competence won't happen if people remain focused on pleasing their superior; this systematically casts managers as parents and employees as children. And finally, purpose is not primarily a com-

---

52 (Anderson, 2017)
53 (Marquet, Turn That Ship Around, 2016)

pany-level thing and cannot be "served" by a superior: it needs to be felt and found again and again by each individual and can only prosper over time if there is consistent freedom and safety to act autonomously.

Where does that lead us? Managers are obviously only able to empower people sporadically. We need to do something more fundamental about the power differential. Maybe we should seek a radical approach and dissolve the hierarchy, allowing a company to become a network of equals. In the next chapter, we'll see how well this works.

Dark Arts

- If we are ever to master companies in the digital age, we need to address the elephant in the room: power.
- Power differentials are corrosive to human relations, to human health, and to the performance of organizations.
- The "governmentality" that we use to run businesses determines who we are, too.
- Hierarchies need two things to work well: stability and a low-complexity environment that makes prediction of performance possible.
- In hierarchies, people tend to focus on solving the wrong problem: pleasing superiors.
- In the digital age, the basic deal between companies and people shifts from "money for submission" to "money for engagement."
- Empowerment is an attempt to patch up the hierarchy for the digital age by telling managers to behave well and hold open a space for "their" employees.
- Hierarchy tends to re-assert itself, preventing empowered, decentralized, liberal practices that are needed to handle complexity and change from spreading.
- The ability of managers to hold multiple mental frames—i.e., dual operating systems—become as important as cool analytical thinking.

Further Reading:

- Earl Shorris (1983) *The Oppressed Middle (Anchor Press/ Double Day)*
- Elinor Ostrom (1990) *Governing the Commons* (Cambridge University Press)
- L. David Marquet (2016) *Turn that ship around* (Penguin)
- Elisabeth Anderson (2017) *Private Government* (Princeton University Press)

■ Chapter 3 Networks: Fine-tuned Degrees of Centrality

The time will come and is inevitably coming when all institutions based on force will disappear through their uselessness, stupidity, and even inconvenience becoming obvious to all.
– Leo Tolstoy, 1894[54]

Our world is full of networks. The human body is a network of cells, the so-cial-political sphere can be pictured as a network, and even physical elements can be pictured as one big network at the quantum level. These are networks that are always shifting in their structure, always reconfiguring. Networks in business have been around since time immemorial. Phoenician traders from the Levant (roughly modern Lebanon) were maintaining a network of com-merce that reached from the North Sea to India already as early as 2000 BCE. The basic nodes of economic networks are people and companies bound to one another by contracts and deals. The network structure has been a core element of the dynamic marketplace for thousands of years.

According to Greg Satell, an author on digital transformation, "a networked com-pany is easy to create: Just stop drawing reporting lines from people to other people." [55] In a networked organization each node—people, teams, or parts of the organization—is free to connect in any way it chooses to whatever other nodes it sees the need to be connected to. In its most extreme form, all nodes would be connected to all others, so there would be no central nodes at all; every co-worker would be connected to every other co-worker. Such an orga-nization can only exist up to a certain size limit. Research has shown that people are able to maintain deep connections to all other co-workers in teams no bigger

---

54 (Tolstoy, 1894)
55 (Satell, 2015)

than five[56] and loose connections in companies no bigger than 150 persons.[57] In a 150-person company, a person might not be able to remember everyone's name, but at least they would have some level of understanding about their job, have a hypothesis about their character traits, share some acquaintances or memories—basically, just enough information to sustain a productive working relationship. There is a limit to the human brain's capacity to connect.

Even extremely distributed technical systems, such as the internet, rely on some degree of centrality. One example is name servers, which are used to convert alphanumeric internet addresses (e.g., **www.google.com**) into standardized numeric IP addresses. Other examples are the standard access points that link regional nets into the global broadband or the governance organizations of the internet such as ICANN or W3C. Even vastly distributed technical networks need some level of centrality.

Human networks need more centrality than machines do, as the human mind is limited to the smaller number of nodes that it can be connected to. A network without centrality is as extreme as a hierarchy, where all nodes are connected by just one node: the CEO. The real question is how much centrality an organization should have.

The question of hierarchical vs. networked company structures is very well researched in business literature on the macro level and in the context of conglomerates, but less so at the micro level inside a company. There are four different types of company networks that are typical approaches to alleviating the shortcomings of a hierarchical company:

1. *A macro-level network.* A network of companies bound together by ownership.
2. *A micro-level network.* A network of people in a self-managed company without a managerial hierarchy.
3. *A technology-centric network.* A network of people and companies held together by technology.

---

56 (Hackman, 2002)
57 The "Dunbar number"; see (Dunbar, 1992)

4. *An ecosystem*. A network of companies and people held together by diverse structures such as ownership, purpose, social relations, and technology.

A network of companies

The hierarchical organization often seems like a large, slow-moving tanker that is hard to steer, so why not empower middle managers to let show their entrepreneurial skill? Instead of a lumbering tanker, a company should become a flotilla of speedboats with a lot of captains bound together by common ownership, a shared mission, and a set of practices that allow the flotilla to coordinate its actions.

The tanker–flotilla metaphor is often used in business as a rationale for splitting up companies. However, mergers and acquisitions do not often result in networked organizations, as they are driven primarily by financial engineering to maximize the value of assets in the short term. It takes much more than financial engineering to build networked organizations. One of the pioneers that undertook to transform itself into a market-centric network of companies was the Swedish-Swiss engineering group ABB.

In 1988 ABB split itself up into hundreds of profit centers and smaller companies in order to achieve entrepreneurial agility. It switched from hierarchical command to the invisible hand of the market to coordinate the actions of its various units. All units were still connected via ownership ties to ABB HQ and its illustrious CEO Percy Barnevik, so a certain degree of centrality did still exist. HQ still set high-level general directions and boundaries, but within those parameters, each individual unit was free to act. HQ did not intervene to cut back on overlapping activities to enforce efficiency, it did not dictate how business should be done, and it allowed internal competition.[58]

---

58 (Peters, Liberation Management , 1992)

In the early 1990s, Barnevik's visionary way of organizing companies earned him rock-star appeal. However, after some very successful years, ABB's performance declined and it reverted back to a more centralized hierarchical organization with some matrix features. Causes and effects in the drama of ABB's organizational experiment are not easy to identify, measure, and untangle, but the general consensus is that ABB ended up with a convoluted set of enterprises that had far too little in common to allow for any coherent action or synergy. In retrospect, it was apparent that just splitting companies into fragments in the hope that the market would do the coordination was not enough. ABB's managers tried many other ways to align their companies, but all attempts tended to increase the bureaucracy to byzantine levels. The anonymity of the market, which reduces all signals to a price, couldn't deliver enough coordination. A network of decentralized P&Ls is toxic.

This is not to say that the market is not able to coordinate actions. Markets were coordinating the world economy then as they are today. However, the market and its price mechanism do not deliver the coordinating power, stability, and foresight that a company needs. The market does a very successful job coordinating extremely specialized world-class companies in specific regions like Northern Italy, Baden-Württemberg in Southern Germany, Silicon Valley, Shenzhen, and other major economic clusters. The clustering of companies creates so many options and positive spill-overs that these markets are often described as eco-systems rather than ordinary markets. The experiment at ABB demonstrated that such eco-systems are very difficult to build up inside companies. However, with improved digital technology, who is to say that the market could not play a central coordinating role in a networked company of the future? Maybe the secret is to mix the market mechanism with digital capabilities to coordinate the flotilla? Some people think that the time is ripe for such organizations and bet their future on it, such as Zhang Ruimin, the CEO of Haier, a global manufacturer whose story and approach we will explore in detail in a later chapter.

A network of people: the self-managed company

A self-managed company is an organization in which everyone shares the same level of power even though they may occupy roles or positions in teams that come with certain individual rights. This type of organization has fewer, and less powerful, central nodes. In a self-managed organization, people connect to one another as needed by the situation, not because it is mandated and planned in the organization chart. A self-managed organization has three great advantages:

1. *Agility.* Its networked structure adapts more easily to changes by reconfiguring itself into new configurations again and again. Every co-worker can change roles, teams, and their own work tasks much more easily. People assign themselves to tasks rather than being assigned.
2. *Complexity capability.* A self-managed organization does not rely on the people in power predicting an optimal structure or predicting who would be a great manager in which position. Instead, no position is permanent, and more weight is placed on the team than on individual authority, decreasing the "blast radius" of bad predictions and enabling dynamic adaptation.
3. *Egalitarianism.* It eliminates the corrosive power differential between people by limiting the arbitrary power any one individual has over another. People can speak up much more freely and have more influence over their work, their team, and the organization.

A self-managed organization solves the three main problems of the hierarchy: the need for stability, the intolerance of complexity, and the systemic corrosion of the power differential. Let's see how this works in practice.

The structure of self-managed companies

A self-managed company is an organization without hierarchical superiors. All people are on the same level. On paper, it takes just six simple steps to transform a hierarchical into a self-managed organization:

1. Take the organization chart of a conventional company hierarchy.
2. Re-define all the boxes as teams.
3. Demote every manager to co-worker.
4. Keep the connections between teams but change the meaning of a link from "subordination" to "communication."
5. Send a representative from every lower-level team to into a higher-level team.
6. Be clear about the decision-making rules used.

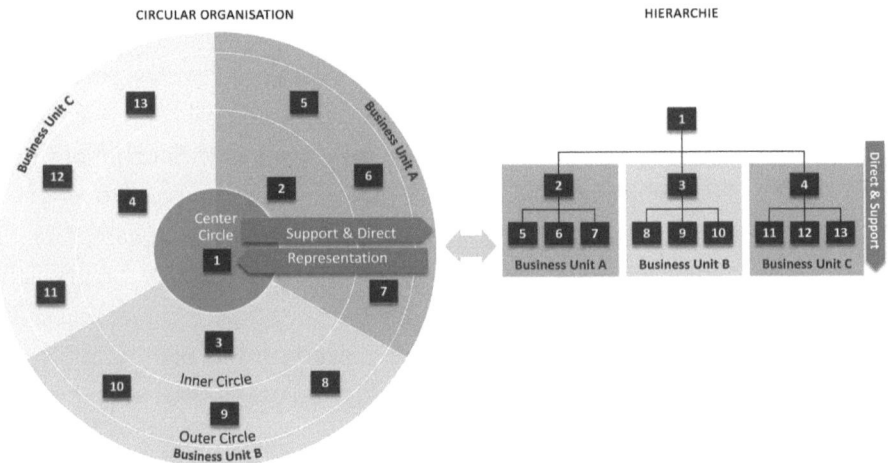

Figure 2 How to turn a hierarchical structure into a self-managed one

What you get from this simple structural transformation is:

- A network of teams instead of a hierarchy of people.
- A lot of self-managed teams.
- New and more complex ways to make decisions, from individual fiat to group decisions.

There are still teams of people in the central and inner circles in charge of co-ordinating the organization, but the members of these teams are chosen and may be substituted on the initiative of the outer circle teams. Furthermore, the members of the two inner circle teams do not have the unilateral power to order teams in the outer circle around. Instead, outer circle teams may pull services from the inner circle teams, if they choose to do so. Inner circle teams are meant to serve the needs of the outer circle teams, not merely order them around.[59]

Still, every once in a while, a company will need concerted action in the form of consistent behavior by a number of outer circle teams. How can this be achieved if the outer circles cannot be ordered around as they would be in a hierarchy? The solution is a power-sharing arrangement between outer, inner, and central circle teams that in some respects resembles a democracy and is not unlike today's company board practices.

The inner circle team has two options. First, it can try to convince outer circle teams to follow its lead and put a proposal for the outer circle teams to vote on. Second, it can retain a right to make decisions about a specific issue. In a self-managed company, a number of fundamental rights are distributed to teams by a constitution or are linked to individual roles. Disputes between teams or individuals are supposed to be solved bilaterally or with the help of a moderator. If this fails, these disputes can be escalated to a panel with sanctioning power. This is comparable to people escalating up the chain of command in hierarchical companies, except that here the panel consists of other co-workers instead of a single manager.

Any team (and any individual team member) has a combination of positional power and democratic power at its disposal to get things done. As long as positional power—"centrality"—still exists, there remains a form of hierarchy. But in this case, the positional power is distributed by the decision of co-workers, the power is held only for a limited duration or with a limited scope, and it may be withdrawn by decisions of co-workers. All this decreases the power differential between people by replacing a regime of open-ended power with a regime of common rights.

The most important unit of the self-managed organization is the team. A team is a group of people that all hold the same rights (with the exception of rights that come with certain roles that a co-worker might have for a period of time). There are various ways to make decisions in a team: absolute voting, relative

---

59 Niels Pflaeging names this a "peach organization" (Pflaeging, 2014)

majority voting, consensus voting, or other more advanced voting mechanisms. Most self-managed teams default to advanced voting mechanisms and may agree on a case-by-case basis to use simpler voting mechanisms for the sake of faster, more efficient decisions.

Every individual is held accountable to the team(s) they are working in. Teams may decide to sanction and dismiss their members within the framework of a self-managed company's constitution. A co-worker may be a member of multiple teams, but usually they work in one team most of the time. The work in a self-managed organization can be imagined as follows:

- Nobody tells you what to do. You pull in the work you want to do yourself.
- Once you take on work, usually by taking on roles for a specific period, you are held accountable for that work.
- If you like your work to be an expression of yourself, you can do that. Should you need others, just convince them to follow you.
- If you fail to contribute enough to the team, other team members will hold you accountable.
- If your team fails to contribute enough to the organization, transparency mechanisms are in place so that the team itself will notice and change its ways of its own accord. Inner circle teams provide the necessary transparency and support.

Many workers in self-managed companies say that though the work itself did not change much under self-management, the social context of the work did. Somehow the emotions connected to certain experiences changed in this new social context, making employees perceive the same experiences in totally different ways:

- From "If I fail, I will get fired" to "Failing helps me grow and become better."
- From "I can get a call and have to go to work anytime, so I never feel as if I have time off" to "My colleagues will only call me when there is really no other solution, and I'd be happy to help them with that."
- From "I need to get this done for my boss" to "I owe it to the team."

A self-managed organization bears some resemblance to a democracy, where all power originates from the people and everyone can rise to a position of power. Then again, most self-managed organizations are *unlike* democracies, as elected representatives in (run-of-the-mill) "representative" democracies, such as a president, chancellor, minister, or mayor, are at the top of a min-isterial hierarchy and assume the role of hierarchs for a couple of years. A self-managed organization is usually much more democratic. First, instead of a limited number of representatives being elected, all representatives on any level are nominated by the people. Every team is able to hire and fire people or assign roles to co-workers within the framework of the decision-making power bestowed upon it (and sometimes codified in a constitution). Second, as a default, decisions are made by the team, although for efficiency reasons the team may grant some co-workers decision-making rights.

Today there are two major standardized organizational models for self-man-aged companies: holacracy or sociocracy. (A lesser-known variant of socioc-racy is collegial leadership. Other models, including scaled agile frameworks, such as Nexus, LeSS and SAFe, share features with those two systems, but are ultimately more multi-project management methods.) These models pro-vide excellent guidelines for running self-managed companies. However, the majority of companies have developed their own specific model of self-man-agement over time. Prominent examples are Morningstar, Gore, Patagonia, Buurtzorg, Haier, and thousands of other self-managed companies, some of which will be discussed in greater detail in later chapters.

A short history of self-managed organizations

Historically, self-management is connected to the workplace democracy movement that started in the 1920s. Experiments with workplace de-mocracy remained on the fringes of broader socialist movements such as worker liberation and unionization. In the heyday of socialism, from the 1920s to the 1960s, socialist parties and unions focused primarily on curbing the excesses of capitalism. The only real attempt to fundamentally change the governance regime inside companies has been communism, an idea far more radical than self-management in its renunciation of all private ownership of capital. There were very few cases of companies outside the social sector that implemented self-management. The most prominent examples were Mondragon, a cooperative in Spain (from 1956), Endenburg Electrotechnic (1960–1970) in the Netherlands, and Semco in Brazil (1980s). With the fall of communism in 1990, socialism has been on the retreat, too. Although worker participation is firmly entrenched in the legal systems of some Scandinavian and central European countries, the cause of liberating workers lost its momentum long ago. This is beginning to change.

The immensely increased complexity of the dawning digital age first made itself felt in the realm of software, where the DevOps movement extends lean and agile into the sphere of IT operations. This led to specialized approaches to software engineering and management, which was a fundamental re-think of traditional, hierarchically dominated ways of organizing work. The Agile Manifesto, put together by a group of frustrated programmers on a mountain retreat in Utah in 2001, captures the spirit behind this thinking:[60]

- Individuals and interactions over processes and tools.
- Working software over comprehensive documentation.
- Customer collaboration over contract negotiation.
- Responding to change over following a plan.

Despite the overwhelming success of self-management at the team- and plant-level, it has failed to scale to company level. Self-management methods tend to be harnessed by the hierarchy but altered to fit its needs, thereby losing much of their potential benefits; as a result, most managers today regard them as just another tool in the arsenal of productivity-enhancing methods. As Deming dryly noted, most managers and companies fail to realize the full benefits of—broadly speaking—lean methods, as they lack a deeper understanding of the underlying "profound system of knowledge," which is to say the mindset, the second operating system.[61]

---

60 (Kent Beck, 2001)
61 (Deming, Out of the Crisis, 2000)

The impetus for self-management today no longer stems primarily from a craving for human rights in the workplace, but from the need for organizational performance. All kinds of organizations, internet platforms, and traditional companies feel that they need new answers for the digital age and have already adapted (or are experimenting with) self-management in parts of their organizations, including Amazon, Netflix, Google, Daimler, Ford, and Michelin to name but a few. In Chapter 9: Configuring Companies with Management Practices, we look at three interesting companies that started on their self-management journey many years ago, but first let us consider the major weaknesses of the self-managed organization.

The viability of a self-managed organization

Nobel-Prize winner Elinor Ostrom, an organizational researcher specializing in analyzing complex rule systems, names three rules that all organizational systems are operated by: *operational rules*, i.e., rules governing day-to-day activities; *collective choice rules*, i.e., rules about who is eligible to participate in decisions; and *constitutional choice rules*, i.e., rules concerning participation in building the framework for the former two types of rules.[62] Hierarchies emphasize operational rules and neglect working on collective and constitutional rules. To build a more liberated company means working more (but not only) on collective and constitutional rules. That feels strange to most people.

The hierarchical way of organizing is everywhere around us, yet most people have no experience with self-managing companies and are quick to discount them. A company without a boss—how can that be? Doesn't that end up in never-ending discussions? What sense does it make to exchange the terror of a boss for the terror of the collective? For most of us, the idea of a boss-less organization seems unrealistic, radical, outlandish, even freakish.

To address these questions, let's start by first looking at what makes working in a hierarchy so attractive to us on a personal level. I think we look for three things from a good boss:

---

62 (Ostrom, Understanding Institutional Diversity , 2005)

1. To make competent decisions
2. To provide the right directions
3. To manage in a way that gets people engaged

Can a self-managed company do these things, too? Can it make the boss superfluous? Can a group make competent decisions? Imagine that all the managers have been demoted and a hierarchy of individuals has been replaced by a network of teams. All of a sudden, the ways groups make decisions is all-important. What we need is good-quality decisions, made with speed and efficiency—exactly what we would expect from a strong leader. Can a collective of teams coordinate itself as effectively as a strong leader? Let's explore this question.

To get a decision right, every leader needs a number of things:[63]

- Full information (i.e., all the facts)
- A valid model of reality
- The capability to predict outcomes
- The motivation to decide in the interest of the company
- The capability to ensure the execution of the decision
- The capability to learn from failure and success

A strong leader is likely to consult with capable and trusted advisors. A strong leader takes in all the information no matter how contradictory, weighs it according to their own model(s) of reality, predicts outcomes, and decides. Afterward, they also encourage learning in the decision-making process. A leader making consistently good decisions is likely to be a leader who takes advice in a process of systematic thinking.

However, an individual decision-maker may lack the ability, the incentive, or the discipline to go through such a process at all. Moreover, in a hierarchy people will limit the amount of information they reveal because of the power differential.

---

63 Decision theory is a complex multidisciplinary field of research. It is easy to get lost in this field, but as an entry-level popular book I suggest (Silver, 2012)

They will choose to reveal only the information, opinions, concerns, or preferences that they anticipate will produce a positive response from their superior. The power differential systematically distorts and corrupts information flow in hierarchies. Consultation with co-workers is a prerequisite for making good decisions, yet there is systematic bias against it in the hierarchy.

Many of the real-life problems that undermine the making of good decisions can be overcome by making decisions in a group. First, the diversity of people in a group leads to a richer set of information, more varied views on reality and—given a proper process—an improved ability to predict outcomes. Second, the myopic self-interest of any single individual will not bias the decision as much. Third, the commitment to executing decisions tends to be higher, as everyone is involved and invested in the decision-making process. Fourth, the group can be a much better place to learn from success and failure of decisions if the group engages in reflective work designs—which we will encounter in Chapter 8: Management Practices for Development.

However, many things can also go wrong in group decisions. Just as the human mind is subject to a large number of biases, groups are prone to other biases that limit their ability to make decisions. The rogue factors in group decisions are the social dynamics within the team. The pitfalls of group decisions include (but are not limited to):

- *Groupthink*. The more homogeneous a group, the less diverse the information that people will bring and the more dissenting information will be suppressed.
- *Extremism*. The less well-acquainted people inside a group are, the more a group tends towards extreme, polarized decisions. Arguments inside a more anonymous group are often won by a skillful agitator or demagogue. Convincing others often requires the sharpening of arguments to such an extent that nuances, contradictions, and moderation are all drowned by simple messages and (apparently) simple truths.
- *Negative politics*. If people choose not to share all the information they have, a group decision becomes biased towards outcomes that

are based only on the information that has been shared. Withholding information or briefing a group in a biased manner is a powerful political tool—just like giving a boss a biased briefing.

- *Too much compromise.* Group decisions tend to be compromises. Things are added to and stripped from a proposal to make a decision acceptable. While compromises are often useful, the outcome can be watered-down solutions that are no longer viable or merely become inconsequential half-measures.

So, who is the better decision-maker, an individual or a group? It is impossible to say what is worse: individual biases that are inherent in human cognition or the combination of individual and social biases that are inherent in a group. However, research has shown that in complex environments excellent teams are able to outperform even individuals with excellent decision-making abilities.[64] However, bad teams also regularly underperform people with bad decision-making skills. In other words, a team can be extraordinarily brilliant or extraordinarily poor—the spread of performance is much wider than in individuals.[65] For example, what some individuals can achieve in a week, others need ten weeks to achieve. For teams, the spread of performance is much wider, sometimes as much as 1:200 weeks. Figure 3 illustrates this point.

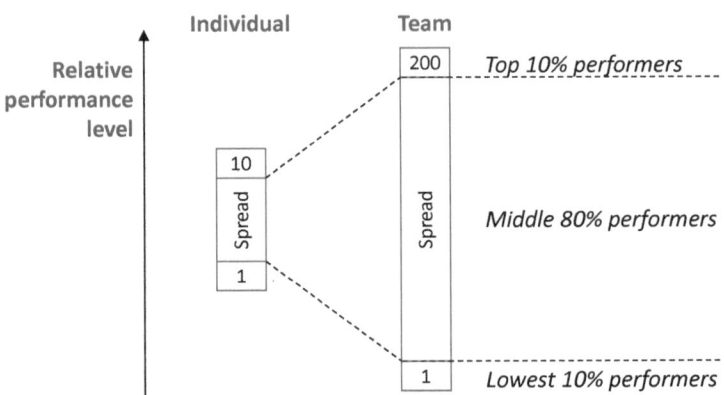

Figure 3 Individual vs. team performance

---

64 (Tetlock, 2016)
65 (Hackman, 2002)

The values given in the figure above are based on fragmentary evidence and cannot be generalized.[66] However, if the conditions for successful teamwork are given, a team is likely to outperform a group of individual actors by several orders of magnitude.[67] Given this performance differential, where should you focus your managerial efforts—on the individual or the team?

If only one could find a way to reliably unlock the performance potential of the team! A significant part of this challenge is to "de-bias" the decision-making processes of a team, and thankfully it turns out that it is easier to de-bias teams than it is to de-bias individuals. For individuals, mental openness, self-restraint, and self-discipline are required if de-biasing is to be successful. De-biasing yourself means opening yourself up to doubts, which is always unpleasant, and in a hierarchy such openness may even make you appear hesitant. [68]

De-biasing groups, however, is much more actionable. According to Richard Hackman, who specializes in team research, de-biasing of group decisions can be achieved by providing an environment that is conducive to excellent team performance:[69]

- *Groupthink* can be limited by making decisions in a more diverse team.
- *Extremism* can be limited by keeping a team stable over a longer period of time, so that people know each other and discuss facts instead of agitating their point of view.
- *Negative politics* can be limited by supplying a psychologically safe environment to speak up, coupled with a strong purpose and clearly communicated performance targets of the organization.
- The tendency towards *compromises* can be countered by keeping performance targets high so that more radical solutions are unavoidable.

De-biasing can thus be built into the work design of a company. It is much easier to adopt work designs in companies than it is to change what goes on

---

66 (Sutherland, 2015)
67 (Hackman, 2002)
68 Good advice on de-biasing can be found in (Gino, 2013); or (Kahnemann, 2011)
69 (Hackman, 2002)

individual decision-makers' minds. One can observe whether or not work designs have been used in a group; whether or not mental steps have been performed in the mind of a human decision-maker cannot be observed, however.

That being said, there are still two important weaknesses inherent in group decisions that cannot be mitigated effectively. First, group decisions take time. The very advantage of group decisions—a careful weighing of information, discussion, and voting—is time-consuming. Therefore, group decisions need to be used sparingly and only for important, complex decisions. For all other daily and routine decisions, it is generally more efficient to let individuals decide. Therefore, in self-managed companies, authority for most day-to-day operational decisions is entrusted to people at the frontline—that is, in the outer circles. Asking for approval from the team or one of the central teams should be an exception.

The second major weakness of group decisions is that providing an environment for effective teams is no minor feat.[70] An organization aiming to fully benefit from group decisions needs to replace individual with collective accountability. In a hierarchy, the central pillar that encourages people to make good decisions is accountability. If you make a bad decision, you will be held accountable. The self-managed company does not have the luxury of this one strong pillar; shared accountability means diluted individual accountability and may result in irresponsible behaviors. It can only work if teams are embedded in an environment that encourages people to take collective responsibility seriously. Such an environment requires a shared purpose, customer centricity, freedom, transparency, learning, supportive leadership, exploration, and practice. Giving up the hierarchy means losing the central pillar upon which coordination rests in hierarchical organizations. New pillars need to be put into place, and we will explore this further in Chapter 11: A Compass to Master Complexity.

This is not to say that individual accountability does not exist in self-managed companies. People are accountable for the commitments they make to their team or their peers. In an effort to pinpoint individual accountability, some self-managed companies invest much more effort than most hierarchical

70 (Hackman, 2002)

companies in defining and maintaining role descriptions.[71] Accountability in a self-managed company is on a collective and individual level, not on a managerial level. No one is accountable for others, but everyone is accountable for themselves and the collective.

In a hierarchy, everyone is ultimately subject to the whims of a manager. In a self-managed company, everyone is subject to the whims of the teams, but no single team holds as much power as a hierarchical manager. In hierarchies, companies can only predict a manager's performance and hope for the best, as we discussed in the previous chapter. The influence over managers is limited to appeals, and a bad apple, especially at higher levels, can cause extreme havoc. A hierarchy can only hope for well-behaved managers, whereas a self-managed company can actively work on maintaining the conditions for its own effectiveness.

Can a group provide the right strategic directions?

Making good decisions is not the same as making good *strategic* decisions. For strategic decision-making, you need to think long-term, understand the strategic intent, and never lose sight of the bigger picture. It takes constancy of purpose. It takes the ability to anticipate, to plot one's moves in advance, to see possibilities, and to maximize one's options with every move. It means accepting losses and trade-offs for the sake of the bigger picture—and taking some clever gambles from time to time.

Generally, individuals (and therefore hierarchies) find it easier to act strategically than a group does. Design-by-committee is often a recipe for mediocrity, whether that design is for a strategy or a product. Given the right setting, teams may be able to come up with better decisions than individuals on a case-by-case basis but may still fail to see the interconnections between decisions. In every team, there is a tendency to compromise, even when more radical moves are really needed to master the situation at hand. Networks are spontaneously creative, but they are not strategic.[72]

---

71 This a central feature of Holacracy. See (Roberston, 2015)
72 (Ferguson, 2018)

It is of critical importance for any company to get its strategic direction right, so should we give up on self-managed organizations? I believe the answer is no. There are a number of caveats in the logic above that often invalidate the superiority of the hierarchy. First, there are not many management positions where deep strategic thinking is actually necessary. Most management positions are about efficient execution and very little about strategizing. Strategy is the realm of top management. Is it worth embracing a hierarchy with all its defects and forgoing the benefits of self-managed companies in the hope that this will enable a few people at the top to make better decisions?

Second, these few people at the top who are supposed to be master strategists might not have any gift for strategy at all. The hierarchy can only do a better job of providing strategic directions if it gets the prediction about a top manager's strategic capability right. Moreover, strategic thinking is not the only skill for which managers are hired: reliability, social conformity, the ability to position and market oneself to decision-makers are just a few of the factors that result in a manager ending up in a top position. Having a "strategic thinker" in a top management position is often just incidental.

Third, strategic decision-making of an analytical kind is really hard in dynamic and complex markets, where having a step-by-step plan is less important than sensing the market and reacting quickly. Here, networks excel over hierarchies.

Fourth, a self-managed organization can mitigate against the lack of strategic thinking by, for example, giving itself a strong purpose that puts decisions into strategic contexts and guides them. This can be done by delegating all strategic decisions to a team of strategists, or even a single person who holds the role of strategist.

In sum, in a somewhat predictable environment it might be beneficial to take the gamble that a clever strategist will end up in a top management position. However, if you think that business strategy is more about evolution than chess, more about adaptability and creative problem-solving than rigid execution, you are better off organizing your company in a more self-managing way.

General Stanley McChrystal, who commanded the US counter-insurgency forces in Afghanistan from 2009 to 2010, said of the complexity of his job: "I stopped playing chess and became a gardener."[73] Maybe you should consider becoming a gardener, or an environment builder, too.

Can a group engage people more consistently?

A good boss engages people. However, a hierarchy can only hope for capable, motivating managers. Once a manager is in a position, there is not much to be done about it. The empirical data says it all: only 15 percent of people are actively engaged at work in traditional companies. People strive for autonomy, and to be treated as a child is scarcely motivating.

In contrast to this, a self-managed company is designed to address the intrinsic motivations of people and should be able to create more engagement. How much more—whether 20 percent or 40 percent—is unknown. Conclusive evidence is not (yet) there at a company-level, and even the Gallup study on engagement level is highly controversial, as shown by Philipp Rosenzweig.[74] However, there is ample evidence at the team-level of the effect of well-tended work environments on people's engagement as well as economic and social outcomes. The main difference is that a self-managed company can actively work on maintaining the conditions for its own effectiveness. It is less about appeals to "good leadership" and more about organizational environment building. If the environment is right, engagement will follow.

We have seen that healthy, effective teams outperform even highly capable individuals in decision-making and engagement. Although teams struggle to be as strategic as individuals can be, there are ways to safeguard against this weakness. All it takes for the magic happen is organizational environment building, a skill which we shall explore in all the remaining chapters of this book. Table 3 compares the performance of the hierarchy and the self-managed organization. Most of the time, organizations will choose a

---

73 (McChrystal, Silverman, Tantum, & Chris, 2015)
74 (Rosenzweig, The Halo Effect, 2007)

combination of both, as we shall see in Chapter 9: Configuring Companies with Management Practices.

Criteria	Hierarchy	Circle
Control	Direct	More Indirect
Stability	Robust	Varying
Clarity	High	Varying
Rationality (Efficiency)	High	Exploring
Agility	Low	High
Capability to handle low complexity	High	High
Capability to handle high complexity	Low	High
Corrosiveness (Biases)	High	Low
Innovation	Low	High
Human growth	Low	High
	Use to execute business	Use to evolve businesses

Table 3 Comparison: Effectiveness of hierarchy vs. circle organization structure

Which organizational system—hierarchy or self-management—is better suited to a company depends on the complexity and the stability of the business environment. The lower the complexity and the higher the stability, the more attractive is the hierarchy. Conversely, the higher the complexity and the lower the stability, the better self-managed forms of organizations perform.

Hierarchy is a great tool for executing business operations in stable, low-complexity environments. If there are few unknowns and changes are limited or predictable, then there is no need to utilize the "wisdom of the collective" and engagement can be induced by traditional rewards and measurement. In all other circumstances, use self-management.

How can we judge whether a business environment is complex or not? It may feel as though complexity is rising, but is it really? Technological complexity is definitely rising, and it pulls companies along on its path to ever-greater complexity. However, the world has always been immensely complex, but only recently has the awareness of this complexity entered numerous scientific fields and the public consciousness. Anthropologists speak of "an ever-increasing circle of our concern" of human consciousness.[75] In a hyper-competitive tech-nological world—populated with attention-starved consumers, set on a stage of global social and ecological fragility—ignoring complexity might no longer be such a clever choice. As Avner Greif, a professor of economics at Stanford University, puts it: "All organizations impose constraints and provide opportu-nities."[76] It is just that hierarchical organizations emphasize constraints more, while self-managed organizations emphasize opportunities more.

Self-managed organizations feel strange and uncomfortable to most of us; it takes some time to get used to them and much more skill to operate them successfully than the hierarchy. With the exception of supervisory boards, group decision-making is alien to businesses. Yet it is one of the best-re-searched areas in the social sciences, and Western society relies on it and has prospered under a regime of group decision-making we call democracy.

The French philosopher Michel Foucault terms the particular set of organized practices and structures through which citizens are governed as "governmen-tality."[77] Every regime of common rights regulates power as well as material and social exchange, and it fosters its own types of mindsets amongst those living within it. The question is: which governmentality do we want? Do we want—or can we afford—to continue with exploitative hierarchy? We have expelled the autocratic hierarchy in favor of democracy in our private lives, but in business, empowerment and the workers' rights movement have failed to dislodge the entrenched hierarchy. Nevertheless, it seems that the weight of companies' ambition for performance, the need to embrace less exploitative practices in business and society, and the ecological limits of the planet are causing nu-merous new forms of governmentalities to blossom in companies in significant numbers. Theodor Adorno, a professor of sociology and philosophy, writes that "systems of ruling immigrate into people".[78] Chances are, society turned a blind eye on the systems we use to run companies for too long.

---

75 (Burke, 1978)
76 (Greif, 2006)
77 (Foucault, 2008)
78 (Adorno, 2003) "Herrschaft wandert in die Menschen ein." Translation into English by the author,

Before we address how to build more liberated organizations, it is necessary to pull an important and increasingly prominent player in to the picture: technology.

The technology-centric network

In this digital age, companies are bound to become networks of companies, people, and technology. It is not only that technology weaves itself into markets, communication, decision-making, business processes, and daily work routines. On top of that, technology is becoming more and more of an independent actor in the economic space, on a par with humans and companies.

Technology makes the networked organization more viable

First, technologies are clearly a game-changer when it comes to the benefits and costs of coordination. Technologies that come to mind are messaging apps, mobile devices, corporate clouds, and transactional back-end systems. All those systems in place today already resemble the nervous system of companies. No organizational theory today can fail to take the tremendous new possibilities in the realm of human-to-machine and machine-to-machine collaboration into account. Interfacing corporate systems to one another, or offering new ways for humans to interact with these systems, means tapping into the nervous systems of companies—and with artificial intelligence advancing, tapping directly into the brains of an organization, too.

The viability of the network versus the hierarchy has always been dependent on technology. Larger companies only became possible with the invention of bookkeeping in the fifteenth century, global companies only became possible with the invention of the telegraph in the nineteenth century, and the digital technologies of today are shifting the underlying vectors of costs and benefits again. Digital technologies enable companies and people to collaborate differently with one another, giving rise to new possibilities for arranging the network of human economic activity within corporate structures and beyond—i.e., creating new "governmentalities."

Free-agent forms of organization, such as Wikipedia, the Apache project (the technology underneath most web servers), or Linux are hugely successful examples of new governmentalities emerging in the digital age. These networked organizations are made up of people who contribute solely of their own volition. Technological progress tilts the scale between hierarchy and network in the network's favor because it makes communication and distributed decision-making easier.

Technology coordinates networks of companies

The second, and more fundamental, point is that technology changes the very nature of human work itself. More and more, technology dictates not only how humans organize but what humans do.

To understand this, it is necessary to look at the way today's digital technologies work. A good example is application programming interfaces (APIs). These are standardized interfaces that enable software programs or users to interact with technology. Technically, these interfaces can take more or less automated forms, such as electronic data interchange, interactive forms on websites, simple FTP servers with data, remote procedure calls (RPCs), or micro-services. For the sake of simplicity, we will group all these technologies under the label API. Although they are as old as software is, they only became ubiquitous and strategic in the last two decades. The rise of the platform business, which is often seen as the most desirable business model to pursue, is very much linked to the rise of APIs.

Most digital companies—among them Amazon, Google, Netflix, and Facebook, but also manufacturers such as Siemens, GE, and Haier—have built their businesses on APIs. APIs offer a way to interact with a company that is standardized, reliable, fast, and efficient, which often eliminates the need for human-to-human interaction. Amazon, for example, conducts nearly all communication and transactions, both internally and with its external marketplace sellers or customers, via API. The principal characteristics of APIs are:[79]

---

79 (Wood, Lauret, Sandoval, & Bill , 2016)

- They allow access to business functions and services in real-time.
- They structure information into clearly expected inputs and outputs.
- Their use is optional and not mandatory if the goal can be achieved in other ways.
- They are immutable: users have to comply with their standards.
- They can be stacked on one another to solve highly complicated problems. These "mash-ups" can then be published to the world as new APIs, starting a cycle of innovation.
- APIs describe the ways in which companies want to be engaged.

Most people regard APIs as cheap, automated ways of interacting, rather like how automated call-center systems are used to qualify a call prior to a human taking over the interaction. But nowadays APIs are even used to coordinate product designers and engineers building new turbines, planes, cars, refrigerators, toothbrushes, or apps. The more companies digitize, the more their interaction with suppliers, partners, and customers becomes a service that can be delivered via an API. A company coordinates its activity both internally and with the outside world according to the nature of the APIs it offers. APIs act as coordinators, aligning the activity of companies and people, and they commit companies and people to courses of action.

It could be argued that it is humans who are coordinating, because they design and publish APIs. While it is true that humans provide a purpose for APIs and influence their design and underlying algorithms, it is also true that those algorithms are becoming more and more complex, interwoven, and intelligent as technology progresses over time. Yet, the complexity of all the APIs of a company like Amazon or Siemens is very hard to understand and control. The more technology progresses, the more humans tend to become influencers rather than shapers of organizational reality.[80]

In a reaction to the increasing complexity and optionality of IT, the people developing and maintaining the systems behind APIs are already becoming more and more decentralized and self-organized themselves. It is no wonder that

---

80 (Harari, 2016)

the agile movement started in software engineering; the options and bene-fits of digital technology are simply too numerous to be controlled centrally by a manager. With the API economy inexorably advancing, the rest of the company will need to learn to master that complexity, too. Just look at a typical Agile, Scrum, DevOps, or Lean team today: IT and businesspeople work side-by-side in a more and more self-managed way. With ever-more-complex technologies making humans focus more on doing things that help to master that complexity, it is clear that technology is dictating not only *how* things are done but also *what* is done.

Technology changes everyone's work

The API economy is not just important for coordinating a company with the outside world; it is also becoming increasingly central to coordinating the inner workings of a company. What started with email and electronic calendars is nowadays supplemented with an increasing array of communication tools such as instant messaging, video conferences, social media, and collaborative workspaces. The functional depth and integration of the software people use to do work is constantly increasing. The day-to-day administration of, for example, expense forms, travel plans, reports and planning applications is now performed using cloud-based apps instead of standalone Microsoft Excel forms. The interactivity of these apps is increasing all the time, so that people can gain more and more value from interacting with software. The push to "electrify and automate" work was the first wave of the industrial revolution. The second wave, which is already making itself felt, is to "cognify and engage" people.

Technology dominates the way humans collaborate—and is likely to do so increasingly as it progresses. This relationship between organizations and technology is known as Conway's law: "Organizations which design systems are constrained to produce designs which are copies of the communication structures of these organizations."[81] As people tend to split up into teams to work on systems, their social interactions—that is to say, the dividing lines be-

---

81   (Conway, 1968)

tween their different areas of responsibility—determine how the system will work. If social relations are deficient while a system is being built, the system will probably reveal these defects.

Today, we see Conway's law being reversed: technology is starting to design organizations, making people do things and organizing itself into structures that are able to benefit from these ever-more-complex technologies, such as agile or self-managed teams. In other words, humans are serving the needs of technology.

In the digital age, managing is no longer just concerned with human interactions. More and more it's about human-machine interaction and machine-to-machine interaction. This adds heavily to business complexity, making the traditional hierarchy a less attractive option.

The omni-networked organization

Imagine an ultra-networked company. First, such a company would itself be a network of companies. Second, these companies would combine hierarchical and self-managed structures. Third, it would run on a technological core, a nervous system that connects and structures how people work both inside and outside a company.

Probably one of the best examples of an omni-networked company is the Chinese conglomerate Haier, a global manufacturer of household appliances with revenue of US$30 billion and 60,000 employees. Haier comprises over 3,000 companies with a maximum size of about 150 people (the Dunbar number), each of which uses a mixture of self-management and hierarchy. Haier employs a backbone of IT systems that defines the way it interacts with its people, companies, customers, communities, and suppliers, to such an extent that the boundaries between who is working in the organization and who is outside become blurred. A person or a company present "on the Haier platform"—be they employee or freelancer, team or company, supplier or customer—can be engaged with in all the ways the designers of Haier's organizational system intended the company ecosystem to be engaged with. The important thing for Haier is that whichever entity is present on the system, it is playing by the rules assigned to that specific entity on a playing field that provides everyone connected to the platform the freedom to act. Omni-networked organizations such as Haier seek to benefit from all four dimensions of the organizational network:

1. *Macro-level.* They employ small entrepreneurial-led companies.
2. *Micro-level.* They use self-management within these companies.
3. *Technology-level.* They use a technology-intensive core to achieve co-ordination and economies of scale.
4. *Ecosystem.* They make the external, vertical, and horizontal borders of companies permeable.

This is of course a daunting, if not impenetrable, task. It requires a map and a compass to design omni-networked organizations, but more on that in Chapter 11: A Compass to Master Complexity. Let's close this chapter with a broader look at the impacts of our current way of distributing power in companies on the economy and society as a whole.

The dual mode economy: A bias towards exploitation

According to Peter Drucker, "The right structure does not guarantee results, but the wrong structure aborts results and smothers even the best directed efforts."[82] In other words, hierarchies exploit. The vast power differentials, the self-interested actors, the asymmetrical information—all of these elements provide hierarchies with a bias towards exploitation and stagnation. That bias is systemic; it can be mitigated somewhat by well-meaning leadership, but it is always there.

Given the size of the technology sector—seven out of ten of the most valuable companies in the world in 2019 are technology companies—and the immense capitalization of the start-up scene, it is overwhelmingly clear that

---

82 (Drucker, 2012)

capital has already given up on traditional, established companies. Established companies are neither agile nor innovative enough to prosper in the digital age, so they remain in a permanent state of exploitation, aggravating the sclerosis and all but ensuring their withering and eventual replacement by more agile competitors. One might call this creative destruction at work.

I am all in favor of creative destruction: let inefficient companies be thrown into the dustbin of history. The problem with creative destruction in a dual-mode economy—i.e., established (and withering) companies exploiting their market while younger companies are innovating—is that it leaves the greater part of the economy and its workers in exploitation mode. The effects of the "double whammy" of running companies by an inherently exploitative hierarchy to execute what is undoubtedly an exploitative strategy—milking the market—is contributing to what we can see every day around us: income equality rising as never before among the working poor, environmental decline, and the rise of authoritarian regimes that pit people against one another. Keeping the majority of the workforce in a business model centered on exploitation is a recipe for disaster for all involved.

If company leaders become focused on exploitation, the agonizing death of companies becomes a self-fulfilling prophecy. If the certain dollar in your hand today is more important than the risky couple of dollars that could be earned tomorrow by investing today, opportunities will be lost. If the corporate mindset is focused on fulfilling forecasts to shareholders, risk-taking will be limited. People inside the company may feel that they could serve customers better were it not for the dynamics of the system that are all geared to producing predictable short-term profits. This will leave people with few freedoms and resources to act on opportunities. Worst of all, this "governmentality" is systematically breeding a culture and individual mindset centered on exploitation; in other words, everyone out for themselves.

If we continue to run companies based on this system of dual exploitation of both people and the planet, we undermine the validity not only of the whole capitalist system, but of life itself. I am not saying that exploitation is not human: clearly it is. There are, however, ways of running companies that are less biased towards exploitation—ways that liberate us from the belief that money for sub-mission is the only way to hook people up to companies, ways that let people engage because they want to be involved in something bigger than themselves. We have a choice to design the business systems we want. The hierarchy is neither agile nor innovative enough for the digital age. Empowerment does not work well in practice, as it can never be applied consistently, if one relies on appeals to managers to refrain from using their powers. The networked company, especially the self-managed company, offers much that the digital age needs (and is favored by the inner workings of technology), but it is much harder to master than running a company through hierarchy.

If we could make empowerment more consistent and therefore impactful, companies could journey more safely towards greater self-management, combining elements of both the hierarchy and the network as required by the situation at hand. I term such companies *liberated companies*. A liberated company is a learning organization that evolves its work designs holistically towards a more egalitarian distribution of power. It aims to free people from oppression and set itself on the trajectory of technology, which will maximize the number of its options over time.

A liberated company internalizes creative destruction in its organizational DNA instead of externalizing it to the invisible hand of the market. It is likely to be more successful economically, socially, ecologically—and ultimately, it is more humane. To be a liberated company does not mean having achieved a certain utopian state; it simply means to continuously strive towards betterment.

In the digital age, liberated companies are likely to outperform any competitor by way of their agility and inventiveness. They can also answer both the need for an environmental and social upgrade of economics ("a green new deal") and meet the competitive performance challenges of the digital age.

Dark Arts

- The defects of the networked organization (i.e., indecisiveness and lack of cohesion) can be overcome by a strengthening of informal ties and effective use of digital technology.
- Self-management is an essential element of a networked organization.
- The hierarchy is the pillar on which coordination of conventional companies rests. If this pillar falls, there needs to be multiple pillars to keep coordination up—organizing becomes more complex and focused on building great environments to work in.
- A hierarchy can only hope for well-behaved managers. A self-managed company can actively work on maintaining the conditions for its own effectiveness.
- A liberated company aims to combine the virality of the network with the stability of focus of the hierarchy.
- In the digital age, a company's organization is not only about human interaction; it is also more and more about human-machine interaction.
- Companies become platforms of interactions, where humans tend to become more influencers than shapers of organizational reality.
- Companies will become more omni-networked over time. Their external, vertical, and horizontal borders will become much more fluid.
- We have the historic chance to leave behind the systematic biases toward exploitation and sclerosis that come with the hierarchy in favor of a more wholesome and liberating model.

Further Reading:

- Peter Block (2003) *Stewardship* (Berrett-Koehler Publishing)
- Frederick Laloux (2014) *Reinventing Organizations* (Nelson Parker)
- Nils, Pflaeging (2014) *Organize for Complexity* (Betacodex Publishing)
- Gary Hamel (2016) *What Matters Now* (Jossey-Bass)

PART II:
A MAP OF WORK DESIGNS

■ Chapter 4: A Map for Organizing in the Digital Age

The future can't be predicted, but it can be envisioned and brought lovingly into being. Systems can't be controlled, but they can be designed and redesigned.
– Donella Meadows, 2001[83]

We have seen that technology favors networked companies over authoritarian hierarchies. At the same time, the new, open, and positive governmentality created by more networked companies will help to overcome the bias towards exploitation inherent in traditional companies. This shift will benefit everyone, including companies, individuals, and society as a whole. However, creating more networked companies is a huge challenge. The remainder of this book is about this challenge. Let us start with a story.

The Tale of Eric and Marc

Meet Eric, the employee, and Marc, the manager. Marc makes a living by chopping and selling wood. Eric has just signed a contract to work for Marc. This makes Eric an employee and Marc a manager. With his signature, Eric has agreed to follow Marc's orders. Disobeying these orders is an option, but it comes at the risk of being fired.

Marc directs Eric to chop some wood, using the most basic form of work design: the direct order. The next day, Marc orders Eric to chop some wood and stack it in a neat pile in the shack. On the third day, Marc is late. Eric sees a stack of wood, and being human and not an automaton, starts to chop it, as he did on day one. Without knowing it, Eric has developed a job description for himself: "My job is to chop wood and stack it." The job description is another basic form of work design. It saves Marc the manager the time and effort of directing Eric.

---

83 (Meadows, 2001)

Unlike a robot, Eric the employee is able to see the work and do it without being given orders. Marc may continue to supervise Eric, but it might be a better use of his time to cart the wood to the market and sell it.

One day, after a heavy rainfall, Eric sees that the roof of the shack where the firewood is stored needs repair. Without being told to, he fixes the roof. Eric uses his judgment of Marc's interest and decides to act autonomously. Marc has not directed Eric to do this, but Eric has developed a sense of purpose in his work and feels responsible for it. Marc comes back later in the day and wonders why Eric has not produced his usual stack size of firewood, but he sees that the shack is repaired. Marc could reprimand Eric for not making the numbers (i.e., not producing the usual stack of firewood), but he decides to praise Eric for having taken the initiative and prioritizing repairing the shack over his chopping duties, thereby embracing another two basic work designs: feedback and delegation. Eric is no longer just following orders, but he is empowered to do other things necessary to keep up the production of firewood.

Why does Marc opt to praise Eric and accept him acting autonomously? Marc, hard-pressed to make a living out of his business, perceives these work designs as being efficient. In his mind, Eric has saved him a lot of trouble, as wet firewood doesn't sell. Marc may not know it, but he has developed the performance hypothesis in his mind that job descriptions, feedback, and delegation produce better results than simply ordering Eric around. Marc benefits from adopting those work designs. Eric likes being responsible, too, which is part of why these work designs are working. But even if Marc didn't care about Eric, he knows he would hurt himself and his business by not employing these practices.

Without knowing it, Marc has developed new work designs based on the things he does or chooses not to do. Being a clever manager, he sticks with those things that bring results and discards those that are wasteful for performance. Like every successful entrepreneur, he is constantly updating his ideas of how work should be done. Over time, Marc might decide to adopt other work designs, such as:

- A regular, weekly meeting to discuss issues.
- Providing a budget to Eric that he can spend on axes or saws.
- A bonus scheme based on Eric's productivity.
- Job sharing, so that Eric assists Marc at the market from time to time to gain a bigger picture of his duties and exposure to customers.
- Annual objective setting and performance review to clarify high-level targets for Eric's work.

Marc allowed Eric to use his own initiative and repair the shack; Eric did this not because he was ordered to but on his own initiative. Marc thus embraced a work design that is stronger than traditional, task-oriented delegation—he delegated decision-making powers to Eric. Marc has reconfigured the work design of his company. Marc the manager will introduce and maintain work designs if he expects that these are helpful for his business.

The point of the story is that every entrepreneur, manager, and co-worker has ideas—which we call work designs—about how work should be done. We use these ideas as heuristics, which in a time-pressed business let us make better, quicker, and more efficient decisions on how work should be done, how to get people to do things, and how to organize and manage tasks.

Every time people collaborate with each other in their day-to-day work, they are using work design: for example, following business processes, conducting meetings, creating reports, giving feed-back, carrying out reviews, providing approvals, making decisions, giving appraisals, and running projects. Work designs are ways of coordinating people's efforts in a team, unit, or company.

Work designs

Work, according to the Merriam Webster dictionary, is "to perform or carry through a task requiring sustained effort or continuous repeated operations."[84] On that basis, "work designs are the patterns of actions used repeatedly to get work done."[85]

---

84   https://www.merriam-webster.com/dictionary/work retrieved on 20 June 2019
85   This way of thinking about companies is what is called in organizational science a neo-institutional view of the company (Maggio & Powell, 2012); or (Scott, 2014).

This way of thinking about companies is based on a "neo-institutional" view of the company, a prosperous school of organizational theory. Work designs are the meaning-laden and action-oriented foundations of organizations—and organizing means to be attending to the configurational logics that produce organized activities.[86]

Four excellent books that describe the foundations for much of what liberated companies are about are Ellen Langer's *Mindfulness*, Brene Brown's *Daring Greatly*, Daniel Kahneman's *Thinking Fast and Slow*, and David Allen's *Getting Things Done*.[87] This book's focus is not on individual but on group-level productivity. Every group, every company, every co-worker and every manager has certain expectations about how work should be done and therefore practices certain work designs. At the group level, two different types of work designs can be distinguished: business processes and management practices. Business processes directly tackle business outcomes. Management practices are more indirect; they focus on the way humans collaborate with each other on the meta-level of work.

The way that business processes and management practices are set up in a company impacts its effectiveness as an organization, as well as the way people and their relations develop or stagnate. Business processes that deny people choices and leave them no space to express themselves can be as detrimental as management practices that do the same. For the sake of simplicity, this book focuses on management practices; we will mostly be using the term "work design," with "management practices" only used where the specific focus is the meta-level of work. The figure below provides an overview.

---

86 I am paraphrasing Scott here, smuggling in the term "work designs." See (Scott, 2014) p. 264-265.

87 See bibliography at the end of this book.

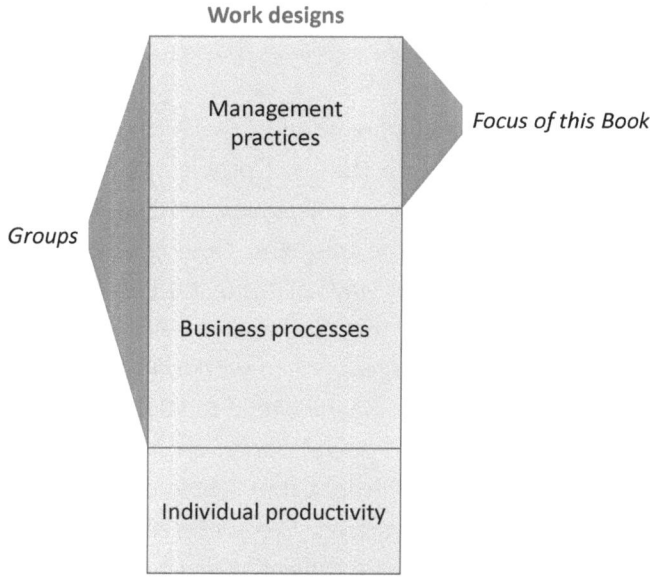

Figure 4 A taxonomy of work designs

The use of management practices is not only unavoidable but is also not limited to managers. They are employed by everyone in the organization who is trying to structure human collaboration on every level. It is therefore important to get these management practices right.

How we acquire work designs

Work designs may be the result of conscious effort, but they are more often acquired—i.e., made one's own—by habit or imitation than by deliberate reflection. Over time, an organization tends to acquire and unify a characteristic set of work designs ("the way things are done here") that become a part of a company's culture—an established, socially accepted, and effective pattern of human collaboration. Work designs are learned through experience, education, and training and are applied to the specific situations we find in a business. There are two caveats to this. First, all work designs are heuristics—a rule for making decisions based on an approximation of the truth. Work designs are practical—good enough, but only occasionally optimal. The notion of "optimal" suggests that reality can be measured, which is usually impossible;

and in any case, the costs of investigating a better solution would outweigh the benefits.

The second problem is far more serious. Once things work to an acceptable degree, we tend to focus on the next problem, such as individual careers, bonuses, satisfying superiors or colleagues, working on strategy, implementing systems, or expanding the business. Getting work done becomes more important than finding better ways of doing it. Peter Drucker's comment that "management is a craft" and that "too few people seek perfection in it" illustrates the tendency of managers not to work on the way they get people to do things.[88] Consequently, companies tend to stick to their current ways even more than individuals do, as social norms always reinforce behaviors. Not only does people's thinking atrophy, but whole companies become resistant to changing their ways of working. Every leader needs to spend some time finding better ways to get work done if they do not wish to become merely an administrative, rubber-stamping bureaucrat. But seeking better work designs is not easy, and the focus on rationality and measurement makes managers systematically vulnerable to blind spots. The "fog of business" makes the causes and effects of work designs very hard to spot.

Work designs are the essence of companies

One of the first people who sought to pierce the fog of business was Frederick Winslow Taylor in the early nineteenth century. Taylorism is at the heart of rational, analytical, impersonal, and scientific analysis of work processes—all of which are hallmarks of a manager's self-understanding. But with their day-to-day focus on measuring and making the numbers and resolving problems, managers have little time to think about work designs. Even if they do have time, the causalities are often unclear and the measurements have a tendency to be hazardous.

Many experienced managers, however, especially at a high level, know that belief, worldview, mindset, abstract systems of work, and company culture matter a lot to companies. In the digital age, more than ever, firms need to learn to work with all these imponderables. The complexity of modernity can

88 (Drucker, The Effective Executive , 2017)

only be mastered by adopting a more complex worldview. If they are to identify their blind spots, managers need to reconcile their bias for action with the need to think more deeply about organizations.

So, what are these blind spots? Professor Robert Kegan, an organizational psychologist, segments a company into four different quadrants based on two dimensions:[89] the level (from individual to organizational), and the degree of tangibility of what people do or feel at work (from work designs to beliefs). The four resulting quadrants are illustrated in Table 4.

	Organizations	Individual

Exterior (Observable)	■ Business performance **Hand**
	 ■ Business objectives
	 ■ Known problems
	 ■ Work Designs
	    ■ Staffing patterns
	    ■ Recruitment and retention
	    ■ Value proposition (for people)
	    ■ Leadership
	    ■ Government structure
	    ■ Goals and targets
	    ■ Resource allocation (capital, time etc.)
	    ■ Patterns of association (teams, meetings etc.)
	    ■ Rewards
	    ■ Forecasting Quadrant I
		■ My role definition
		 ■ Individual capabilities **Head**
		   (What I know, what I can do)
		 ■ Individual problems and challenges
		
		 Quadrant II

Interior (Beliefs)	■ Mission/ deep purpose of the organization ■ Org. culture ■ Org. health (vs. performance) ■ Collective developmental maturity ■ Collective immunity to change Quadrant III	■ Personal values and motivation ■ Hardwired personality preferences ■ Individual developmental maturity ■ Individual immunity to change Quadrant IV
	Heart	

Table 4 The four quadrants of organizations

The first quadrant holds the more tangible structures, which managers and organizers work with every day to coordinate people and units working in a company. The second quadrant describes how an individual experiences their place within the organization: the job, their own capability, and the problems and challenges they face, all of which are to a great extent determined by the work designs used to run the overall organization. The work designs of a company, found in quadrant one, systematically impact quadrant two. A work design that restricts local autonomy impacts the way people are able to

---

89 Based on (Kegan & Laskow, 2016). Another, similar structure is Scott's "three pillars of institutions"; see (Scott, 2014).

do their job, and so too does every purchasing guideline, every management approval, every assignment, every project, every HR regulation, every way of management—in other words, every work design.

The third quadrant describes a company's culture, which is the aggregate of beliefs and worldviews that people in the company tend to hold collectively as a result of the norming of social groups. These beliefs allow them to stick together and work productively and create consistency and reliability. While it is arguable that work designs are an expression of a company's culture, it is also built through the practices used to run the company. Work design (quadrant one) and beliefs (quadrant three) are therefore interdependent.

The same is true for the beliefs that individual co-workers hold, which is found in quadrant four. Everyone's personal values and motivations are (and may remain) different, but through the process of social norming they tend to align over time. People bring their whole person to work, with all their preferences and worldviews, and they find a home at work by aligning those preferences and worldviews with the workplace, which means they take the values of the company home, too. Systems change the mindsets of people over time—and work designs are what the system is built from. The reverse causality is also true: organizational beliefs (or individual beliefs held at a high hierarchical level) determine work designs. However, work designs are much more tangible and practical to work with. Changing work designs—for example, the way decisions are made or meetings are run, and how information is made available—requires rational thought, decision-making, and implementation. Changing beliefs, on the other hand, requires much, much more. It requires a shift in human minds, a revision of beliefs often caused by some deep and lasting experience and insight. Such shifts are difficult to effect, measure, and sustain.

Every work design comes with underlying beliefs. The way feedback is given, or status is reported, or meetings are run, or vacations are scheduled—all aspects of the work design have some impact on beliefs. Over time, the way that work is done becomes the way people *expect* that work to be done, and an element of order and reason emerges. A work design becomes morally acceptable and deemed to be good (or at least a necessary evil).

What this book proposes is to change companies by changing work designs. Whether you want to start a revolution or just introduce minor improvements, it will always involve doing things differently—which in turn will lead to new insights and beliefs and ways of thinking. All the beliefs in the world are useless if no action follows from them, but any action will lead to experience and results that might change beliefs. To move the hand is easier than to move what is inside the head and the heart; if you can get the hand to take new actions reflectively and mindfully, there will be enough food for the head and heart to get them going, too. All it takes to start is just a bit of curiosity to open oneself to new mindsets.

Robert Kegan recognizes two things. First, organizations can be changed by starting work at any of the four quadrants. Second, every new effort needs to address all four quadrants simultaneously. It needs to address the hand (quadrant one), the head (quadrant two), and the heart (quadrants three and four). In his work, Kegan makes extensive use of work designs in quadrant one that help get new thinking going.[90] He proposes sharing impressions and feelings in a group, which may feel like group therapy and out of place in businesses—too softheaded, "psycho-babble," or "all talk and no action," and so on—yet these reflective work designs are levers to influence people's beliefs. All work designs impact what is going on in the heads and hearts of people, even such mundane things as status reports and meeting formats. Consequently, all work designs should be set up in such a way as to foster the "right" individual beliefs (Q4) and company culture (Q3), and to get people thinking in new ways (Q2). The configuration of its work designs determines much of what a company is about and what it can achieve; its every aspect can be set up in such a way as to improve the effectiveness of its organization.

It is reasonable to ask whether companies have a right to intrude into people's hearts and heads for the sake of effectiveness rather than focusing on simply their hands and heads. The only case where manipulation of people is universally accepted is when it helps them become more autonomous, more able, and

90 (Kegan & Laskow, 2016) Chapters 4 and 5

more willing to express themselves. This may sound more like psychotherapy than work, but doesn't any manager need to pick a point on a scale between the two poles of tough accountability or human kindness? Let's explore that next.

Better work designs may invite people into the workplace more fully

Most books (including this one) about agile start-ups, high-performance teams, self-management, innovation management, design thinking, or digital companies call for one thing: embracing people more fully. In their own way, they all suggest reconnecting the belief system of the heart and the intuition with the rational head through the experience that the hand offers. But it is possible to focus too much on people's needs. A company, after all, exists to perform a particular mission and requires people to submit to a common will, irrespective of their individual points of view. People need to commit to a certain course of action even if they disagree with it: accountability, alignment, and commitment remain the cornerstones of any successful company.

Every company is a sociotope of performers and slackers, introverts and extroverts, the engaged and apathetic, the honest and the liars, yet people still need to be motivated and engaged, aligned with the company's targets, and held accountable for what they do. A good manager gets the best people, gives them clear goals and the authority to achieve those goals, then stands back and holds them accountable for the results. Even in self-managed teams, individual accountability is a must; each person needs to live up to their promises. However, accountability becomes toxic if it is used as a mechanism to apportion blame. If all failures are seen as negligence or incompetence, people will try to define their accountabilities as narrowly as possible. Shirking responsibility becomes the norm and taking action becomes the exception. A workplace that focuses only on results will therefore quite quickly become dysfunctional. In business, the causality of results is often uncertain and cannot be fully attributed to individual work efforts. "Result-only" workplaces may appear tough, action-oriented, and averse to anything soft, but ultimately—especially in a more complex digital economy—they are doomed.

Accountability alone is not enough. It needs to be supplemented with a tolerance of failure coupled with a willingness to look beyond results and consider efforts. Accountability and fairness need to go hand-in-hand. Although fairness is subjective and riddled with the dilemmas of justice, there is a proxy to measure the degree of fairness in a workplace. It is called "psychological safety," a shared belief that a workplace is a safe place for interpersonal risk-taking.[91] William Kahn, an organizational psychologist, describes it as "a workplace where it is safe for a co-worker to speak up and act without fear of negative consequences for one's self-image, status, or career."[92] In such a place, people are not punished for their views and elicit them freely. If people assume that their open words will be viewed fairly by all others (including superiors), they feel accepted, respected, and therefore more willing to shoulder accountability. Amy Edmondson and Edgar H. Schein, two of the most prominent organizational psychologists of our time, produced a framework that shows the interplay between accountability and psychological safety (Figure 5).

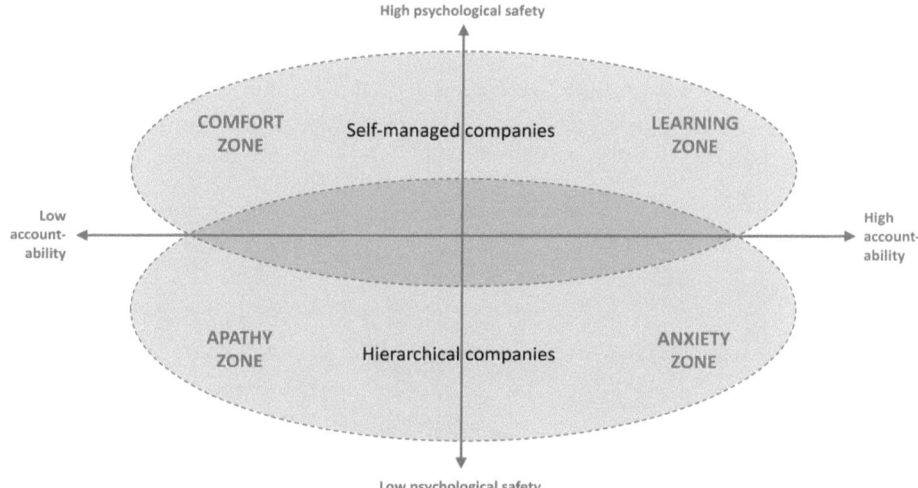

Figure 5 The four zones of engagement

In a strongly hierarchical company, it takes a lot of self-restraint for superiors to maintain a work environment that is psychologically safe. Subordinates have a strong need to please their superior, who may not always be willing to hear all

---

91 (Edmondson A. C., Psychological Safety and Learning Behavior in Work Teams, 1999).
92 (Kahn, 1990).

those critical, contradicting, supposedly "silly" comments. Hierarchical compa-nies often find themselves either in the apathy or the anxiety zone. The apathy zone is characterized by low engagement, whereas engagement is much higher in the anxiety zone, where the constant threat is to "deliver the results or else." In such workplaces, many choose a path of defensiveness and submission.

Then there is the comfort zone—a workplace where people take care of each other and listen to each other gladly, but are not held accountable for results. Here understanding is so rampant that words crowd out actions and people hesitate to hold themselves or anyone else accountable. These companies are good places to be but bad places for performance.

Things get done in all four zones. In the apathy zone, they are done in a slow-moving, administrative way; in the anxiety zone, in an exact but rather uninspiringly rigid manner; and in the comfort zone, very inconsistently. But only in the learning zone are things done professionally and in a positive spirit. The tendency for people to speak up in the pursuit of their clear account-abilities creates a natural bias towards learning. The learning zone is exactly where liberated companies want to be: a great place for results and a great place for people.

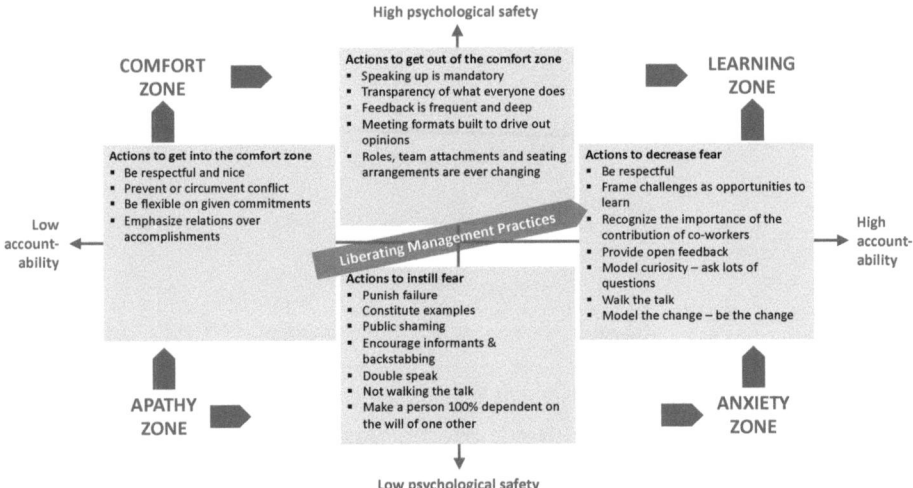

Figure 6 The four zones of engagement – actions

Figure 6 suggests some actions for transiting from one zone to another.[93] Running a company is not a choice between being "tough on" or "kind to" people. The best companies do both: they assist with accountability of teams and of individuals and they make it safe for people to speak up and declare themselves accountable. Liberated organizations can have both accountability and kindness.

Why work designs are a great vehicle to affect change

So work designs can be used to influence the head and the heart of companies, and they have a number of features making them a great vehicle for change. Work designs can be:

- Copied from one company to another.
- Combined with other work designs that reinforce one another, creating a configuration of work designs that is much stronger than the sum of its parts.
- Easily understood, learned, and implemented.
- Experimented, experienced, scrutinized, and modified.

Work designs might be the most tangible way humans are able to think of and tinker with organizations. Companies can be changed and even transformed by adopting, adapting, and discarding them. They can be observed in meetings, in approval forms, in calendar schedules, in company policies, or just by watching the way people act in groups. They are portable "best practices" for human coordination, "bricks of human collaboration" which can be used to configure companies in overall configurations that lend themselves to rational analysis. And if work designs are scaled and adopted for long enough, there is every chance that the less tangible aspects of human work—principles, beliefs, and culture—will be reconfigured, too.

If companies were to start changing and never stop experimenting with their work designs, they would enter a process of constant re-configuration and management would become a business process like any other, subject to continuous

---

93 Based on (Edmondson & Schein, Teaming, 2014).

and deliberate improvement. If organizational development becomes an act of evolving configurations of work designs, a leader's focus shifts towards environment building. A leader fosters the continuous self-evolution of a company not by providing a work environment, but by enabling the process of its evolution.

Dark Arts
- Everyone is using work designs—there is no way not to. The thing is to become aware of them and seek better ones for the situation at hand.
- Companies are can be changed best by addressing the heads, hearts, and hands of those in it by using a set of work designs that support each other and incorporate a consistent set of values and behaviors.
- To speak up is not natural in hierarchies. It must be learned and requires constant renewal.
- Psychological safety needs to be coupled with high accountability to create the creative abrasion that allows clever solutions to spread.

Further Reading
- Robert Kegan and Lisa Laskow (2016) *An Everyone Culture* Harvard Business Review Press
- Amy C. Edmonson and Edgar Schein (2014) *Teaming* Jossey-Bass
- Amy C. Edmondson (2018) *The Fearless Organization* Wiley

■ Chapter 5: The Liberated Company Map

Freedom that depends on the restraint of the powerful is no freedom at all.
One needs to restrict some people's freedoms so that they are forced to
act in a more public-spirited way.
– Jamie Susskind, 2018[94]

So far we have identified the main feature of the terrain that defines regions on the map of organizations in the digital age—the way power is distributed in companies. We zoomed into the map and found specific locations—work designs. Before identifying their places on the various regions of the map, let us first organize them.

The nine types of management practices

There are many ways to categorize management practices. Henry Fayol, a director of an early nineteenth-century French coal-mining company and a father of the field of organizational theory, came up with five different functions of management: planning, organizing, coordinating, commanding, and controlling.[95] A contemporary group of researchers specializing in the research of management practices came up with eighteen categories,[96] and recently, the writer Aaron Dignan came up with a useful similar map.[97] I believe that every management practice can be attributed to one of the nine categories shown in the 3x3 matrix of Table 5.

---

94 (Susskind, 2018), Chapter 10
95 (Fayol, 1917)
96 (Bloom, van Reemen, Genakos, & Sadun, 2012) see **https://www.nber.org/papers/w17850.pdf.**
97 (Dignan, 2019)

		Coordination ☞	Intelligence 🧠	Emotions ♡
🕴	**Action**	**Organizing** How we organize	**Decisions** How we make decisions	**Meeting** How we meet
🔍	**Control**	**Directing** How we set directions	**People** How we treat people	**Transparency** What we share
📈	**Development**	**Projects** How we do big new things	**Learning** How we learn	**Feedback** How we reflect

Table 5 The nine types of management practices

This is of course a simplification, but it is a useful one. The aim is to provide a map, which is an approximation of reality that is useful for orientation, not to achieve academic exactness.

In attributing a management practice to a type, we need to decide its main purpose. Take an elementary practice such as managerial feedback. Traditional feedback sessions conducted by superiors with their subordinates are certainly about reflection, learning, and transparency, but the prime purpose is often really control. So "managerial feedback" goes into the "control" group, although it is clearly a multi-purpose tool. Another example is status reporting. Does this practice fall into the "control" or "transparency" group? I assigned it to "control," as this is what I think the primary purpose of more traditional status reporting is. I recognize that these decisions are arbitrary. Categories are good for mapping, and mapping is good for orientation, but the true complexity is certainly greater than any map can show.

The rows of the matrix are ordered by the directness of the effect that a management practice has on the work itself, in descending order. In the first row are the types of work designs that are there to regulate how actions are done in a company: organization, decision, and meetings. The second row contains those types of management practices that are needed to control actions: directing, people, and transparency. The third row contains those practices that provide dynamics to a system: projects, learning, and reflection. Looking at the matrix by column shows us the hand, the head, and the heart: the categories we have seen in Robert Kegan's holistic view of the company. The first column contains the three categories focused on coordination (the hand), the second those focused on analyzing (the head), and the third those focused on emotions (the heart).

Putting management practices into nine rough categories for the sake of introducing some order into this diverse field is all well and good, but the true value of the map comes from linking management practices to the working environment in which they perform best. We now come to the "liberation level."

Liberation level: a measure of the size of the power differential

The success of a management practice is very much dependent upon the way power is distributed in a company. For an autocratic company, even participative decisions—a practice that calls for managers to involve co-workers in their decision-making—will already feel mildly radical, while decision-making by consensus or objection integration will feel totally out of place. Companies can be categorized by the size of the power differential between people, by what I call "liberation level." The lower the liberation level, the more power is concentrated in managers. The higher the liberation level, the more power is shared and the more people are able to be true to themselves. The scale goes from level 1, the classical hierarchy, to level 4, the self-managed organization. Between those extremes sit level 2, the empowered organization where employees have a certain limited amount of freedom and say in how work is done, and level 3, the supportive organization, where managers focus on the provision of a working environment but otherwise largely refrain from intervening. Up to and including level 3, the hierarchy is still in place, but managers assume a more and more liberating, supportive role (see Figure 7).

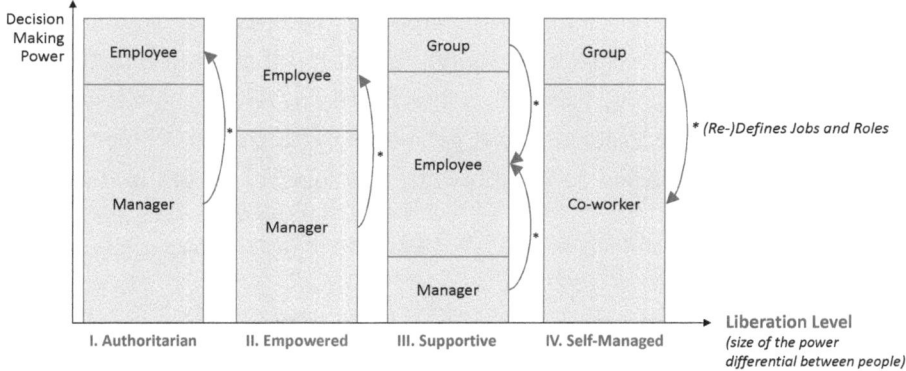

Figure 7 Decision-making at different liberation levels

At level 1, managers make most decisions. At level 2, they involve employees more in decision-making. At level 3, managers take on a supportive role and let groups manage themselves more. Level 4 represents the self-managed organization, where managers are non-existent and groups take over.

This four-level liberation model is not unlike other models of organizational maturity. It bears a close resemblance to Renis Likert's Model of Management Systems[98] and shares commonalities with Ron Westrum's 2004 model[99] and Frederick Laloux's 2014 model.[100] Table 6 compares the models.

	Likert	Liberated	Westrum	Laloux
Levels	Exploitative Authoritarian	Authoritarian	Pathological	Red
	Benevolent Authoritarian	Empowered	Bureaucratic	Yellow
	Consultative	Supportive	Generative	Orange
	Participative	Self-Managed		Green
				Teal
Scale	The amount of control a company exercises over its members	The size of the power differential between people	How organizations process information	Stages of human consciousness

Table 6 Development stages of organizations: Four Models

In level 1 companies, managers are in command and people need to subordinate themselves to them. With increasing maturity, people subordinate themselves less and less to their superiors and more and more to their mission within the company. Failing to subordinate oneself to the mission, or to live up to one's responsibilities, will get people into trouble in more mature companies, just as failing to comply with the superior would in lower-level companies.

---

98 (Likert, 1961)
99 (Westrum, 2004)
100 (Laloux, 2014)

Each management practice has a certain maturity level at which it works best. For example, managerial feedback is a practice that works best at level 1 because it was invented by the hierarchical organization—a competent superior greasing the cogs in the machine. Other practices like Kanban boards work best at level 3, because people need to be willing and competent enough to attract work to themselves instead of being assigned it. It is not that Kanban boards won't have some benefit at other stages; rather, the benefits will be more limited according to the difference in maturity levels.

While a company can be described as being at a certain liberation level, there may be units within it that are at a different maturity level. There is a danger in deviating too much from the prevalent culture of distributing power. Imagine an authoritarian, level 1 company. To get from level 1 to level 2, it takes a more enlightened manager to empower his direct subordinates. If the same manager decides to go to level 3 or even level 4 while the rest of the organization is still at level 1, they will face tremendous difficulties. To the hierarchical level 1 mindset, level 2 seems "boldly modern," level 3 seems "quirky and somewhat irresponsible," and level 4 makes the manager look like a fanatical anarchist. Every company has its primary modus operandi, the main maturity level at which it operates, and the cultural norm that it tends to adopt as a default.

The authoritative hierarchy is the default model on which society operates today. Over time, the liberation level is likely to fall to that default level, especially if no one is paying attention to the way work designs are used. To deviate from the default takes mindful thinking and energy.

The danger of using management practices too boldly

However, mapping management practices by type and liberation level is still not enough. Some management practices are extremely demanding in terms of a company's overall maturity level. For example, adopting self-service targets (level 3) or objection reduction (level 4) in a level 1 company can do real damage to everyone involved, as neither co-workers nor manager are ready for such a massive power shift away from managers and to co-workers. There are, however, small "work hacks" that provide a benefit but do not really hurt anyone, even if they fail. For example, daily stand-ups or retrospectives (both level 3) do not come with great risks for the initiator or the group. If these are undertaken in hierarchical companies at level 1, nothing bad will happen— they will just be less effective as people won't open up. A third criterion is therefore needed to order the map of management practices: severity level, which is defined as the risk of using a practice out of context. The higher the severity, the less advisable it is to use a practice outside its assigned liberation level. The higher the difference between the liberation level of the organization and the practice, the more careful you need to be.

The benefit of any one management practice is limited

While management practices can be attributed—with a pinch of salt—to a type, a liberation level, and a severity, there is no attribute to describe their potential benefits. The benefit of a single management practice is very hard to measure and depends on the situation a company is in. [101] For example, one good retrospective might make all the difference for a project, just as one good decision taken by consultative decision-making (level 3) might make the difference between success or failure of a major initiative. Overall, the benefit of implementing a single management practice is limited. What matters more is the organization's overall configuration of work designs—i.e., those practices that reinforce one another and rejuvenate the organization with similar underlying values.

The Liberated Company Map

The Liberated Company Map orders this diverse set of management practices along three dimensions:

- *Type of management practice.* The nine major quadrants are arranged in a three-by-three matrix.

---

101 A group of scientists dedicated to researching the effectiveness of management practices can be found at https://worldmanagementsurvey.org

- *Liberation level.* Each type is subdivided into four sub-quadrants. All level 1 practices can be found in the top left quadrant. Level 2 practices are in the top right quadrant, level 3 practices in the bottom left quadrant, and level 4 practices in the bottom right quadrant.
- *Severity.* Each line in a sub-quadrant lists a management practice, ordered by severity level. The most severe management practices are listed first; those lower in the lists tend to be less risky choices.

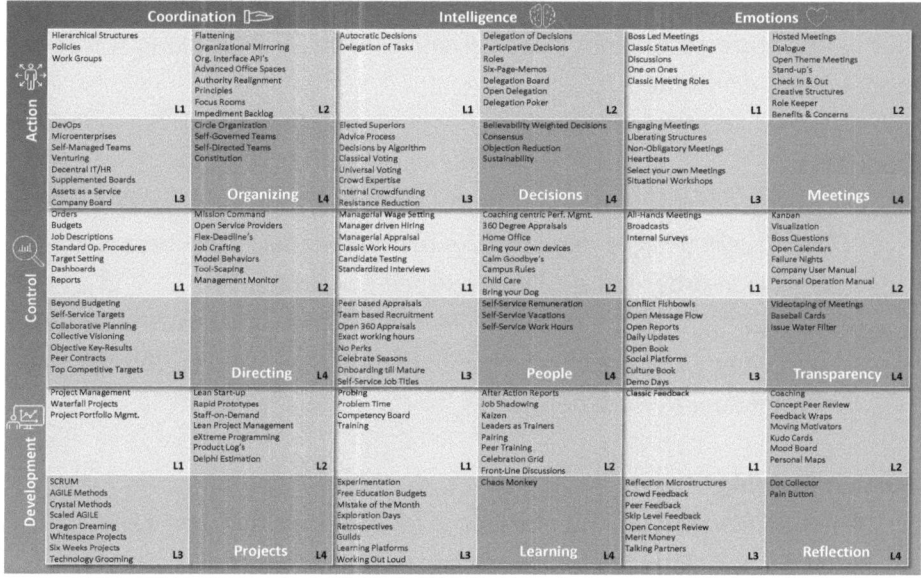

Figure 8 The Liberated Company Map

The Liberated Company Map is rooted in a neo-institutional view of organizations.[102] It should provide orientation, but it is not intended to be an accurate or academically rigorous framework. A company is a complex system; there are no standardized definitions of management practices and the attributes I have assigned are necessarily subjective. The Map can be used to discuss new, potential beneficial practices, to diagnose maturity levels, to point out inconsistencies between work designs of different maturity levels, and to plan new alternative configurations of work designs. The intention is not to create a compendium of all management practices, but rather to encourage thinking

---

102 (Scott, 2014) (Maggio & Powell, 2012); (Zucker, 1983)

in management practices terms. The goal is to package and label them according to the needs of the organization and treat them like any other actionable element. Any company can be described by marking the management practices it uses on this canvas. We will carry out this exercise extensively for one traditional and three very innovative companies in Chapter 9: Configuring Companies with Management Practices.

In the next three chapters, we look first at how level 1 "authoritarian" companies work before considering the alternatives that can be utilized if power is more equally distributed.

Dark Arts
- In its essence, a company is nothing other than a set of work designs.
- These work designs need to fit with one another in the best way possible in order to be collectively self-reinforcing.
- Work designs can be described by their primary purpose (category), by the degree of power-sharing (liberation level), and by the risk that a malfunctioning work design has for the company (severity).

Further Reading
- Renis Likert (1961) *New Patterns of Management* McGraw-Hill
- Frederick Laloux (2014) *Reinventing Organizations* Nelson-Parker
- Richard W. Scott (2014) *Institutions and Organizations* Sage Publications
- Aaron Dignan (2019) *Brave New Work* Portfolio

■ Chapter 6: Management Practices for Action

Management is the most creative of all arts, for its medium is human talent itself.
– Robert McNamara[103]

The first three categories of management practices are those most closely related to actions: how to organize, how to make decisions, and how to conduct meetings.

Management practices for organizing

How work is allocated to people is quite fundamental: who should do what? In a classical organization, the answer is provided by hierarchical command. The superior determines which jobs there are and assigns people to them. The hierarchical way of organizing has been so universally adopted by companies that most people take it for granted. Gerald Fairlough, a former Shell executive and a writer on liberated organizations, speaks of the "hegemony of the hierarchy": the hierarchy has such a monopoly of our mind that we are hard-pressed to imagine a different form of organizing ourselves,[104] although there are about 200 others. Admittedly, the hierarchy is an immensely consequential practice and one not easily changed, but it is still only a management practice and can be discarded if there are better alternatives. The hierarchical way of organizing is not a law of nature.

The smallest work unit of a classical hierarchical organization beyond the individual is a workgroup. In a workgroup, tasks are executed on behalf of a superior, and the superior monitors and manages the work process and prog-

---

103 Robert Mc Namara, US Secretary of defense from n a 1961 to1968, ina convocation address at Millsaps College, in Jackson, Mississippi. Cited in (Rosenzweig, Robert S. McNamara and the Evolution of Modern Management, 2010)
104 (Fairlough, 2007)

ress, designs the team and its work environment, and sets its overall direction. Workgroups are not teams, however. Workgroups rely on individual efforts that are coordinated by a manager. In contrast, teams do not rely as much on managerial coordination. To qualify as a team, a team must monitor and manage its own work process and progress. Hackman distinguishes four types of groups in the workplace (Figure 9).[105]

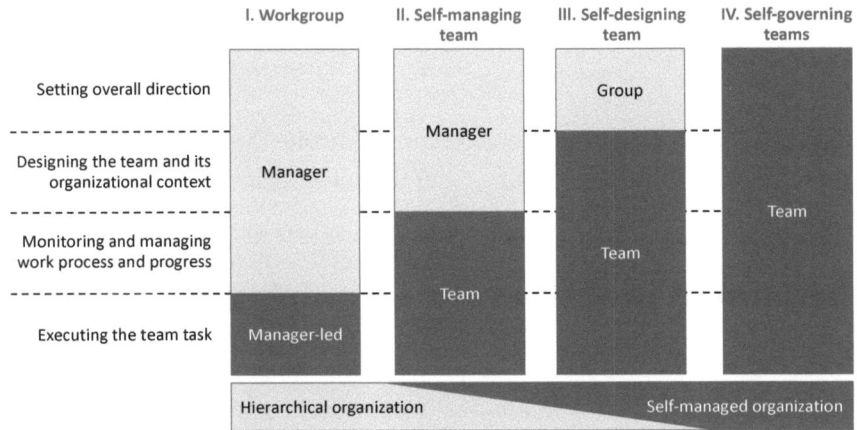

Figure 9 Group types

A soccer or basketball team is a team, not a workgroup. The coach determines a team's composition, deployment, and tactics, and ensures a good environment for the team, but during the game the coach stands on the sideline and is not directly involved in what is going on on the pitch. Players decide all the details: to whom they pass, where they run, how long they hold the ball, when to shoot, etc. Teams are "self-managing" in the sense that they monitor and manage their work themselves; managers remain on the sideline to set the overall direction and look after the environment the team is working in.

There are good business reasons for not misidentifying workgroups as teams. First, workgroups do not rely on relations between co-workers. Consequently, many artificial and therefore inefficient team-building exercises become redundant (or, at worst, hypocritical). Second, and more

---

105 (Hackman, 2002)

important, is the realization that what makes a great workgroup is not the same as what makes a great team. A workgroup needs an environment that allows everyone to do their individual best. Workgroups are not so much dependent on people building relations with each other as they are on good processes and workflows. They need the right level of authority, resources, and competence to do their work, whereas deeper investments in relationships are only really necessary in teams. In workgroups, it is better to invest in eliminating impediments to the flow of work.

Another typical management practice of level 1 organizations is policies. Policies lay down codified rules for some (or all) people in the organization, and offenders are disciplined. Coordination by policy (also known as bureaucracy) is efficient, broadly speaking, but too many rules may stifle individual initiative.

Severity	Liberation level			
	I. Authoritarian	II. Empowered	III. Supportive	IV. Self-Managed
Very high (Fundamental)	• Hierarchy			• Circle organization • Self-governed teams
High	• Policies	• Flattening • Organizational mirroring • Organizational interface APIs	• DevOps • Microenterprises • Self-managed teams • Venturing	• Self-directed teams
Moderate	• Work groups	• Advanced office space • Authority realignment • Principles	• Decentral IT/HR • Supplemented boards	• Constitution
Low		• Focus rooms	• Assets as a service • Company board	
Very low (Work Hack)		• Impediment backlog	• Hierarchy of purpose	

(CHASM — vertical label between "Supportive" and "Self-Managed" columns)

Table 7 Management practices: Organizing

Level 2 companies seeking to empower their employees employ management practices such as:

- *Flattening.* Keeping the number of hierarchical levels low and therefore the leadership span (number of subordinates to superiors) high.
- *Organizational mirroring.* Organizing from a customer perspective. This usually leads to cross-functional teams.
- *Organizational interface APIs.* Every part of an organization can be understood as delivering certain outputs based on certain inputs. Increasingly, software rather than people is doing the processing and

delivering outputs in the form of services such as HR, IT, marketing, or purchasing, opening up the inner workings of a company to everyone (either inside or outside the company).

- *Advanced office spaces.* The physical work environment is a work design in itself—i.e., open space, neighborhoods, campuses, and other concepts.
- *Authority realignment.* Reshuffling decision-making authorities between superior and subordinate through structured discussion.
- *Principles.* A set of guiding statements that show a company's values and behaviors, ranging from bullet lists such as Amazon's "14 principles"[106] to books filled with stories, such as Netflix's 2009 "culture book."[107]
- *Focus rooms*: Rooms for between one and three people that may be used by anyone at any time, no reservations necessary. These are spaces for private conversations and deep, focused work.
- *Impediment backlogs.* A way of capturing all things requiring improvement and taking action on the one that is holding a team back the most.

Many other management practices could also be listed here. You will find more resources for further investigation listed in the Appendix.

On level 3, "supportive," the hierarchy is still intact but managers adopt a supportive role, enabling the company to better use the following management practices:

- *DevOps.* A combination of software development and systems maintenance operations. It starts from the needs of technology (see Chapter 1) but ends up reshaping the way humans organize around technology, going beyond the realm of IT and ultimately impacting many more business areas.
- *Microenterprises.* The practice of splitting units into independent organizational units when they become too big to be managed easily (which is often when they exceed the Dunbar number of 150 persons).

---

106 https://aws.amazon.com/de/careers/culture/ (retrieved 15 June 2019).

107 **https://de.slideshare.net/reed2001/culture-1798664/9-At_Netflix_we_particularly_value** (retrieved 15 June 2019).

- *Self-managed teams.* Teams that are responsible for executing as well as managing and monitoring work processes and progress. Team managers focus on designing the team and setting general directions.
- *Venturing.* A practice that imitates the way venture capitalists seed and foster start-ups. At a corporate level, most major companies are already on the road to master venturing. More mature organizations seek to give everyone the opportunity to venture—i.e., become an entrepreneur or link up with one while staying with the company.
- *Decentralized IT/HR.* With the digital revolution, IT is the primary tool for getting work done; likewise, people recruitment and development becomes a core function of every team. Therefore, IT and HR should shrink and retain only some basic service functions.
- *Supplemented boards.* Company boards (or other key panels) are supplemented with elected members. Candidates may be internal or external. These panels may make decisions by other means than usual— e.g., advanced voting mechanisms, advice process or consensus.
- *Assets as a service.* The way assets are placed at the disposal of co-workers determines much of their work environment. With pay per use, many assets can be turned into a service, like a business process-level intervention.
- *Company board.* A Kanban board to visualize the company's work design experiments. It tracks ideas, experimentation, testing, and integration of work designs into the overall work design configuration.
- *Hierarchy of purpose.* Thinking of companies as hierarchies of purpose rather than hierarchies of functions will often result in more cross-functional teams.

Maturing to level 4 means abandoning the conventional hierarchy and fully embracing self-management at the company level. There is a steep chasm between levels 3 and 4, as power is being redistributed from individuals to a collective. When a company embraces self-management, the following management practices become more feasible:

- *Circle organization.* A non-hierarchical way of organizing self-managed teams. There is a central circle (often the owner), an inner circle (support units such as finance and IT) and the outer customer-facing circle. Many other non-hierarchical networked regimes are also possible.

- *Self-directed teams.* Resembling self-managed teams, but with the added feature that the team sets its own targets.
- *Self-governed teams.* Resembling self-directed teams, but with the added feature that the team decides its own composition.
- *Constitution.* Codifying the hard governance structures, decision procedures, functions, and rules of an organization.

At level 4, management practices for organizing work must fill the vacuum of the discarded hierarchy and deal with the distribution of power. A number of frameworks describe models of more distributed, egalitarian leadership: "prepackaged" systems, containing many management practices in themselves, such as sociocracy and Holacracy; more open systems such as collegial leadership; or custom-made organizations, such as those described by Laloux or Carney/Geetz.[108]

Many of the more liberating management practices need to be accompanied by changes to the way decisions are made. Let's explore that next.

Management practices for decision-making

In most conventional companies, decision-making is a personal skill of the superior rather than a management practice. A superior is entitled to make decisions on anything within their area of accountability, from the biggest to the most trivial matters. In autocratic decision-making, there is no need for the superior to make their thinking transparent, except at the request of their own superior, which often results in decision-makers failing to give decisions due deliberation and "shooting from the hip." The potential lack of both transparency and rigorous thinking causes many problems, including flawed decisions, misinterpretations, and people feeling left out.

It is generally recognized in management literature that proper delegation of tasks is effective, as it frees up time for managers to focus on higher-level

---

108 (Laloux, 2014).; (Carney & Geetz, 2016)

or higher-value activities. Delegation lets others build competence by giving them tasks they aspire to. However, just like autocratic decision-making, delegation is very much dependent on the individual skill, style, and willingness of the manager.

Severity	Liberation level			
	I. Authoritarian	II. Empowered	III. Supportive	IV. Self-Managed
Very high (Fundamental)	▪ Autocratic decisions		▪ Elected superiors	▪ Believability weighted decisions ▪ Consensus
High	▪ Delegation of tasks	▪ Delegation of decisions ▪ Participative decisions	▪ Advice process ▪ Decisions by algorithm (AI) ▪ Classical voting	
Moderate		▪ Roles ▪ Six-page memos	▪ Universal voting	▪ Objection reduction
Low		▪ Delegation board ▪ Open delegation	▪ Crowd expertise ▪ Internal crowdfunding ▪ Resistance reduction	▪ Sustainability
Very low (Work Hack)		▪ Delegation poker		

Table 8 Management practices: Decision-making

More transparent decision-making often produces better decisions and smoother implementations through:

- *Delegation of decisions* as well as tasks.
- *Participative decision-making* with intensive engagement by others before, during, and after decision-making.
- *Temporary and flexible distribution of responsibility*, which is a more permanent form of delegation that is much easier to redistribute than jobs.
- *Six-page memos*, authored by the team, without any slides, read in silence at the beginning of a decision meeting to provoke clarity of thought.
- *Delegation board*, which is a team exercise to get everyone's views about the subject and extent of delegation.
- *Open delegation* providing transparency and the opportunity to object, volunteer, or add crucial information.
- *Delegation poker*, a game-based approach to determine the authorization level between a superior and co-workers.

The "empowering" practices listed above engage coworkers but still leave the final call to be made by the superior. Supportive organizations go a step further: they do not only leave bigger decisions to employees more often; they go deeper into the decision-making process. They concern themselves with questions like:[109] Who has the right to determine that a problem exists at all? Who has the right to participate in a decision? Who determines that a choice needs to be made now? Who defines what an acceptable solution is? Decision-making practices of supportive companies can be listed as follows:

- *Elected superiors*. They hold their posts for a specific duration.
- *Advice process*. A co-worker has decision-making authority, subject to consulting with others and explaining their reasoning. This powerful technique has the advantage of a single decision-maker while creating bonds of obligation.
- *Decisions by algorithm (AI)*. Supplements and sometimes replaces human decision-making with artificial intelligence.
- *Classical voting*. Majority, consensus, qualified majority or other mechanisms.
- *Universal voting*. Determines the most appropriate type of decision-making on a case-by-case basis.
- *Crowd expertise*. Delegates solution-finding to the crowd rather than people inside the organization.
- *Internal crowdfunding*. A stock market for innovation that allows employees to bid on alternatives or ideas.
- *Resistance reduction*. A voting mechanism that selects the alternative with the least resistance, thereby revealing preferences.

Most level 4 self-managed companies utilize the decision-making practices of supportive companies. There are, however, some practices that are so advanced that they particularly lend themselves to self-managed companies:

- *Believability-weighted decision-making*. An advanced "elitist democracy" where pre-determined weights reflect experience and track record of the individual voter.

---

109 Problems described scientifically in "The Garbage Can Model of Organizations," i.e., the nature of any organization to muddle-up solutions, personal dispositions, and problems into one messy garbage can. See (Cohen, March, & Olsen, 1972)

- *Consensus.* A majority is required to approve a given course of action, but the minority agrees to go along with it subject to modification to remove objectionable features.
- *Objection reduction.* A more structured form of consensus decision and key feature of Holacracy. If no valid objections exist, a decision is made to avoid stalemate.
- *Sustainability.* By adding sustainability to the factors that need to be considered in all major decisions, it becomes a permanent feature of daily business.

Management practices for meetings

The advanced mechanisms discussed above share one central feature: they are dependent on excellent meeting structures. Meetings are the place where collective intelligence is harnessed, yet they are often boring, a waste of time, inconsequential, something to be endured. Exciting or effective meetings are rare.

There are many reasons for the meeting overload that is so common: insufficient delegation; the need to appear active; the measurement of self-worth by the crowdedness of one's schedule; and too many corporate initiatives. In day-to-day business, many meetings are such a chore that many people "tune out" and lose the very discipline needed to make a meeting successful.[110]

Companies should strive to make meetings a place where all people share their thoughts and opinions freely. They should strive to create "Ideal Speech" situations, a term coined by the Philosopher Jürgen Habermas who attaches four conditions to such situations:[111]

1. Every subject with the competence to speak and act is allowed to take part in a discourse.
2. Everyone is allowed to question any assertion whatsoever.

---

110 For an excellent narrative on meetings, see (Lencioni, 2007))
111 (Habermas, 1990)

3. Everyone is allowed to express their attitudes, desires, and needs without any hesitation.
4. No speaker may be prevented, by internal or external coercion, from speaking out.

Successful meetings require effort and structure. Group psychologists have found that the quality of human interchange in meetings depends on the way participants prepare; the way meetings are opened; the framing of subjects discussed; the conversation structure; the psychological safety of the situation; the way different viewpoints are extracted; the way synthesis is done; and the way actions are assigned.

All these points must be considered each and every time if meetings are to be more than a recurrent irritation. In classical organizations, bosses lead meetings; they are the ones entitled to invite people, set the agenda, decide on the meeting structure, and provide the discipline which is crucial to make a meeting a success. Of course, the quality depends significantly on the boss's skill level in moderating meetings. Unstructured meetings tend to degenerate into discussions with people trying to make an argument to convince others of their point of view. Those with strong views—and a position in the hierarchy that make stating a strong view safe—tend to "win" a discussion. In unstructured discussions, people tend to talk *at* instead of *to* each other.

Another frequently used meeting type in level 1organizations is the status meeting. In these meetings, information is shared, some discussions take place, and actions are assigned, but there may be prolonged discussions, a single participant (often the boss) may talk most of the time, or there may be no commitment to action (or inconsequential follow-up).

Severity	Liberation level			
	I. Authoritarian	II. Empowered	III. Supportive	IV. Self-Managed
Very high (Fundamental)	▪ Boss led meetings	▪ Hosted meetings		
High		▪ Dialogue	▪ Bar camp ▪ Engaging meetings ▪ Liberating Structures	
Moderate	▪ Classic status meetings ▪ Discussions ▪ One-on-Ones	▪ Open theme meetings ▪ Stand-up's	▪ Non-obligatory meetings	
Low		▪ Check-In/ Check-out ▪ Creative structures ▪ Role keeper	▪ Heartbeats ▪ Select your own meetings ▪ Situational workshops	
Very low (Work Hack)	▪ Classic meeting roles	▪ Benefits & concerns ▪ Improv card storytelling ▪ Integrative engagement index		

Table 9 Management practices: Meetings

Many management practices listed on the Liberated Companies Map are linked to certain meeting structures, especially in the "reflection" and "learning" categories. The quality of its structure determines the effectiveness of any meeting.[112] Figure 10 explains different levels of meeting structure, from unstructured at the top to highly refined at the bottom.

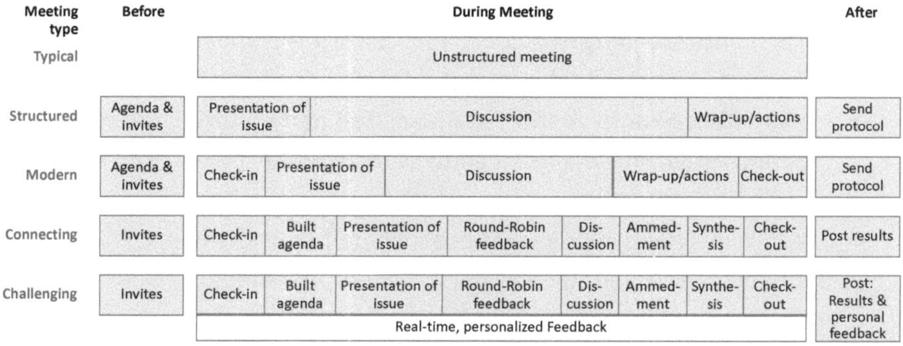

Figure 10 Different levels of structuring meetings

A meeting can be structured in different segments of phases, each with its own purpose, rules, main actors, and participant roles. It can have its own frames, seating arrangements, and resources (sticky notes, whiteboard, cards, apps, etc.). Each segment can have its own microstructures, like a meeting inside a meeting.

---

112 For a taxonomy of meetings, see (Keith, 2018)

Meetings that are set up and conducted professionally are very effective tools for doing business. The easiest and most effective way to counter the lack of facilitation skills in a boss is to assign a meeting host whose function is not the logistical arrangements of the meeting, but the securing of good communication by structuring the meeting appropriately.

Another effective way to improve meeting structure is to learn how to have a dialogue. A dialogue is a basic communication technique centered on listening and inquiry without advocating one's own thoughts. Instead of making a discussion a central element of most meetings, dialogues give everyone an option to open up, participate, and learn. Other important methods used in more empowered company environments are:

- *Open theme meetings*. A free-ranging format where the agenda is developed at the start of a meeting and people vote to extend time-boxed slots dynamically, enabling meetings to focus on things that really matter to the participants.
- *Stand-ups*. A short meeting or meeting segment done with all participants standing in a circle and utilizing a standardized set of questions in a round robin to get everyone to speak up.
- *Check-in/check-outs*. A short standardized early-morning or start-of-meeting ritual where a team gathers to allow for focus, priming, and people to speak out.
- *Creative meeting structures*. These include brainstorming, thinking hats, Synectics, Lego Serious Play, Delphi method, nominal groups, and morphological analysis.
- *Role-keeper*. Roles are assigned to participants at the start of the meeting, e.g., facilitator, devil's advocate, optimist, creative visionary, fact-finder, emotional medium, etc.

A great many work hacks address the meta-level of meetings or segments of meetings, including:

- *Benefits and concerns*. A quick way to wrap up the meeting where everyone states their feelings about it.

- *Improv storytelling.* A gamified storytelling technique that uses illustrated cards to reframe a problem or a decision.

The more liberated a company, the more important meetings become as the collective takes over from the individual manager.[113] The "1-2-4-ALL" structure, a part of a set of dozens of meeting microstructures labeled "Liberating Structures" by Keith McCandles and Henry Lipmanovic,[114] is a great example of a microstructure usable in many meetings. Its purpose is to engage every participant simultaneously by generating questions, ideas, and suggestions. In the first minute of a meeting, everyone reflects on a specific question posed to the whole group. The next two minutes are spent in a discussion with another random person. After that, four minutes are spent sharing thoughts in a four-person group. At the end, each group shares their insights with the whole group for a total of 5 minutes. The whole structure usually takes about 10 to 12 minutes to complete. It relies on the four elements typical of all efficient meeting structures: a specific question, highly refined scripting, strict time-keeping, and minimal facilitation. The result is high engagement by everyone because no one can withdraw without co-workers noticing.

Although a single round of 1-2-4-ALL is certainly action-packed, 12 minutes is not much time to produce anything. Now imagine that you run multiple rounds of 1-2-4-ALL to drill down on some central idea, or you combine it with other more conventional meeting structures (such as brainstorming, discussions, or townhalls) or other liberating or agile structures (such as retrospectives, TRIZ, or Troika Consulting). Although this may sound like structural meeting overkill, good meeting structures are easy to understand once they are experienced. They quickly become a norm, raising the quality of human collaboration without much effort. Once people have been initiated into the structure, they can apply it themselves without much external help.[115]

---

113 For a plethora of helpful meeting structures, see (Lipmanowicz & McCandles, 2014). See also **http://www.liberatingstructures.com.**
114 (Lipmanowicz & McCandles, 2014)
115 There even is an app for it which can be found by searching for "liberating structures" in App stores.

Figure 11 compares conventional meeting practices with liberating structures. The great thing about liberating structures is that they give control to the group. With everyone contributing actively, it energizes and fosters more creative solution-finding.

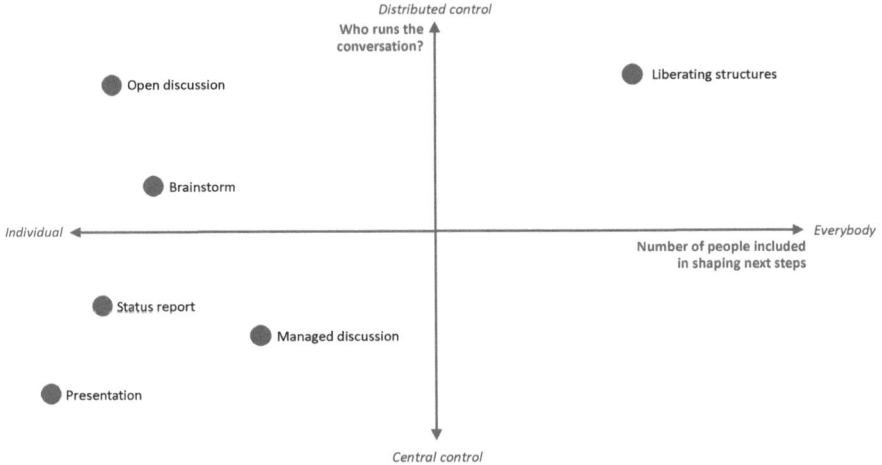

Figure 11 Conventional vs. liberating meeting microstructures[116]

Other techniques at level 3, the "supportive" company, are:

- *Bar camp.* Similar to Lean Café, but the whole meeting runs in several parallel break-out groups. People facilitate the meetings they want to happen and vote with their feet for which sessions to attend.
- *Engaging meetings.* Structures that allow for surprises and improvisation, such as "fishbowls" where intense communication occurs in an inner ring, while an outer ring observes, questions, and makes suggestions.
- *Non-obligatory meetings.* This tests whether meetings—or the presence of individual participants—are actually needed.
- *Heartbeats.* Conventional status meetings are replaced by written monthly summaries of actions that are posted to the entire company.
- *Select your own meetings.* Everyone may participate in every meeting. This requires transparent meeting schedules.
- *Situational workshops.* Everyone (or a pair or a team) briefly shares a single challenge and people decide after the meeting whether and in

116 (Lipmanowicz & McCandles, 2014)

what form to take action. The objective is to efficiently "pull in" rather than to assign actions.

Every organization relies on organizing, decision-making, and meeting practices. Which one is your team or company using? Why? How consistently are they used? Does it work?

■ Chapter 7: Management Practices for Coordination

If you expect people to be acting in concert
you will get a lot of acting and a bad concert.
– Peter Block[117]

Coordination management practices are about directing, looking after people, and providing transparency.

Management practices for directing

There is no shortage of management practices for directing people in classical hierarchies. The most basic mechanism is the order. Higher-ranking people are, within the limits of the law, entitled to tell people what to do. People may grumble and bend orders somewhat, but by and large, they will follow them. In a world where anything can be achieved by giving orders, there are three skills a manager needs to master most: ordering the right things, giving clear orders, and giving the right order to the right person. Orders are sometimes disguised as wishes or preferences, but attentive co-workers can nonetheless be relied on to act on those unsaid orders.

Other directing management practices at level 1 that are mainstays of today's corporate culture are target-setting, budgeting, dashboard, standard operating procedures, reports, and job descriptions.

---

117 (Block, Stewardship, 2003)

Severity	Liberation level			
	I. Authoritarian	II. Empowered	III. Supportive	IV. Self-Managed
Very high (Fundamental)	• Orders	• Mission Command		
High	• Budgets	• Open Service Providers	• Beyond Budgeting • Self-Service Targets	
Moderate	• Job Descriptions • Standard Op. Procedures • Target Setting	• Flex-Deadlines • Job-Crafting • Model Behavior	• Collaborative Planning • Collective Visioning • Objective-Key Results (OKR) • Peer Contracts (IOU) • Top Competitive Targets	
Low	• Balanced Scorecards • Reports	• Management Monitor • Tool-Scaping	• Organizational Dashboards	
Very low (Work Hack)		• Subjective Event Tracking		

Table 10 Management practices: Directing

A more empowered control management practice is known as "mission command." Pioneered in the second half of the nineteenth century by Erich von Moltke, a Prussian general, it was perfected by the end of World War I, used at scale in World War II by the German army, and remains part of the command doctrine of all modern Western armies. Mission command means giving an order based on a high-level description of the overall targets, the intent behind the order, and boundary conditions. An order given as a mission still follows the "I want you to do X" formula, but the X itself is a higher-level objective. The reasoning behind the order is explained in sufficient detail that the recipient knows why it has been given and is free to use everything at their disposal in the way they deem best to work towards the "commander's intent." Mission command emphasizes the "why" behind an order over the "what" and the "how." It requires four things of the commander and two things of the person receiving the order. The commander needs:

- Clarity of thought to be able to state the order at a high level and make it fit into the overall higher-level intent.
- Willingness to explicitly set out their thinking and assumptions.
- Thinking on strategic, operational, and tactical levels, identifying the interconnections between those levels, and having a solid grip on the possibilities and alternative options.
- Superb prioritization skills to distinguish primary targets from potential "sacrifices." There are two types of sacrifice: secondary

targets one is willing to forgo as long as the primary target is secured; and resources, such as people, time, money, that will not be available for other purposes.

The recipient of a "mission order" needs both competence and awareness of the context in order to be able to make decisions on the spot that work towards the commander's intent.

Although mission command appears to only be applicable to large high-level missions, it also works very well on a tactical level. The literal translation of the German *Auftragstechnik* is "task tactic," which hints at its usefulness even for day-to-day orders. If the superior and subordinate share a high degree of trust and understanding of what they are trying to achieve together, there is no need to give exhaustive briefings. Mission command is most beneficial if the work environment is arranged in such a way that orders can be given briefly and efficiently while giving the recipient liberty to turn the intention into reality. It will only work with transparency, decentralization of authority, a shared purpose and understanding, and trust between people.

Mission command is an egalitarian way of giving orders in which each side respects the other. Ordering, with its autocratic associations, implies a large power differential, and mission command is only possible if the power differential is much smaller. The person giving the order is willing to be questioned while the recipient is challenged to think for themselves and determine the best way to work towards the intention. Giving clear directions is important for all companies, but mission command remains useful even for self-managed companies.

Other directing management practices on level 2 include:

- *Open service providers.* Units are free to source some or all central services (IT, HR, FI), which may foster better service as internal monopolies disappear.
- *Flex deadlines.* Varies targets and scope instead of moving deadlines. This invites prioritizing and trade-offs while still maintaining accountability. Consequently, budgets become more important than estimates.

- *Tool-scaping.* Evolving the tools used inside a company towards more integration, more transparency, more interactivity and engagement. The use of all kinds of software applications, collaboration platforms, conferencing software, social media, and servers frequently develops haphazardly within companies. Consciously and constantly evolving the increasing use of digital applications may be beneficial.
- *Model behavior.* A 4-step practice helping people towards a new behavior: (1) answer a question in a group; (2) prioritize and discuss; (3) identify wanted behaviors; (4) act accordingly and show the behaviors. This turns the doctrine that behaviors follow mindsets on its head and puts the behavior first so that the mindset can follow.

At level 3, the "supportive" company, there are a number of practices that encourage more bottom-up participation:

- *Beyond budgeting.* The classic budget process tries to do three conflicting things—target setting, forecasting, and resource allocation—leaving no room for failure and causing manipulative and risk-minimizing behavior. A better solution may be to establish three different types of budget process, driven more by the need to experience and learn than by the need to predict.[118]
- *Self-service targets.* Under the right circumstances, with high levels of social cohesion, people who set their own targets tend to challenge themselves even more than their superiors would.
- *Collective visioning.* Companies, units, processes, projects, and teams can all benefit from a shared vision. One way of achieving this is to write a short narrative (in no more than 30 minutes), share it, extract common themes, then vote on the themes to prioritize and synthesize the vision.
- *Collaborative planning and budgeting.* Budgets are self-assigned by business units (and given certain high-level guidelines and priorities) after the impacted departments have been consulted. Conflicts are resolved by bilateral or multilateral arbitration.

---

118 (Bogsnes, 2016)

Then there are more tactical work-hack practices that allow for effective control:

- *Objective key results (OKR)*. A framework for defining and tracking objectives and their outcomes. OKRs were invented at Intel and made popular at Google.
- *Peer contracts*. A formalized agreement between co-workers, called IOUs in some companies. Morning Star, a pioneer of self-management, calls them "CLOUs" (colleague letter of understanding). Peer contracts should always be transparent and able to be seen by all co-workers at any time.

Again, there are no specific practices at level 4. All that is needed is already available at the lower levels. At level 4, the control model depends heavily on effective social norming, seasoned with a pinch of direction and control offered by inner-circle teams.

Management practices for people

The second category of management practices for coordination, which fall squarely into the realm of today's HR departments, are those used to administer people: pay, working time, appraisal, recruitment, and perks.

| Severity | Liberation level | | | |
	I. Authoritarian	II. Empowered	III. Supportive	IV. Self-Managed
Very high (Fundamental)	• Managerial wage setting			• Self-service remuneration
High	• Manager-driven hiring • Managerial appraisal	• Coaching-centric Per. Mgmt.	• Peer-based appraisals • Team-based recruitment	• Self-service vacations
Moderate	• Classic working hours	• 360-degree appraisals • Home office	• Exact working hours • Open 360-degree appraisals	• Self-service work hours
Low	• Candidate testing • Standardized interviews	• Bring Your Own Devices • Calm Good-Bye's • Campus rules • Childcare	• Annihilation of perks • Celebrate seasons • Onboarding till mature • Self-service job titles	
Very low (Work Hack)		• Bring your dog		

Table 11 Management practices: People

People management practices get a bit more interesting at level 2, the empowered organization. If managers choose to empower people, they need to give them more choices. Nevertheless, the wish to influence people is still there, so managers need to adopt a more coaching-like approach. Most companies do not have the luxury to hire people for their coaching abilities, but must instead work with the managers they have. Michael Bungay-Stainer, a coaching expert, states the four main difficulties of coaching:[119]

- Coaching takes up more time than more direct, judgmental ways of directing or appraising people.
- Some managers do not want to be coaches: listening patiently is not for everyone.
- Managers lack belief in coaching, or the persistence or ability to do it.
- Even if a coaching approach is mandated in an organization, the actual application and quality of coaching techniques is very hard to measure.

Other management practices and work hacks available for empowered organizations are:

- *360-degree appraisals.* A structured review of a person by peers, subordinates, and superiors, often as a variation of the traditional annual review.
- *Home office.* Freedom for people to choose their work environment.
- *Bring your own devices.* Technology is inexorably and increasingly blending people with their devices and integrating work and life. Divorcing people from their own devices—effectively extensions of themselves—and forcing them to use devices mandated by IT will become increasingly anachronistic.
- *Calm good-byes.* A dismissal opens a vacuum. People should be given time to say goodbye, and a manager should post a follow-up note explaining the reasons for the dismissal so that there are no lingering unanswered questions.
- *Campus rules.* A number of practices aimed at ensuring longer uninterrupted intervals of work: for example, silence at the workplace (like in a library); office hours for experts or managers (instead of

---

119 Paraphrased from (Bungay-Stainer, 2016)

open-door policies, which often lead to interruption); asynchronous communications first, real-time ones second; and the prioritization of focus more than interruptions.

- *Childcare.* How much does it cost to have a room and a qualified person available to look after children in an emergency compared with having a parent call in sick? Often all parents need is a temporary option to bridge gaps. The idea is to "welcome humanity" into the workplace.
- *Bring your dog.* Further in the spirit of integrating work and life, dogs could be brought into the workplace. There are measurable psychological benefits.

In more supportive, level 3 organizations, the power shifts from managers to teams. Teams are responsible for appraising each team member themselves. Removing the power to reward and sanction performance from a manager is a very significant step. Netflix has abandoned managerial appraisal in favor of peer-based appraisal. Co-workers can be appraised by anyone, at any time, in a very lightweight format based on three questions: What to start? What to stop? What to continue? Dozens of other forms of appraisal rest on the same underlying principle that no individual has the sole power to appraise others. Appraisals and the managing of individual performance becomes a collective duty.

Other "people" practices of supportive companies are:

- *Team-based recruitment.* The team, not a superior, does the hiring and decides who will work with them. The manager may or may not have the power to veto the decision.
- *Exact working hours.* Overtime is discouraged in an attempt to foster more productivity, healthy working hours, and a focus on getting the work done rather than just being present.
- *Open 360-degree appraisals.* Often used in small group settings, this is a 360-degree appraisal where the process or results do not remain private. The feedback is given in public and the results are openly displayed and discussed.

- *Annihilation of perks.* Perks are signs of privilege associated with a specific position in a company: parking spaces, big offices, latest gadgets, working hours, special coffee, or (generally speaking) the luxury to follow the rules only if one chooses to. Removing these signs of authority helps create more open, adult-to-adult relations.
- *Celebrate seasons.* Change working days or hours according to the season—for example, 4 days a week in summer, 5 days for the rest of the year, and extra hours in winter. The point is not to work less, but to blend work with life better.
- *Onboarding till mature.* New recruits are onboarded by letting them join a project or unit of their own choosing and remain there pending a positive evaluation.
- *Self-service job titles.* An alternative to traditionally prescribed job titles. Everyone gives their job a name they think expresses it best. Social pressure tends to lead to reasonable outcomes, while people both think deeply about their mission inside the company and express their aspirations.

At level 4, the self-managed company, the last remaining powers of management shift towards co-workers. At this level, dealing with remuneration presents interesting challenges. Many authors advise against changing pay practices for as long as possible and keeping them simple and transparent in all cases.[120] Classical hierarchies enjoy tinkering with the renumeration system; in contrast, self-managed organizations are more about the ability of people to attach their intrinsic motivation to the service of the company.

"Self-service remuneration" can be achieved in four steps: (1) inform everyone of the average percentage increase available for payroll across the entire organization; (2) get everyone to answer a couple of questions about their own performance and the situation the company is in; (3) get everyone to bid for what they feel is an appropriate increase; and (4) discuss in the group and use a decision method like consensus, objection reduction, resistance reduction, or the advice process.

---

120 (Block, 2003)

Similar structures can be used to determine working hours and vacations for individuals and teams:

- *Self-service vacation.* A variation of self-service remuneration wherein the number of days off can be self-determined and pay is reduced accordingly. The timing of vacations must still be agreed with the team, but the number of days is not defined in the contract and can be changed dynamically.
- *Self-service working hours.* Similar to self-service vacations. Everyone picks their own time to work.

Many of these "self-service" or team-based practices, if introduced in isolation, have a limited chance of success. Level 3 or 4 management practices are much more likely to succeed if flanked with other practices on the same or neighboring levels. One of the biggest enablers of many advanced practices is transparency.

Management practices for transparency

Transparency helps people to better understand what is going on in a company, which helps build trust and leads to better decisions. Transparency is like fertile soil where creative minds and purpose seekers can find rich nourishment. Yet, most companies approach transparency on an "all you need to know" instead of an "all there is to know" basis. There are three common reasons for this restriction. First, creating transparency costs time and effort. It is not enough to just publish data—people must have the time and competence to make sense of it, too. Second, information is power, and creating more transparency therefore means giving up power. Third, it is often unclear what somebody can do with their new insights. If there is only one way to do a job and there is no opportunity to change anything, insights will not lead to actions. Non-actionable insights may even frustrate people.

In classical hierarchies, information is disseminated primarily by a superior via word of mouth. Management is, according to Professor Henry Mintzberg, largely an oral profession.[121] There are occasional broadcasts (usually through

---

121 (Mintzberg, 2019)

email), but people tend to pay much more attention to managers' spoken words than their carefully crafted written statements.

	Liberation level			
Severity	I. Authoritarian	II. Empowered	III. Supportive	IV. Self-Managed
Very high (Fundamental)				• Videotaping of meetings
High			• Conflict fishbowl • Open message flow • Open reports	• Baseball cards
Moderate	• All-hands meetings • Broadcasts • Dashboard	• Kanban • Visualization	• Daily updates • Open book • Social platforms	• Issue water filter
Low	• Internal surveys	• Boss questions • Open calendars • Failure nights	• Culture book • Demo days • 10X factor meetings	
Very low (Work Hack)		• Company user manual • Personal operation manual		

Table 12 Management practices: Transparency

Empowered companies recognize the benefits of an "all there is to know" stance and invest more in it. Office spaces in such companies are often decorated with large-scale printouts, walls full of post-it notes, or well-sketched flipcharts. Visualization of anything, from mundane issue lists to arcane values, display not only openness but also the willingness of people to stand for something, to express themselves, and to be scrutinized. Physical visualization in office spaces or floors is especially powerful as passersby cannot help but see it. Good visualizations, unlike screens which have to be called up, naturally slide into view without much effort. Like advertising, they take hold of both subconscious and conscious sides of the brain.

A key visualization technique that combines many different purposes and is easily understood is the Kanban board, which visualizes tasks, targets, progress, workload, and responsibility in a table. What makes a Kanban board special is that it comes with a set of processes, defining:

- What should be tracked (one card per work item).
- How to prioritize and assign work (by a pull system).
- In which stages work should be done (typically in columns like "To be done," "Started," "To be tested," and "Done").
- Who is working on what (by names noted on a card).

- A regular interval and a structure for the team to meet and update the chart together.
- The maximum amount of work in progress that should be going on a certain stage at any point of time (the work in progress or WIP limit).
- The bottlenecks experienced by the team (by looking at how many cards are stuck at a certain stage or with a certain person without much movement).
- What has been achieved (in the "Done" column).

A Kanban board is a light, configurable, and extremely effective way of tracking tasks. It can be configured to track and coordinate almost anything in businesses, whether on an individual, team, or company level. It is a truly multi-purpose tool that will remain useful for the entire lifecycle of a company, no matter its size.

Other examples of work hacks that drive transparency for level 2 companies are:

- *Boss questions.* The boss posts his questions openly for all co-workers to read and comment on. This is the inverse of patronizing.
- *Open calendars.* Everyone has full visibility of each other's calendars.
- *Failure Nights.* A meeting where managers (or co-workers) ask four questions, each to be answered in a single sentence, about their latest failures: What did you learn? At what cost? What is the good in the bad? How high is the return on failure?
- *Company user manual.* A manual on how a company works, written from the perspective of a "user." Useful not only for onboarding and alignment, but also for making changes visible.
- *Personal operation manual.* A written statement of how one wants to be communicated with and worked with. To avoid sounding self-centered and self-righteous, humor, humility, and self-deprecation are advisable.

Supportive companies at level 3 find it easier to be open and accept the pain that comes with transparency. They relax control of communications and use more flexible, engaging meeting formats, such as:

- *Conflict fishbowls.* Two or more people discuss their conflicts openly in front of an audience.
- *Open message flow.* Everyone may drop in on everybody else's communications at any time (for example, by replacing email with open Slack channels, Trello Boards, etc.).
- *Open reports.* Reports of all meetings (protocols, action lists) are published for all to see on a message board or a web platform such as Slack.
- *Daily updates.* A journaling technique in which every morning everyone in the organization publicly posts answers to three questions: What did I do yesterday? What is to be done today? What are the things or feelings preoccupying me? Like a management one-and-one with yourself, daily updates are not about control or criticism, but self-reflection and openness.
- *Open book.* Educating co-workers in financial literacy and openly communicating business figures so that everyone can understand the company's financial underpinnings.
- *Social platforms.* A cloud platform that allows more egalitarian social interaction. Today, there is no real alternative to managing the virtual self. Some even say that in a digital world, the virtual self is more and more yourself—at least in the eyes of others.
- *Culture book.* A regularly maintained collection of stories displaying the organization's learnings and values. These can include narratives or drawings that describe real events, and they serve to replace statements of corporate values.
- *Demo days.* Teams display their ideas in a crisp, entertaining, and inspiring way (similar to hackathons). The main purpose is to foster transparency, encourage new ideas, and increase engagement.
- *10X Factor meetings.* Monthly all-hands meetings with a series of five-minute presentations of individuals' contribution to the company, watched and rated by everyone.

A few additional practices at level 4, the self-managed company, demonstrate how radical dedication to transparency can be painful at times. The first is the highly controversial practice of videotaping and streaming every meeting for anyone in the organization to view. This requires people to be true to their words in every situation or risk being exposed as a liar or hypocrite. An organization practicing universal videotaping could well turn out to be a dystopian surveillance state making people feel constantly on guard that they are acting politically correct. Instead of being liberating, transparency can become a cage.

Another practice is called "baseball cards." The cards, based on self-description, feedback, or psychometric testing, describe individuals' traits (both good and bad), expertise, and working style. While they invite self-reflection, these cards may strike at the heart of one's self-image, so in order for them to work, the willingness to feel the pain of openness and self-reflection must be strong.

Do universal videotaping of meetings or "baseball cards" based on psychometric data push transparency too far? Whatever the verdict, the fact that these practices are technologically feasible and already being used hints at future possibilities. They may be alien to many people, but could we use the upsides while avoiding the downsides? Isn't this amount of transparency in an age of voluntary self-tracking inevitable? Time will tell.

■ Chapter 8: Management Practices for Development

One of the great tragedies of all time is people
holding opinions without ever putting them into the open.
– Ray Dalio, 2018[122]

Most companies largely opt out of developmental management practices. They believe that systematic learning and reflection is not necessary and, beyond occasional training sessions, can be safely left to the individual worker. In the same vein, projects are just mechanical, analytical exercises to get from A to B; they are merely lists of somewhat dependent tasks that can consequently be planned and executed in a top-down, analytical fashion. This disdain for developmental practices contributes to the static, sclerotic environment in which so many companies find themselves.

In the digital age ambiguity reigns and change is rampant, making it indispensable for companies to invest in developmental management practices. Yet, in hierarchical companies with lower liberation levels, these practices tend to be ineffective. There is no better way to learn than exploring in a diverse team, guided by one's own intrinsic motivation.

Management practices for projects

Whenever a company puts considerable effort and collaboration into changing its way of working from the status quo to a future state, a project is called for.

At maturity level 1, typical managers approach projects as they do the rest of their work—analytically. The analytical breakdown of projects is typically done in seven steps: (1) determine the status quo; (2) determine the desired

---

122 (Dalio, 2018)

state; (3) determine the deltas between the status quo and the desired state; (4) determine the actions needed to eradicate the delta(s); (5) order and group the actions in a logical manner; (6) assign the work; and (7) check the execution and adapt action plans if necessary. Popular classical project management methods, such as PMi or Prince2, do not waste too much time on steps 1 to 3; they take the project goals as given and focus on the execution part, steps 4 to 7. The emphasis is on getting to the desired state, B, not questioning it.

The classic way of organizing projects when a company can pinpoint, in detail and with certainty, what is best at a future point of time is the so-called "waterfall project." A blueprint is written that describes the future state in detail, and work starts only after the blueprint is approved. A steering committee holds the project manager and the team accountable to the letter of the blueprint, but the steering committee must understand the blueprint and be absolutely sure that this is what they really want before they approve it.

Severity	Liberation level			
	I. Authoritarian	II. Empowered	III. Supportive	IV. Self-Managed
Very high (Fundamental)		• Lean start-up		
High		• Rapid prototypes • Staff-on-demand	• SCRUM	
Moderate	• Project management • Waterfall projects	• Extreme programming • LEAN project management	• Agile methods • Crystal methods • Scaled AGILE	
Low	• Project portfolio mgmt.	• Product logs	• Dragon dreaming • Six-Week projects • Technology grooming	
Very low (Work Hack)		• Delphi estimation • Value poker		

Table 13 Management practices: Projects

However, in a digital economy, predicting a certain desirable future state is becoming harder and harder, especially at the level of detail necessary for blueprints of waterfall projects. The project team finds itself determining the results of its own work while actually doing the work. In the digital age, a purely analytical way of looking at projects is no longer sufficient. Developing software has always been quite different from construction work, like building a bridge. Software is immaterial and involves many human-made abstractions that are much more bendable than the concrete pillars of a bridge. The time-tested waterfall project still has its place, and blueprints are still valuable, but a more evolutionary approach to project targets and a more empowering approach to project teams are needed. These practices can be found at higher liberation levels.

Let's start with the lean family of methods. Since the spectacular quality and success of Japanese carmakers in the 1980s, the term "lean" has become fashionable and is used to describe production systems that employ self-managed teams. The metaphor inherent in the word "lean" plays perfectly to the paradigm of efficiency that is so prevalent in companies. Over the last three decades almost all companies have enacted some major lean initiatives, but more often than not the concept has been corrupted. Many ordinary cost-cutting measures have been labeled "lean"—which is quite an irony, as the essence of lean is autonomous, self-managed, and learning teams and not lay-offs of people. Sadly, many managers have failed to understand this distinction.

Lean is a precursor to today's agile models, which are already also being corrupted by hierarchies, hijacked as an exploitative method for more control and productivity. In productivity terms, companies often appear to benefit from agile and lean, although they usually fail to utilize the full potential of these methods—especially when it comes to quality, evolutionary innovation, increased agility, and more sustainable team efforts. Managers are, by and large, oblivious of the detail and the fundamental principles underlying these methods.

Other practices at level 2 are:

- *Lean startup.* Focuses on the fast delivery and improvement of a "minimal viable product" (MVP) in fast iterations.
- *Rapid prototypes.* Techniques for circumventing constraints by building throw-away prototypes. The target is to demonstrate central concepts, not to deliver viable solutions immediately.
- *Project Parliament.* A parliament, consisting of project team members and representatives of the involved business units, is charged with making significant decisions based on secret voting. The idea is to get problems and opportunities discussion out into the open, more than a project manager and steering committee ever hope for.

- *Staff on demand.* An automated way of directing people towards a common goal, enabled by technology and social insights. Geared toward accelerating the norming, storming, forming, and performing phases of teams.
- *Extreme programming.* A software development method focusing on working in pairs in a test-driven development process. It can also enrich many business projects.
- *Lean project management.* A set of rules for approaching work in a team-centric, learning way. Very similar to agile methods but with a greater focus on tackling waste in processes.
- *Product logs.* Looks at a project as a product that needs to be built with a required list of features that can be debated, prioritized, refined, morphed, delayed, and neglected as needed.

Agile is both a set of values and a toolbox. These can be used to "flavor" more conventional projects (e.g., stand-up meetings) and come up with tailor-made methods. Agile methods work best at level 3. Although they can be used at lower liberation levels, they are bound to conflict with the values and behaviors of the hierarchy. Level 3 examples include:

- *SCRUM.* A rigorous, packaged application of agile methods providing a scripted environment to solve complex problems using autonomous teams. More orderly situations may lend themselves better to waterfall projects.
- *Crystal methods.* A lightweight, scalable agile project method developed by a co-writer of the Agile Manifesto, Alistair Cockburn. Although SCRUM (developed by other co-writers of the Agile Manifesto) won the publicity battle, Crystal provides a toolbox for those wanting to escape the rigidity of SCRUM.
- *Scaled agile.* A catch-all for methods that apply agile in large, multi-team projects, such as LeSS, SAFe, Nexus. These methods have yet to be adopted significantly in the market, perhaps because they are thought of from a bottom-up perspective (the team) and ignore the larger lessons of organizational theory.
- *Dragon Dreaming.* A lesser-known, gamified, and somewhat spiritual method of running small projects.

- *Whitespace Projects.* An approach to encourage and facilitate „under the radar" projects that unfold without management's specific approval.
- *Six-week projects.* All projects are six weeks long. Anything requiring effort beyond that should be a product (which itself is built across a number of 6-week projects). The key is to finish what has been started at the end of every six weeks.
- *Technology grooming.* A variant of project portfolio management, where technology, not products, is the subject of a screening and development process. This works better with more mature organizations, as it requires the capability to run experiments.

There are no specific management practices for projects at level 4, but there are many work hacks, one of which is estimation techniques. All managers are responsible for allocating resources, deciding what should or should not be done. Decisions about projects tend to be the costliest for managers, so a better understanding of how teams (or suppliers) arrive at estimates can be crucial. Most project managers use a combination of bottom-up (asking the specialists) and top-down (picking a number based on experience) thinking processes. Here are two interesting techniques that can supplement the process, increase the quality of results, and accelerate the formation of the team:

- *Delphi estimation.* A time-consuming approach to estimation or prediction, but possibly the best technique in existence today. The estimate proceeds in several stages, where independent experts see the work of other experts, comment on it, and adapt their work in consequence.
- *Value poker.* Gaming cards are used to improve everyone's perspectives. It is fast, but not as effective as the Delphi estimate.

Management practices for learning

Let's start with two assertions. First, a company cannot learn—it is the individuals within the company who learn. Second, learning is not the primary target of a company—learning is only needed from time-to-time by a limited number of people in the organization.

Both these assertions are only true up to a point. It is the collective memory of an organization—consisting of work designs, management practices, and social norms—that allows it to remember what worked and what did not. Consequently, the better (or worse) that companies can perform, the better (or worse) this collective memory (sometimes described as company culture) can absorb positive learning and "unlearn" outdated norms or work designs.

Second, the more stable or predictable the environment in which a business operates, the less learning is necessary. Conversely, in a digital environment that is inherently unstable and dynamic, learning quickly becomes the only critical and sustainable competitive advantage a company can have. By 2019, this is more or less conventional wisdom. This is, however, often misunderstood as a call for especially clever leadership; a call for learning at the top level or for the chosen few—for example, those people in product design. All the top executives traveling to Silicon Valley, all the innovation labs and corporate campuses built to entertain an elite set of product designers or software engineers, all of it shows that learning is still interpreted as a necessity for the few—i.e., for those doing the thinking. The rest of the organization is there to execute what those clever business leaders and product people came up with. The dichotomy between strategy and execution is still dominant in most organizations.

Yet innovation science shows us the great dangers of limiting learning to the elite. Innovation relies not so much on intelligence, but very much on diversity and serendipity. Elite groups are, by definition, not diverse. They are therefore susceptible to groupthink, which is fatal to any innovation effort. Serendipity, on the other hand, is an advanced notion of luck. It is a combination of the facts that luck favors the prepared and that unexpected things happen in unexpected places if one is open to seeing, listening, and recognizing. A business that confines learning to an exclusive and elite group is a business that struggles to see, listen, and recognize innovations.

By and large, company leaders follow the established thought patterns of the industrial revolution: thinking happens at the top. They may try to create learning environments with something of the flavor of a start-up for software engineering and design people, but the rest of the organization is geared to executing what other people have thought out.

In the digital age, change is happening at so many levels and at the same time. It is not only the ability and opportunity to recognize change that matters, but also the speed of execution and scaling. It is often argued that in a digital economy, strategy and execution become one. If strategy can't be fixed for meaningful periods of time, it needs to evolve through rapid execution at rapid intervals.

Learning needs to become more pervasive at all levels of the organization. Yet learning is such a boring term, conjuring up an image of being taught something in a rather tedious process, like in school. Few of us enjoyed that. Learning could be so much more exciting in companies than it was at school. In school, learning is done for its own sake, for the inherent value of knowledge and thinking. In companies, learning is ultimately an exercise in advanced problem-solving. Learning in classic hierarchies, however, is often on-the-job training. Training, moreover, is usually deficit-oriented: a job requires a certain skill and the person assigned to it has to be brought up to the required skill level by training. The whole notion of learning in business is seen by many managers as all but synonymous with training. Ask a manager what management practices he uses to encourage learning, and they will probably point to "an average of five days of training per person per year." Regardless of the number, the focus on training as the only learning practice is lamentable.

At level 1, learning is driven by a manager who assigns people to training or educates them themselves. Probing is the practice of discussing an issue in an intense private session with a subordinate. Good probing can reveal very meaningful insights while also strengthening the relationship. Yet, it is not easy to manage this listening, coaching, and communication exercise without being seen as a micro-manager. Probing can also be done in a workshop setting; problem-time is a carefully scripted probing practice.

Another example of a level 1 learning practice is the competency board, which is a public noticeboard that displays competency levels of people. At Decurion, a hotel chain, this board displays fifteen competencies with five levels each. Qualification, a test, and positive peer approval are needed to achieve these levels. It is visible to everyone in the company and aims to spark a desire in co-workers to progress their competence.

Severity	Liberation level			
	I. Authoritarian	II. Empowered	III. Supportive	IV. Self-Managed
Very high (Fundamental)				
High			• Experimentation • Free education budgets	• Chaos monkey
Moderate	• Probing • Problem time	• After action reports • Job shadowing • Kaizen • Leaders as trainers • Pairing • Peer training	• Mistake of the month • Exploration days • Retrospectives	
Low	• Competency board • Training	• Celebration grid • Front-line discussions	• Guilds • Peer reviewed journal • Learning platforms • Working-out loud • Historian	
Very low (Work Hack)		• Good catch logbook	• Dispute resolver	

Table 14 Management practices: Learning

At level 2, the focus shifts away from the manager as the driver of learning towards peer-to-peer learning between co-workers:

- *After-action reports (AARs).* This is a reflection exercise based on three questions: What happened? What did we expect? What can we learn from this gap? It can be done after a one-hour meeting or a multi-year project and is more impactful if the AAR is available for all to see (cf. transparency practice *open reports*).
- *Job shadowing.* A person is assigned to follow another person for days, weeks, or even months so both can work, learn, and develop together. It can be difficult to do, but it is important not to degrade one person to the role of a bystander or an intern doing easily delegated daily chores.
- *Kaizen.* A group of methods and beliefs to foster continual improvement of work teams, Kaizen calls for iterative work in cycles (e.g., plan-do-check-act, PDCA) with stepwise, evolving goals. Kaizen is at the heart of agile and lean methods but can be applied in isolation.

- *Leaders as trainers.* Fosters connections and lets a leader discover flaws in their thinking.
- *Pairing.* Similar to job shadowing but based on tasks rather than whole jobs. Pairing has the advantage of being less time-consuming and more intensely focused on a specific task. The responsibility for the task should be with the pair.
- *Peer training.* Co-workers take turns teaching each other. Encouraging people to train each other might be a better, more engaging, and cost-effective option than using external trainers.

Less severe, work hack-style practices are about promoting awareness of things that people might learn from:

- *Celebration grid.* A way of reflecting on the silent evidence of failures and successes—i.e., successes that were based on people doing the wrong things and failures that were based on people doing the right things.
- *Frontline discussions.* A group of randomly selected workers are asked: "How would you solve X?" on a regular basis (quarterly, for example). Management attends these discussions, but they are preferably silent.
- *Good catch logbook.* A ledger or cloud platform accessible to all where every success, failure, and learning are recorded by everyone. Can apply to a team, a group of teams, or even companywide.

At levels 1 and 2, the understanding of learning is rather traditional: there is generally a curriculum, which describes what is to be learned, and a pedagogy, which is a way of organizing the learning process. At level 3, the curriculum becomes dynamic. Management or HR are no longer the designers of learning curricula; things that are to be learned find themselves through the intrinsic drive of the people inside the organization. Regarding pedagogy, learning is no longer just training events but is woven into the fabric of everything that a company does by way special microstructures built into meetings and other regular practices.

The most important learning practice of all is experimentation. Experimentation is a great deal more than testing, although traditional companies often confuse the two. It is about systematic, yet meandering, learning. It includes the careful formulation of a hypothesis, the crafting of a good experimental setting in which to perform statistically rigid tests (often based on time series), and a reliable method of analyzing, discussing, and disputing the findings. At the same time, experimenting in business is a pragmatic, fast-paced, action-driven activity, not a scientific exercise; as such, it needs to use heuristics (assumptions as short cuts). Successful experimentation is hard for lower-maturity companies, as failures must be seen as learning opportunities that may lead to brutally open discussions. Finding the right balance between an action-biased business and a thorough scientific mentality can be challenging.

Other practices for learning at level 3 are:

- *Free education budgets.* People are free to spend on education without any approval—to procure books, training sessions, or conferences, for example. The spending is visible to everyone; moreover, the effectiveness of education often increases and budgets often decrease.
- *Mistake of the month.* Highlighting mistakes in a monthly ceremony encourages the taking of well-intentioned risks. It showcases the desired behaviors and makes the organization more open to failure and learning.
- *Exploration days.* Scripted themed events allowing people to work outside their assigned jobs.
- *Retrospectives.* Structured learning sessions (postmortem or AAR) after an activity has been performed for a while; it is woven on a small scale into minor daily work routines.
- *Guilds.* Self-organized communities of interest that focus attention in an area that doesn't warrant a dedicated team.
- *Peer-reviewed in-house journal.* Experiments done or concepts proposed are peer-reviewed and published in-house to promote transparency and knowledge. This emulates the academic way of

working and encourages workers who like to engage in critical and systems thinking to work together and prosper. It resembles *peer* or *open concept review* but is more rigidly applied.

- *Learning platforms.* Web-based learning systems, often using gaming or social contexts.
- *Working out loud.* Everyone makes a request to a group, which tries to use its combined knowledge, resources, and connections to help fulfill it, thereby fostering a culture of giving.
- *Historian.* Organizations invest very few resources in their past. Learning from the experience of previous initiatives can be made systematic by allocating the role of historian in charge of tracking and researching what has worked and what has not.
- *Dispute resolver.* Structured guidance on dispute resolution can be supported by a checklist, an app, and mediators.

Management practices for reflection

Reflection is central to the performance of an organization. Letting others know how they are doing provides direction and momentum to an individual's effort. A classic trinity of management practices rooted in the machine metaphor is:[123]

- One-to-one meetings between an employee and a superior are there to gather information, like the dashboard of a car.
- Delegation, jobs, and roles are there to tell an employee what to do, like a steering wheel.
- (Classic) feedback is telling employees how to do their work, like the gas and the brake pedals.

Giving feedback based on observed behavior is a critical skill in traditional, low liberation-level companies. Giving feedback in an appreciative, sensible, fair, emotionally intelligent way that challenges the employee to perform highly is a very valuable skill for any manager. However, there are many major potholes to navigate.[124]

---

123 (Horstman, 2016).
124 (Sanford, 2017)

- Feedback tends to silence people. Criticism implies judgment and we all recoil from feeling judged. Psychologists such as Daniel Goleman contend that threats to our self-esteem and sense of self-worth in the form of criticism can feel like threats to our survival.[125]
- Feedback often says more about the feedback-giver than the recipient. Most feedback is more about the giver's self-projection than about the truth. Bad judgments are common in a business environment where there is pressure on time and results.
- The quality of feedback can't be measured. With no good way of establishing its effects or whether it was well-received, it is very hard for a manager to get better at it.
- Feedback is about being right and the other person being wrong.

Severity	Liberation level			
	I. Authoritarian	II. Empowered	III. Supportive	IV. Self-Managed
Very high (Fundamental)			• Reflection microstructures	• Dot-collector
High	• Classic feedback		• Crowd feedback • Peer feedback • Skip-Level feedback	• Pain button
Moderate		• Coaching • Concept peer review	• Open concept review	
Low		• Feedback wraps • Moving motivators	• Merit money	
Very low (Work Hack)		• Kudo cards • Mood board • Personal maps	• Talking partners	

Table 15 Management practice: Reflection

Empowered, or level 2 companies tend to lead by coaching. While feedback is centered on giving advice, coaching is centered on providing open questions that encourage self-reflection. Good coaching is non-judgmental and appreciative, and less tainted by the individual mindset and observations of the coach. While there is mixed evidence about the effectiveness of coaching as a leadership style (measured by overall performance of an organization), it is undoubtedly one of the best ways of revealing people's potential. Good coaching is hard. It is an indirect way of leading that requires personal skill and restraint.

---

125 (Goleman, 1995)

Carol Sanford argues that "feedback is colored by projection and barbed by annoyance—it lets people shut down."[126] Yet feedback is indispensable: how can you lead a company or a unit if you are not supposed to tell people how they are doing? Companies at higher levels of maturity have found two answers to this.

The first is to create a culture where candid feedback is universally given, so people know how to handle it and tend to take feedback as a learning opportunity and less as an existential threat. The second is to shift from feedback to self-reflection. Companies at higher maturity levels provide both management practices that encourage a feedback culture and an environment that encourages self-reflection. This type of company environment is supported by a belief in both critical and systems thinking. Critical—or Socratic—thinking adheres to the objective analysis of facts to form a judgment. It is rational, skeptical, unbiased, factual thinking that is at the same time self-directed, self-disciplined, self-monitored, and self-correcting. It seeks to overcome myopia and groupthink. Given its focus on rationality, there is little opposition to critical thinking in companies.[127]

Systems thinking encounters more resistance. Systems thinking can be described as awareness of the whole organization—its heart, hand, and head—with all its complexity, uncertainties, and changing interdependent causalities. In systems thinking, all viewpoints have merit and there is no monopoly on truth. That doesn't mean there is no truth, but truth is more often than not uncertain and partial. To be open about one's doubts is often seen as inappropriate for a manager.

A company founded on the beliefs of critical and systems thinking is one that appreciates an abundance of feedback and self-reflection. One of the best ways to build these beliefs into an organization's culture is to adopt management practices, such as the following level 2 practices:

- *Concept peer review.* Instead of discussing concepts with superiors, peers first review and provide feedback on concepts regularly.

---

126 (Sanford, 2017)
127 A basic list of six questions demonstrates the power of Socratic thinking in a nutshell (**https://en.wikipedia.org/wiki/Socratic_questioning**), retrieved on 21 June 2019.

- *Feedback wraps.* A five-part asynchronous written feedback (usually by email or platform message) that describes context, lists observations, expresses emotions, sorts observations by value, and ends with suggestions. Fast and open feedback wraps are a more regular and appreciative form of feedback.
- *Moving motivators.* A card-based practice useful for team formation and coping with a major change. Each card represents one value—e.g., honor, relatedness, curiosity, power. People are asked to rank their values and put the cards on the table while explaining their reasoning. They then shift their cards to signify how a proposed change impacts their values at work.
- *Mood board.* People can post feelings, questions, and comments about a subject in any way they choose. The board can be used in a meeting or at any time in the office space, arranged as a table, a graph with two axes, or just a wild collage of text and images.
- *Kudo cards.* A form of "thank you" notes.
- *Personal maps.* Knowledge about a person is a prerequisite for giving useful feedback. A written record—in the form of a mind map, for example—may help a person remember details such as spouse's name, birthdays, tastes, key traits (though it shouldn't be done in secret).

At level 3, the focus moves further from external (other people providing feedback) to internal consideration (self-reflection), as well as from centralized (down the chain of command) to distributed feedback (everyone providing feedback to everyone). The most important management practice at this level is *reflective microstructures*, where reflection is woven into the existing work design. For example:

- A team status meeting starts with a check-in routine, with everyone asked to say what is on their mind.
- A workshop ends with people sharing what they have learned, their remaining questions, and their level of confidence going forward.
- A planning meeting lets people split into pairs to share their thoughts about alternatives, and present the commonalities and differences to the group. For example, by using the 1-2-4-ALL meeting microstructure.

Some companies have so much spiritual zeal—often by virtue of their founder—that their people take part in stand-alone reflective exercises.[128] These companies emphasize the spiritual nature of their community. Liberated companies might choose to follow this practice or leave the spiritual sphere to the individual. This author is skeptical of attempts to foist spiritual journeys onto people; while it may create outward submission to the spiritual regime, it will not necessarily result in inner conversion.

Other practices to encourage feedback in supportive (level 3) organizations include:

- *Crowd feedback*. Why elicit feedback only internally? Customers, suppliers, or partners can deliver valuable insights. Enabled by digital technology, crowd feedback can be built into every business process giving "outsiders" the opportunity and motivation to engage.
- *Peer feedback*. A way of decentralizing feedback is for people to invite other people to give them feedback at regular intervals. Feedback is given in a round-table session with all (preferably up to five) feedback givers.
- *Skip-level feedback*. Feedback is given to the boss's boss at regular intervals or for specific purposes. Skipping levels gets frontline and management more connected, while still providing enough context to make the exchange meaningful.
- *Open concept review*. A variant of *concept peer review*. Concepts are posted on a discussion board, and everyone (or a group) in the organization is expected to provide feedback.
- *Merit money*. Co-workers express positive feedback by rewarding one another with a fixed sum of money for any action they think worthwhile. Rules specify the number of rewards an individual may award per period and transparency to prevent people gaming the system.
- *Talking partners*. An assigned pair of co-workers meets daily or weekly for about 15 minutes to talk about whatever is on their mind at work. Partners change periodically.

---

128 Examples can be found in the *Augenhöhe* films, which depict medium-sized enterprises in Central Europe, banks, manufacturing, engineering companies, see **https://vimeo.com/122321254** retrieved 19 June 2019. (German language website: **https://augenhoehe-film.de**)

A company that weaves feedback and reflection into daily business routines through its management practices is going a long way towards building critical and systems thinking directly into its work design. The arbitrariness of feedback ("colored by projection and barbed by annoyance")[129] is overcome by doing more of it and distributing it widely so that it becomes a way of being.

Bridgewater, a hedge fund and a very progressive organization that we will analyze in more detail later in this book, has an extreme feedback culture where feedback is enveloped in critical and systems thinking. Two of its reflective management practices are:

- *Pain button.* Sharing how your feelings have been hurt on a cloud platform accessible to everyone and open for comments.
- *Dot collector.* Performance evaluation during meetings or at any other time. Each person can be given a performance rating and any number of comments for all to see in real-time, so there is no time delay between performance and evaluation. A healthy and stable environment is needed for this to work well and to avoid the blame game.

Working at Bridgewater is both demanding and rewarding. Learning opportunities are boundless, but the openness and candidness of feedback exposes any personal weakness for all to see. While it may feel dystopian, it shows what is possible and what the future holds.[130]

Dark Arts
- Work designs offer tangible and actionable ways to change hearts and minds in companies.
- Slot new management practices into your organization or drop existing ones to grow people and better organizations.
- Much can be said in favor of reducing power differentials, but "empowered" or "supportive" practices that are still based on the hierarchy may provide a better choice to start the journey.

---

129 (Sanford, No More Feedback, 2019)
130 An interesting – if curious – fact is that James Comey, the FBI director fired by President Trump in 2016 over the Russia investigation previously worked for Bridgewater.

- In the digital age, when you are thinking about:
    - o *Organizing*: Think (self-managing) teams.
    - o *Decision-making*: Think advice process.
    - o *Meetings*: Think liberating microstructures.
    - o *Directing*: Think mission command.
    - o *People management*: Think peer appraisals.
    - o *Transparency*: Think visualization and Kanban.
    - o *Projects*: Think agile methods.
    - o *Learning*: Think advanced problem solving, e.g., experimentation.
    - o *Reflection*: Think reflective microstructures.

Further Reading
- Peter M. Senge (1990) *The Fifth Discipline* (Currency)
- Jurgen Appelo (2010) *Management 3.0* (Addison Wesley Professional) and (2016) *Managing for Happiness* (Wiley)
- Stanley McChrystal, et al (2015) *Team of Teams* (Penguin)
- David Marquet (2015) *Turn the Ship Around* (Penguin)
- Brian Robertson (2015) *Holacracy* (Penguin)
- Carol Sanford (2017) *The Regenerative Enterprise* and (2019) *No More Feedback* (Interoctave)

PART III:
COMPANY CONFIGURATIONS

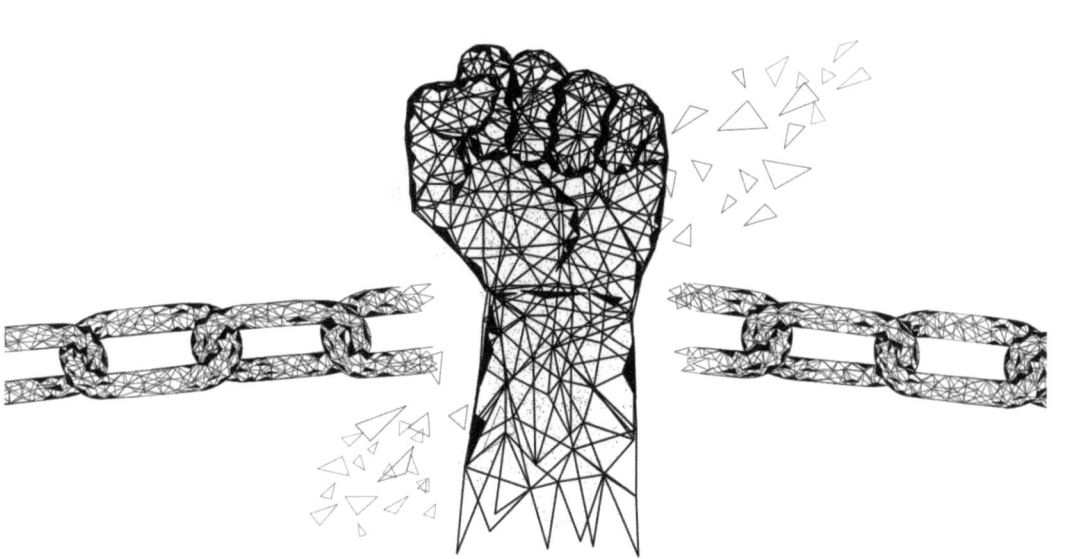

■ Chapter 9: Configuring Companies with Management Practices

A company is a product: Do people who work here know how to use the company? Is it simple? Complex? What's fast, what's slow about it? Are there bugs? What's broken that we can fix quickly and what's going to take a long time?
– Jason Fried and David Hansson[131]

Every company uses work designs. It doesn't matter whether these are consciously adopted or just happen to be there. People might not be aware of the existence of work designs, but as soon as any number of people collaborate, the use of work designs is inevitable. Work designs are a list of product features, the product being the company itself.

However, most leaders tend to limit their thinking about organizations to issues of structure, business processes and this or that piece of management wisdom or fashion. Some leaders, those more inclined to think holistically, are aware that any decision about a particular work design represents at the same time a choice of the corporate values and culture that are embodied in it. Yet very few managers understand how to bring some rigor into the process of configuring companies with work designs.

The central question is: What does a good work design configuration look like? Despite all the advice provided in business literature or elicited by consultants, science has found no recipe for organizational success. Companies and markets are too complex to allow an answer that is simple enough to be useable. As a business practitioner, it is easy to feel lost and abandoned amidst the plethora of advice, conflicting evidence, and dilemmas to be solved. This

131 (Fried & Heinemeier, 2018)

makes management a field that is very susceptible to fashions, beliefs, simplification, and motivational calls for action.

While it would be foolish to run a business based on simplistic advice, truthful advice is inconclusive and unhelpful. The only way forward is to try new things, observe the effects, and continuously fine-tune ways of doing things in a group. A helpful way of doing this is to map the current work designs of an organization onto the Liberated Company Map. This map can be a starting point in a quest to find better solutions. To see how this might work, let's take a look at how other companies configure their work design. We look at one rather traditional company and three that are at the forefront of organizational design.

A cartography of the management practices of four companies

The idea of configuring companies is not new. The term "configuration" was first used in organizational research as early as 1973, but at that time it was limited to playing around with different forms of hierarchies.[132] Configuration is the art of describing stages and their effects and is found in all social sciences. It is also regarded as a unifying school of thought in the realm of strategic management.[133] In this chapter, we explore the work design configurations of four different companies. Since the maps presented in this chapter represent a simplified order superimposed on the complex subject of companies, they are only partially accurate. However, even a geographical map is just an approximation of the physical features of a territory. The vagueness of the map of management practices is a reflection of the much vaguer territory of companies. It is much more like an early Renaissance map that can be used by explorers: there are plenty of opportunities to explore the uncharted areas and to complete the whole picture. The key is to take the initiative, go out, explore, and configure companies to make them a better place to work for everyone.

---

132 (Galbraith, Designing Complex Organizations , 1973)
133 (Mintzberg, Strategy Safari, 2008)

The four companies mapped in this book are all successful companies even though they each operate in totally different sectors. However, it is not so much the sector that determines which work designs a company is using, but rather its aspirations, as the analysis in this chapter will demonstrate.

	Retailer	Bridgewater	Haier	Buurtzorg
Main idea of USP	Location	Superior decisions	Entrepreneurship	Service mastery
Sector	Retail	Finance	Manufacturing	Home care
Digital driver	Omnichannel	VUCA	IoT	Platform
Purpose	Shareholder value	Shareholder value	Customer service	Betterment
No. of employees	46000	1700	76900	14000

Table 16 Company background

Three of the four companies are extremely successful organizational pioneers, ranking among the most inspiring companies in the realm of management and organization. The fourth, a retailer, is a good, well-rounded, conventional company. It is not a bad place to work, with solid economic results and low attrition rate. As such, it is very representative of many well-run traditional companies.

There are two criteria for marking a work design on the map. First, the work design must be adopted widely in the organization. Second, it must be central to the way the system works. Only if these two conditions are met can a work design be considered "adopted" and marked in bold. Consequently, any practices that are not widely adopted or not central to the organizational model will not be marked. Of course, there is no such thing as a universal measurement that can be applied. However, if there are sizable pockets inside the organization that are using a certain practice, those practices will be listed in non-bold letters to indicate development.

Map I: Retailer - a classic configuration

The configuration of management practices used by a more traditional organization, a major multi-billion-euro revenue European retailer, is illustrated in Figure 12.

	Coordination	Intelligence	Emotions
Action	Hierarchy Policies Work Groups L1 / L2 / L3 / Organizing L4	Autocratic Decisions Delegation of Tasks L1 / L2 / L3 / Decisions L4	Boss Led Meetings Discussions Classic Status Meetings *One on Ones* Classic Meeting Roles *Hosted Meetings* *Liberating Structures* L1 / L2 / L3 / Meetings L4
Control	Orders Budget Job Descriptions Standard Op. Procedures Target Setting Reports L1 / L2 / L3 / Directing L4	Managerial Wage Setting Manager-driven Hiring Managerial Appraisal Classic Working Hours L1 / L2 / L3 / People L4	All-hands Meetings L1 / L2 / L3 / Transparency L4
Development	Project Management *Agile Methods* Waterfall Projects Project Portfolio Mgmt. L1 / L2 / L3 / Projects L4	Training L1 / L2 / L3 / Learning L4	Classic Feedback *Coaching* *Moving Motivators* L1 / L2 / L3 / Reflection L4

Figure 12 The management practices of a European retailer

This successful retailer is feeling the pinch of the new digital competition. To be "Amazonized"—i.e. to be whittled down in revenue and profits into insignificance—is a major threat in today's retail economy. About 90 percent of sales are generated from traditional stores, yet the company still relies on a command-and-control way of managing its business:

- *Organization*. Hierarchy and policies used to organize actions. Work is assigned by managers to subordinates.
- *Decisions*. Managers make decisions and may delegate parts of the execution.
- *Meetings*. It is agreed they should have an agenda, start and end on time, and results should be captured in meeting minutes, but little further thought is given to meetings.

- *Control.* Like most traditional organizations, the company is heavy on control. People are supposed to do their job as described by a manager.
- *People.* Managers appraise people for compliance.
- *Transparency.* The company operates on a "need to know basis." There are no practices for transparency except the biannual all-staff meeting at business-unit level.
- *Projects.* Traditional waterfall projects delivered by traditional project management and facilitated by a small corporate project portfolio management team. Agile methods are tinkered with in some parts of the organization to mixed results.
- *Learning.* Deficit-oriented. People are trained to overcome any perceived skill gaps that prevent them from doing their job properly.
- *Reflection.* Managers are expected to give corrective feedback.

Overall, the company has been relying on broadly the same set of management practices for years, even decades. Compare the Liberated Company Map (Figure 8) to Figure 12 and it becomes clear that the retailer is missing out on many practices. Indeed, most managers are probably not even aware of their existence, or have only a rudimentary understanding of certain practices, let alone of the interdependencies between different practices. Typically for traditional hierarchical companies, the lack is greatest in the fields of decisions, meetings, transparency, learning, and feedback. In contrast, directive and people practices are quite numerous and occupy most of the managers' time. When managers are supposed to know better and organize the work, there is no need for more elaborate practices in the other categories, especially those on the outer axis of "Development" and "Emotions." Management's blind spot is clearly visible.

The fundamental credo of this particular configuration of management practices is that competent managers ensure that everyone does their assigned job. In Part III of this book, I will make the case that every company needs to hold a set of ideas to configure itself well in the digital age. Using a simplified version of this framework, the five basic ideas of this retailer can be described as:

1. An idea of technology that is ... nowhere to be seen.
2. An idea of performance centered on the competent manager.
3. An idea of rule based on hierarchical control.
4. An idea of work based on static jobs and a division of people into two classes: thinkers (managers) and doers (employees).
5. An idea of life that sees work as a job to be done with loyalty and competence.

That configuration has worked well for the retailer in past decades. In the age of Amazon, however, the continued lack of development and intrinsic motivation leaves the company struggling to adapt to the realities of the ever-changing digital marketplace. Economic results are still good but have stagnated a bit over the last couple of years. This is a good company, yet management is struggling to come to grips with shaping its future.

Map II: Bridgewater - an all-out learning configuration

Bridgewater is all about learning. For a global hedge fund, it is all-important to get the big decisions right—i.e., the ones involving billions of dollars. Consequently, Ray Dalio, the founder and guiding spirit of the company, has configured it with work designs that strive to get one thing right: making big decisions. Learning is the sustainable advantage that Bridgewater seeks in order to make ever-better decisions.

Bridgewater can be characterized as a hierarchical organization that relies not on direct orders but on mission command. Through its management practices, Bridgewater strives to develop people from a socialized mindset ("team players") to a self-authoring mindset. It wants people to become autonomous, independent problem-solvers. A framework of adult development, proposed by Harvard researcher Robert Kegan, whom we met before, underlies Bridgewater's choice of work designs. In his 2018 book, Ray Dalio describes his organization as "a machine to produce good decisions through the optimal use of the collective power of self-authoring minds."[134]

---

134 (Dalio, 2018)

Let us look at how Bridgewater achieves this, category by category (see Figure 13).

Section	Level	Coordination	Intelligence	Emotions
Action	L1	Hierarchy; Policies; Work Groups	Autocratic Decisions; Delegation of Tasks	Boss Led Meetings; Discussions; Classic Status Meetings; One on Ones; Classic Meeting Roles
	L2		Delegation of Decisions; Participative Decisions	Hosted Meetings; Dialogue; Check in & out; Creative Structures
	L3	Decentral IT/HR	Advice Process; Decisions by Algorithm; Classical Voting	Engaging Meetings; Situational Workshops
	L4	*Organizing*	Believability Weighted Decisions — *Decisions*	*Meetings*
Control	L1	Budget; Job Descriptions; Standard Op. Procedures; Target Setting; Dashboards; Reports	Managerial Wage Setting; Manager-driven Hiring; Managerial Appraisal; Classic Working Hours; Candidate Testing; Standardized Interviews	All-hands Meetings; Broadcasts; Internal Surveys
	L2	Mission Command; Model Behaviors; Tool Scaping	Coaching centric; Performance Mgmt.; 360 Degree Appraisals	
	L3	Self-Service Targets; Collaborative Planning	Peer based Appraisals; Open 360 Appraisals; Onboarding till Mature	Open Reports; Daily Updates; Social Platforms
	L4	*Directing*	*People*	Videotaping of Meetings; Baseball Cards; Issue Water Filter — *Transparency*
Development	L1	Project Management; Waterfall Projects; Project Portfolio Mgmt.	Probing; Problem Time; Training	Classic Feedback
	L2		After Action Reports; Kaizen; Frontline Discussions	Coaching
	L3		Experimentation; Mistake of the Month; Retrospectives; Learning Platforms	Reflection Microstructures; Peer Feedback; Skip Level Feedback; Talking Partners
	L4	*Projects*	*Learning*	Dot Collector; Pain Button — *Reflection*

Figure 13 Management practices of Bridgewater

Organization

Bridgewater has not abandoned the traditional hierarchical structure. It focuses much more on learning and reflective practices, while expecting managers to empower employees so that people can take charge of their own development. Managers are to refrain from ordering and requesting obedience; instead, they should use *mission command*. Personal development at Bridgewater is decentralized: everyone is a coach and a mentor, as well as being coached and mentored.

Decisions

This is the area where Bridgewater is very special and very focused. Most decisions are still made by individuals and hierarchical superiors, but the most important decisions are made using a unique process called "believability-weighted decision-making." In a very structured meeting format, decisions are made by voting on alternatives. The number of votes that everyone gets depends on their track record of making good decisions. More experienced, more competent, more knowledgeable people with better track records get more votes than novices without much experience in the subject that is to be decided upon. Hierarchical rank does not matter—but competence in the subject to be discussed does.

The thinking behind believability-weighted decision-making is that voting is good, as it allows an organization to use collective intelligence, but it is better still if the voting is done by competent people—an idea that is as reasonable as it is fraught with difficulty and danger. Who determines the competence levels or the individual believability of people? At Bridgewater, that competence level can be set by a superior, it can be voted upon by a group, it can be established by data analysis (for example, on the basis of CVs or psychometric testing), or it can be a combination of these three methods.

Believability-weighted decision-making is an attempt to make high-stakes decision-making in companies more effective. In democracies, anyone proposing this kind of decision-making would be rightly accused of Orwellian elitism. Every national assembly, even the founding fathers of American democracy, struggled with this issue: "Surely, we can't give equal voting rights to the plebs, the uneducated masses! We aristocrats/bishops/merchants/educated people need to lead." In a company setting, the jury is still out on the believability-weighted decision-making idea. Ray Dalio is sure that this kind of decision-making is a huge part of the reason why Bridgewater is—by some measures—the most successful hedge fund in the world.

More conventional decision-making practices are also used at Bridgewater, like participative decision-making, delegation of decisions, and the advice process. Routine decisions, those that can be safely trusted to a number-crunching machine, are routinely engineered into algorithms. Especially in the financial sector, machines are making many decisions on their own, or at the very least are an integral part of a combined machine-human decision-making process. While other companies haphazardly approach decision-making-by-machines (often as minor features of this or that process), Bridgewater has elevated algorithmic decision-making into a work design.

Meetings

Bridgewater is strong on meeting structures. It recognizes that everyone must be heard. It employs a time limit of a maximum of two minutes of uninterrupted talk in small meetings. It also expects people to make themselves heard, too: staying silent is not an option. Even in large-scale meetings, people are obliged to give feedback about their feelings and the performance of other meeting participants, using an online app that displays the feedback in real-time while the meeting is still in progress. People are supposed to be open-minded and assertive. Meeting structures drive these two behaviors to the fore.

Control

Bridgewater employs most of the usual practices of a hierarchical organization: target setting, budgets, dashboards, standard operating procedures, job descriptions, and reports. The most significant practice to align and control the work of people at Bridgewater is mission command, although Ray Dalio doesn't call it that. The nature of mission command fits the overarching target of creating and utilizing self-authoring minds perfectly, as it is squarely based on the independent problem-solver. On top of mission command, people are also expected to pick challenges themselves. The self-authoring mind writes their own destiny in service of the mission that a superior or the company has defined.

Bridgewater uses "toolscaping" intensively to supply its people with integrated tools to manage the business. Far beyond the usual communication and business process supporting systems, it goes so far as to provide apps for interpersonal conflict moderation and interpersonal transparency, as well as cloud systems to stream videos of meetings. It appears that founder and CEO Ray Dalio takes a personal interest in an ever-expanding integrated toolset.

People

Bridgewater emphasizes three kinds of people practices: testing, coaching, and feedback. Testing is pervasive. New hires remain in a special "onboarding" status for as long as reviews are not good enough for them to be allowed to move into the regular line organization. Dalio writes that a 30 percent attrition rate is acceptable, and onboarding can take up to 18 months. Even people inside the organization are re-evaluated regularly by co-workers at all levels and through the use of psychometric testing. Dalio speaks of "oiling the machine," a questionable and telling metaphor for his utilitarian outlook on people.

Performance management is centered on *coaching*. Being a manager at Bridgewater means being a coach; without outstanding listening skills and the ability to effectively question, no one at Bridgewater would be able to climb the ranks, or indeed, retain their job for long.

Transparency

Transparency at Bridgewater is highly valued:

- *Videotaping*. Every meeting is videotaped and accessible for everyone.
- *Issue filter*. Everything people feel about the company and job is supposed to be captured in a system for all to see.
- *Baseball cards*. Every person is described with a small number of key personal attributes determined by psychometric testing and co-worker feedback.
- *Open reports*. Every report is available to everyone. Classified reports do exist but are a rare exception.
- *Daily updates*. Every day, everyone in the organization posts their answers to three questions: What did I do yesterday? What is to be done today? What are my reflections—i.e., the things or feelings that are most in my mind? These posts can be seen by everyone in the organization.

Bridgewater is definitely operating on an "all there is to know" basis, not on a conventional "need to know" basis. Its overarching target is to supply all the information that "self-authoring" minds at all levels can process, learn, and use to provide feedback or come up with better decisions. This degree of openness is radical and can easily appear dystopian. Is a workplace where the light of transparency is everywhere and there are few dark corners to hide and rest still a place for humans? Is this degree of transparency making people show compliant behavior on the outside while keeping their true views to themselves? Many people are quite skeptical about Bridgewater's configuration of work designs, while others, like philanthropist Bill Gates, appear to be supportive of Dalio's practices.[135]

Projects

Little can be obtained from the sources about any special work designs for projects. However, it seems fair to speculate that Dalio's outlook on projects is bound to be determined by the three cornerstones on which he built Bridgewater: elaborate decision-making, learning, and radical transparency/feedback. This means Bridgewater would be expected to use more mature work designs for its projects, like agile methods, but I found nothing to substantiate this claim.

Learning

Dalio's core idea for his company is learning. He wants Bridgewater to be a meritocracy of ideas, a place where the best ideas are produced and where people that consistently produce these great ideas rise to the top. He even provides a formula for this: "Idea meritocracy = Radical truth + Radical transparency + Believability-weighted decision-making." The target is to create a culture of learning, where failure is allowed and the resulting pain is distilled by (brutally honest) reflection into learning. Everyone is expected to teach everyone all the time in a work environment saturated with learning opportunities.

Reflection

Reflection in an environment of "radical truthfulness" means ignoring social impulses to dampen one's critique to the point of being perceived as unkind and rude. Dalio calls this way of giving feedback "tough love." As well as re-

---

135 A critique can be found at **https://www.nytimes.com/2017/09/08/business/dealbook/bridgewaters-ray-dalio-spreads-his-gospel-of-radical-transparency.html**, retrieved 5 June 2019.

flective microstructures, peer feedback, skip-level feedback and talking part-ners, two more radical practices stand out from the host of opportunities for self-reflection at Bridgewater: the "dot collector" and the "pain button."

Bridgewater clearly puts the collective interest of the company ahead of the individual interest of comfort and self-preservation. Bridgewater is a very challenging workplace where employees need to display an uncompromising willingness to learn. There is nowhere to hide from personal injury of the ego in a place of radical openness and radical transparency. Unlike other elitist organizations, no one is able to rest on their laurels. Its central ideas are:

- An idea of technology that sees technology and people as co-workers.
- An idea of performance centered on making ever-better decisions.
- An idea of ruling based on a hierarchy that nurtures people to become self-authoring.
- An idea of work based on never-ending, relentless growth in a machine of learning.
- An idea of life based on mental awareness.

You might feel fascination or abhorrence at these radical practices, but one thing is for certain: they are a great experiment.

Map III: Haier - an entrepreneurial avant-garde configuration

While Bridgewater is about learning, Haier is about entrepreneurship. Haier has changed its management practices radically, first in the face of China's rapid development and evolving place in the global economy. Back in the 1980s, CEO Zhang Ruimin, who still holds the position today, famously staged a ceremonial destruction of washing machines with sledgehammers to draw attention to quality problems. With the digital revolution, Haier needed to reinvent itself once again, this time destroying its hierarchical way of working and radically changing the configuration of its management practices.[136]

---

136 (Cao, 2018)

	Coordination ☞ (L1)	Coordination (L2)	Intelligence 🧠 (L1/L3)	Intelligence (L2/L4)	Emotions ♡ (L1/L3)	Emotions (L2/L4)
Action (top)	Policies; Work Groups	Flattening; Organizational Mirroring; Org. Interface API's; Principles		Delegation of Decisions; Participative Decisions	Discussions	Hosted Meetings
Action (bottom)	Microenterprises; Self-Managed Teams; Venturing; Assets as a Service; Company Board	Circle Organization; Self-Governed Teams; Self-Directed Teams — *Organizing*	Elected Superiors; Crowd Expertise	*Decisions*	Engaging Meetings	*Meetings*
Control (top)	KPI Dashboards; Reports	Mission Command; Model Behaviors; Tool-Scaping			All-hands Meetings; Broadcasts; Internal Surveys	
Control (bottom)	Self-Service Targets; Collaborative Planning; Top Competitive Targets	*Directing*	Peer-based Appraisals; Team based Recruitment; Open 360 Appraisals; No Perks	Self-Service Remuneration — *People*	Open Book; Daily Updates; Demo Days	*Transparency*
Development (top)	Project Management; Waterfall Projects	Lean Start-up; Rapid Prototypes; Staff-on-Demand; Lean Project Management	Probing; Problem Time; Training	After Action Reports; Kaizen	Classic Feedback	
Development (bottom)	Technology Grooming	*Projects*	Experimentation; Learning Platforms	*Learning*	Crowd Feedback; Peer Feedback; Skip-Level Feedback	*Reflection*

Figure 14 Management practices of Haier

Haier's management practices are all about encouraging entrepreneurship. Everyone inside and even outside the Haier organization is encouraged to fulfill their entrepreneurial potential. The whole Haier group is set up like a platform to which entrepreneurs can attach themselves and co-prosper no matter where they come from. The founder has dubbed this management model *Rendanheyi*. *Ren* stands for entrepreneur, *dan* for customer value, and *heyi* for the integration of *ren* and *dan*: the entrepreneur drives customer value while embedded and supported by the Haier platform. Let's take a look at this configuration category by category (see Figure 14 Management practices of Haier).

Organization

Haier is a fully networked organization of independent microenterprises with a maximum size of about 150 people each—the Dunbar number. A microenterprise is part of one of three circles. The outer circle of microenterprises is free to act independently in the market. It is supported by an inner circle of specialized support microenterprises that provide IT, HR, finance, and many other services but have limited power to direct frontline microenterprises.

The third, central circle is in charge of the strategic direction of the whole enterprise. Consequently, microenterprises in the outer circle are free to use the inner circle's services or not, just as they would use the services of any other external supplier.

Note what is missing under "organization," for example, reports. While Haier does of course use reports, they are merely tools, not something fundamental to its management model.

Decisions

Decisions are made in each microenterprise as in a typical, level 3 "supportive" organization. A microenterprise is led by a manager who is supposed to adopt an egalitarian, servant-leader approach to management. The leader can be toppled anytime by a 2/3 majority vote; anyone can propose anyone as a new leader, but the final selection of leaders is made by the central circle team.

Meetings

Haier uses hosted meeting and engaging meeting structures. An example is its weekly OEC meeting (Overall–Everyone/Everyday/Everything–Control/Clear), a collaborative planning, reporting, and alignment meeting where co-workers reflect on their targets and results and come up with actions in front of the group.

Control

Targets are set by everyone independently without managerial interference. These targets should be closely connected to customer value (*dan*) and seek to aspire to "top competitiveness." All targets are made public on the Haier cloud platform and need to be negotiated with the leader of a microenterprise or representatives of the inner circle in a second step. Technically speaking, the way targets are set at Haier is a bottom-up process with strong boundary conditions, using transparency to create social pressure. This process is influenced—but not dictated—by hierarchy.

People

The people management practices used by Haier are typical of a level 3 supportive company; peer-based appraisals across all levels are visible to everyone in the microenterprise. Remuneration is set in a transparent manner with a fixed and a variable amount based on the self-served targets and the performance of the microenterprise. Perks such as job titles or any kind of individual privileges are frowned upon. Hiring is peer-based.

Transparency

Transparency is hugely important at Haier. The company has invested heavily in cloud systems to capture and make accessible all information that a co-worker can ask for. For people to make sense of the data, financial literacy (i.e., open book) is encouraged and seen as an important element in promoting entrepreneurial behavior. Haier also uses engaging meetings (especially the OEC meeting) to inform people and encourage them to speak up.

Projects

The type of project management practiced by Haier is not completely clear from available sources. Haier's extraordinary focus on the customer and quick, iterative action suggests that the company embraces the lean start-up way of working. The inner circle microenterprises, the service platforms, and the large investments in cloud systems make it easy for Haier to embrace a staff-on-demand approach, enabling operations to be quickly scaled. Haier's core business is all about the internet of things (IoT). The company's operations, reflecting that dominance, wouldn't be possible without modern cloud technology.

Learning

Learning in Haier's self-organized microenterprises is entrepreneurial, evolutionary, action-oriented, and customer-driven. Microenterprises are tightly knit communities that know their reputation and money is at stake if they (and their co-workers) do not rise to the challenge of the aspiring targets, the *dan*. Experimentation and a form of *Kaizen*, i.e., evolutionary improvement, are essential practices.

Reflection

Reflection is everywhere at Haier. Everyone is supposed to give feedback to everyone, including via the Haier cloud platform. Microenterprises have the right to investigate and evaluate the performance of inner-circle enterprises, bringing any grievances to the attention of inner-circle leaders as well as the whole Haier community. Most importantly, the customer is invited to give feedback on everything that Haier does. Haier's products capture customer feedback via their sensors and are directly connected to the Haier platform, which in turn is connected to every individual worker. This way, customer feedback, instead of ending up in a soulless, abandoned data warehouse, arrives directly on the doorstep of every co-worker, whose targets are linked to customer satisfaction.

Haier's management practices are all configured to encourage entrepreneurship. They are based on these five ideas:

- An idea of technology that is all but based on putting the company on the trajectory of technology, i.e. making everything possible to satisfy the wants of technology as discussed in Chapter 1.
- An idea of performance centered on borderless entrepreneurship.
- An idea of ruling based on networked, self-organizing microenterprises.
- An idea of work based on customer-driven, aspirational targets.
- An idea of life that frames work as a struggle to serve the customer.

Haier does not mandate the practices to be used within its microenterprises in detail, but it certainly encourages them to adopt a supportive, level 3 stance to manage themselves. However, entrepreneurs (i.e., all workers within microenterprises) enjoy the freedom to adopt their own work design configurations. Haier mandates certain boundary conditions but leaves the detailed design up to the microenterprises to determine in light of their local circumstances. Variety is welcomed and seen as productive. CEO Zhang Ruimin appears to be fully aware of the value of decision-making and learning practices, but he does not mandate them in every microenterprise. A couple of years ago, Haier acquired GE Appliances, a major American competitor. Although Haier did not mandate its way of working there, the former GE Appliances now appears to be running on the Haier platform, having adopted much of the work design configuration of its parent.[137]

Map IV: Buurtzorg - an egalitarian configuration

Our fourth example is something completely different. We now shift from the lofty heights of European retailing, global finance, and manufacturing to an organization providing home care to the sick and the elderly.

Buurtzorg (Dutch for "neighborhood care") is an extraordinary organization.[138] Since its founding in 2006, it has seen remarkable growth, with about 14,500 co-workers in 2018, exceptional client and co-worker satisfaction, and unheard-of levels of productivity and efficiency. Just as Haier or Bridgewater are market leaders in their fields, Buurtzorg is a leader in the health care field. In an aging society, the practices that Buurtzorg uses with such remarkable success may be much more significant than those used to produce household appliances or clever capital investment.

Buurtzorg has attracted much attention in modern business literature. It is a company that has managed to defy conventional thinking for the last 12 years and exceeded all expectations. It provides much better care for patients than was ever deemed possible, at lower costs and with a consistently happy and engaged workforce. At the heart of Buurtzorg's approach is self-management. There are over 1,000 nursing teams, each with a maximum of 12 nurses,[139] supported by a tiny headquarters of about 80 staff and an outsourced

---

137 https://www.bloomberg.com/news/articles/2019-02-08/six-sigma-gives-way-to-rendan-heyi-at-ge-s-appliance-business (retrieved 16 July 2019).

138 Most information about Buurtzorg is sourced from (Nandram, 2015). A good overview of Buurtzorg can be found in this blog article: **https://medium.com/@Harri_Kaloudis/a-first-attempt-at-a-systematic-overview-of-the-public-record-on-buurtzorg-nederland-part-a-ff92e06e673d**, (retrieved 10 June 2019).

139 In addition to 10,000 nurses, there are 4,500 home care workers.

IT system operated on a pay-per-use basis. There are no managers and no hierarchical reporting lines. Let's see how this works.

Figure 15 Management practices of Buurtzorg

Organization

Buurtzorg's management paradigm has been described as "integrating simplification."[140] It is based on:

- *Self-governed teams.* Each team is free to recruit or dismiss team members, to set their own directions, to decide what to work on, and how to do it.
- *Circle organization.* The 80-strong circle teams have some shared services, including basic HR, legal, coaching, and IT, but do not direct the individual teams.
- *Microenterprises.* No team is bigger than twelve persons. Teams are split once they grow over that threshold.

---

140 (Nandram, 2015)

There are five principles underlying Buurtzorg:

1. *Client focus*. The patient's well-being comes first and always.
2. *Professionalism* of the nursing teams.
3. *Autonomy* of every team member to judge and do what is best for the client. Everyone is a "body, mind, and social health entrepreneur."
4. *Web-based platform* for efficient coordination and learning.
5. *Serving others*, be they patients, co-workers, or local communities.

Buurtzorg bases everything on the importance of small teams. That makes its organization remarkably simple. The other eight categories of management practices are basically about integrating the teams so that consistently good health care and economic results are delivered.

Decisions

In the 1990s, many people had the seemingly great idea to "professionalize" health care. Professionalization meant using industrial-age management tools that were in vogue at the time—specialization, outsourcing, measuring, benchmarking, process design, best practices—all with an eye to achieving higher productivity and more consistent, error-free levels of quality. It did not work out this way at all. Today in Western economies, health care is much costlier and arguably not much better than before.

The academic brilliance used in business and process design seems worthless when used on such a complex subject as health care for people. Buurtzorg has demonstrated that a holistic view of the patients, the autonomy to spend as much time as needed with a patient, and an ethos of competence serves everyone better. Where "professionalization of health services" relied on mandated, top-down processes (where people are ordered to do this or that), no one in Buurtzorg's teams is ordered to do anything. Everything is decided either by oneself or—if needs be—consensually by the team.

Consensus is not well-liked in most businesses. It reeks of indecision, of everlasting time- and motivation-consuming bickering. But it does a great job at Buurtzorg in getting people to feel valued and act as autonomous masters of their work. The time spent talking, explaining, and lobbying appears to be a good investment. It helps people light the fire inside them and devote themselves to service.

Some decisions are voted on. The headquarters might put this or that decision to the vote or the team themselves might decide in consensus to vote on a case-by-case basis. Or it might empower a single team member to make a decision about a specific question (i.e., the advice process).

Buurtzorg's teams use seven roles to delegate tasks to their members: nurse, housekeeper (facility manager), informer (controller), developer (project manager), planner (scheduler), team player (contributor), and mentor (in charge of onboarding new team members).

Buurtzorg aims at sustainable home care solutions. Therefore, it engages with the local community, neighbors, shops, friends, and relatives. Its team members are part of the fabric of local communities. Nurses aim to mobilize people as soon as possible and render themselves and their services superfluous. At Buurtzorg, people are enabled and expected to do what is best for their patients rather than keep them in a perpetual state of dependency. Locally embedded, self-governed teams go a long way to solving the dilemma of economic incentives vs. quality of service in the patient's favor.

Meetings

At the heart of Buurtzorg is the weekly team meeting. At the beginning of this meeting, every team member is expected to say what they need from this meeting. The agenda for the meeting is thus built on the spot, according to actual needs. At the end of the meeting, people are asked if they got what they needed. Several days a year, the Buurtzorg Congress is held. The Buurtzorg Congress uses engaging meeting formats, such as agenda building, breakout sessions, run-and-select-your-own meetings, and other microstructures. Except for the two meetings mentioned above, there are no other mandated meetings. Teams are free to meet other team members or other teams, if they think it necessary. Meeting structures at Buurtzorg are minimal, simple, and efficient. A lot of care is given to get these few but central meetings right. Right from its founding, Buurtzorg has invested in an online platform and a central coaching team that educates nurses in communication skills, such as discussions and dialogues.

Control

There is one last vestige of hierarchical power: founder Jos de Block. There have been instances where de Block has served as the decision-maker of last resort, but overwhelmingly he refrains from meddling in the autonomy of the 1000+ teams. The coaching team is supposed to stick to its guns, too: it is there to coach and not to direct. With one coach looking after about 50 teams, it is hard to do anything more, anyway.

The practice that Buurtzorg uses to remain in control of teams can be characterized as mission command. Buurtzorg demands a 60 percent utilization rate of invoiceable hours from its teams. It leaves the team with all the freedom to decide how to achieve this goal. Provided that this goal is met, and patients are served well, a team will not hear much from the rest of the organization. If the utilization rate is consistently below the target, a coach will engage with the team to mediate a solution, but not to mandate one. On the other hand, any team or team member can engage with the rest of the organization, as needed: Work is all "pull" and very little "push."

Tool-scaping and dashboards are used as critical glue for organizational coherence. Transactional systems support functions such as billing and purchasing. Communication systems enable team members to exchange information in forums, wikis, and so on, as well as providing education on care practices or business subjects. Information systems provide a dashboard about a team's performance with some selected benchmarks about how other teams are doing. As in other companies, there are lots of systems. The difference at Buurtzorg lies in the way that the systems—the "tool-scape"—have evolved and been pragmatically developed by an independent software provider. That software provider has been with Buurtzorg from the beginning and developed the tool-scape on a pay-per-use base, taking on entrepreneurial risk and investing in the prosperous future of Buurtzorg. In contrast to this, most companies rely on centrally planned and mandated systems. At Buurtzorg, systems can't be mandated—they have to be embraced by nurses if the software integrator is to earn anything.

Besides high-level target setting (mission command) and IT systems (tool-scaping and dashboards), Buurtzorg relies on social norming to control the activities of the teams. Each new team member needs to immerse themselves into the culture of Buurtzorg. New teams are built by splitting existing teams to guarantee that the longer-serving team members will seed Buurtzorg's culture into the new team. Everyone is expected to show the behaviors important to Buurtzorg and embrace its principles and practices. This is not a choice: either comply or leave.

There are no standardized jobs at Buurtzorg, just the seven roles which shift from time to time. People are actually encouraged to build their own jobs and make their work fit their talents and preferences, a practice known as job crafting. Additionally, within the constraints of the team's mission (the overall aspiration of Buurtzorg for excellent home care and the 60 percent utilization target), teams and individuals can pick their own targets (i.e., self-service targets). Buurtzorg exemplifies many of "beyond budgeting" practices.

People

Teams are self-governing—i.e., they are in charge of recruitment, dismissals, vacations, and working hours. They are supposed to appraise each other regularly (peer appraisal). This appraisal is about personal development and is not in any way tied to targets or money. There is very little fuss about remuneration. Nurses are paid under a union agreement according to their educational level with a standard annual increase and bonuses based on the areas worked in. Remuneration is all about being fair. Motivation comes from client service, from local communities, from the relations inside the team, and from professional mastery. Variable bonuses and shares are not needed, nor are any special perks or titles. There are no special office spaces, reserved parking, or company cars.

Transparency

Transparency is valued highly. At the team level, regular team interactions and close proximity between all team members in the local community all but guarantee transparency. At the corporate level, the IT platform with its designated set of benchmarks creates visibility of other teams' issues and performance, as well as the overall status of the company.

Buurtzorg as a company is not hard to understand at all. There are, for example, no complicated supply chains to monitor and no multi-million assets that need to be utilized. At Buurtzorg, it is all about people. The IT systems provide social platforms for people to engage with one another and information is rarely restricted (i.e., open book and open reports). While benchmarking is done between teams, teams are not ranked and there is no competition for the top spot. To prevent competition from creeping in and undermining the spirit of cooperation, team rankings are not publicly available. If a team feels itself to be below par in any aspect—perhaps triggered by one of the overall, averaged benchmarks—it may engage with a coach who points the team in the direction of another team from whom it might be good to learn.

Projects

Buurtzorg is itself a never-ending project. Its networked structure of autonomous, self-governed teams adapts according to the needs of their clients and changing legal or administrative requirements. The team itself pulls in services from HQ or other providers and decides on new initiatives with other teams— such as trying new treatment methods, for example. Teams are unlikely to feel the need for elaborate project management techniques.

It is a different picture at HQ. One can see from the way they work with the external software company that rapid prototyping and lean, evolutionary, thoroughly customer-focused projects with few formal approvals and documentation are the way projects are practiced.

Learning

Every team member is free to follow their own learning drive. The pain, the relief, and the happiness experienced by patients is an excellent motivator for learning, especially in a such a purpose-driven organization. Functional, individual, and team-based training is encouraged and often delivered by other team members (peer training). There are no training budgets. A team decides for itself about spending money on training (free education budgets). Specialist nurses—for example, those specializing in artificial hearts—may group together in communities of interest (guilds). Individuals and teams are autonomous; they may experiment in any way they see fit and share insights on the IT platform (learning platforms) with others. They can decide to share their insights on Buurtzorg Discovery Days (exploration days) with the rest of the organization, or they can seek to get directly in touch with everyone else in the organization, including the founder (frontline discussions).

Medical professionals can only stop learning to the detriment of their clients. In an open organization such as Buurtzorg where there are no firewalls between teams, a team that stops learning will be identified and challenged, and—most importantly—will probably already have challenged themselves.

Reflection

The dominant form of reflection at Buurtzorg is peer feedback. Everyone is expected to share their observations with their team, be that in the course of their work or during meetings (reflection microstructures). With no power differential, people are not afraid to speak up. Giving up the hierarchy makes giving feedback a lot more natural and honest.

The central ideas of Buurtzorg can be summarized as follows:

- An idea of technology that is centered on using it to help foster human collaboration.
- An idea of performance centered on competent co-workers.
- An idea of ruling based on self-management.

- An idea of work based on its inherent meaning.
- An idea of life based on caring for one another.

Bridgewater, Haier, and Buurtzorg have all gone to extraordinary lengths to make their configuration of work designs contribute to their central ideas. All of these companies are extraordinarily successful in their markets. There might be a causal relationship.

■ Chapter 10: Comparing Company Configurations

Organizing means to attend to the configurational logics
that produce organized activity.
– Richard W. Scott, 2014[141]

This chapter is by far the most speculative in the book. We are now going to compare the four companies described in the last chapter.

The Liberated Company Map is based on heuristics. It is not a mutually exclusive framework—there is overlap between management practices, and it is not collectively exhaustive. In fact, there might be other practices which are not on the map. We must therefore be careful not to over-interpret any findings. In order to "prove" anything substantively, we would need a bigger, better sample and a much more solid, scientific version of the Liberated Company Map. Having said that, let's see what we can find by zooming out of the map and comparing different configurations.

The ideas behind the four companies discussed in the previous chapter are very different (see Table 17). Perhaps the biggest difference of all is that Haier, Bridgewater, and Buurtzorg have clear ideas, whereas in most traditional companies the underlying ideas are hard to spot—or, at worst, they are random, incomplete, or simply erroneous. Even more important, a random co-worker in those three companies asked to name those big underlying ideas would probably be able to describe them in their own words. In a more traditional company, even top-level managers will stammer and fall back on meaningless jargon. The most important idea of all may be simply to have an idea.

---

141 (Scott, 2014)

Main idea of:	Retailer (Hierarchy)	Bridgewater (Empowered)	Haier (Supportive)	Buurtzorg (Self-Managed)
Technology	none	Co-existence of technology and people	Trajectory of technology	Utility to foster human collaboration
Performance	The competent manager	Making ever better decisions	Borderless entrepreneurship	Competent co-workers
Ruling	Hierarchy	Hierarchy nurturing the self-authoring mind	Self-managed microenterprises	Self-management
Work	Two types of people: Thinkers & Doers	A machine of learning	Customer driven & aspirational	Inherent meaning
Life	Loyalty and competence	Mental awareness	Service	Caring

Table 17 The central ideas

Analysis by number of work designs

In general, a low number of work designs indicates a work environment that is easy to understand and work in, provided that these work designs are consistent. More self-managed companies may make work more self-fulfilling, but not necessarily easier.

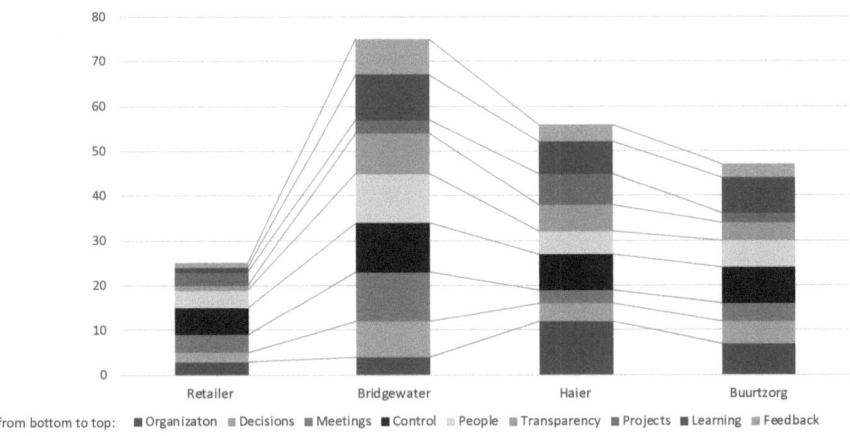

Figure 16 Number of work design per company and category

Thesis I: More self-managed companies need a higher number of work designs than more hierarchical companies

The three more self-managed companies appear to use double or even three times the number of work designs that the conventional company does. The hierarchically organized retailer uses 25 work designs compared with 75 at

Bridgewater, 56 at Haier, and 47 at Buurtzorg. The more liberated companies seem to need more work designs, whereas a hierarchy vests all powers in managers, so there is no need for elaborate work designs. Removing the key pillar of coordination—hierarchy—means adopting more work designs in order to continue coordinating a company properly.

Even Buurtzorg, which made simplicity a key feature of its overall work design, uses twice as many practices as the traditional company. Does this mean it is more difficult and regulated to work in more liberated companies? It is certainly more complex to find your way on your own rather than being told what to do. More liberated companies offer more possibilities, which can be overwhelming to some co-workers.

Thesis II: Empowered companies may need a disproportionately large number of work designs

Bridgewater is a hierarchical company that seeks to empower people, which makes it a liberation level 2 company. It employs by far the highest number of practices, 75. It appears that to maintain the hierarchy while empowering people to the mental level of the "self-authorizing mind" requires a lot of discipline. This discipline is instilled through mandated management practices, which may explain the high number of work designs. Vestiges of the hierarchy can also be found at Haier. Each of its microenterprises is headed by a boss, although that boss might be toppled by a 2/3 majority vote. Haier, which is more of a liberation level 3 (supportive) company, uses the second-highest number of work designs.

Thesis III: The step from a traditional hierarchy to an empowered company will disproportionately increase the number of work designs

Not all empowered companies have such an extraordinarily high aspiration for the intellectual development of co-workers as Bridgewater. The total number of work designs is, however, bound to rise with the step from liberation level 1 to level 2. In this transition, work designs are piled on in order to give the managers a structure through which they can perform their job. Many HR managers know that more empowerment is good for a company and its people, and they subsequently push for the adoption of new work designs—typically 360-degree feedback, skip-level feedback, and corporate value exercises. Empowerment can only exist where managers consistently hold a space that allows people to make their own choices. As a result, empowered companies need to use more work designs to regulate this space into existence.

Thesis IV: Overall, the number of work designs rises with the liberation level until a company adopts self-management

A more liberated workplace may be a more complex one. Coworkers are no longer told what to do and need to find their way without the guidance of a boss—meanwhile, potential anarchy is reined in by more work designs. The rising number of work designs is a price that needs to be paid for liberty. However, the number of work designs may drop once a company has crossed the chasm to level 4, the self-managed company. Of course, our sample is too small to make generalizations, and more quantitative research is certainly needed. But at least there is a logical argument to be made: once the hierarchy is abandoned for self-management, fewer management practices are mandated as middle management no longer needs to be enticed to hold open the space for more self-management. Middle management is dissolved, and the number of rules can drop (see Figure 17). To put it another way, self-management thrives on a low number of rules that are simple enough for everyone to understand.

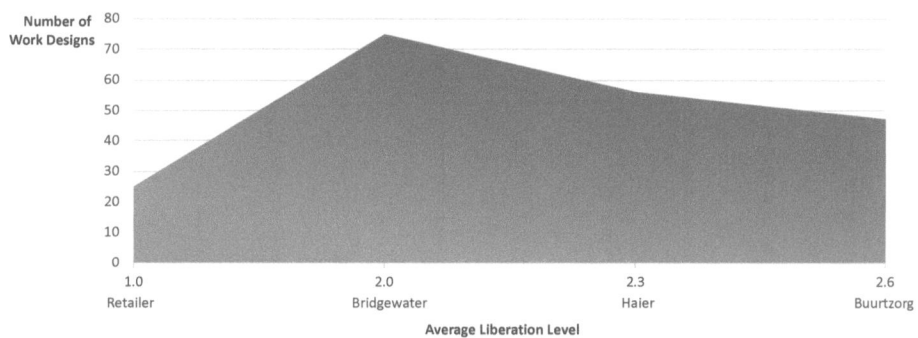

Figure 17 Number of work designs vs. average Liberation level of practices

Analysis by liberation level

Zooming in closer, companies are not "liberated" per se. Although they can be classified as traditional, empowered, supportive, or self-managed, this is a simplification, a generalizing label. Companies often use work designs from all levels, though they may use more from some levels than others. The classification of management practices by the four liberation levels only provides high-level guidance. It is the configuration of work designs to the specific needs of the situation that matters.

Company	Traditional	Empowered	Supportive	Self-Organized
Retailer	100%	0%	0%	0%
Bridgewater	43%	20%	29%	8%
Haier	21%	29%	43%	7%
Buurtzorg	13%	28%	45%	15%

Table 18 Share of practices per level and company

The average liberation level is a simple weighted average of all the levels of work designs that a company is using. The weighting factors are: 1 for traditional work designs; 2 for empowered work designs; 3 for supportive work designs; and 4 for self-managed work designs.

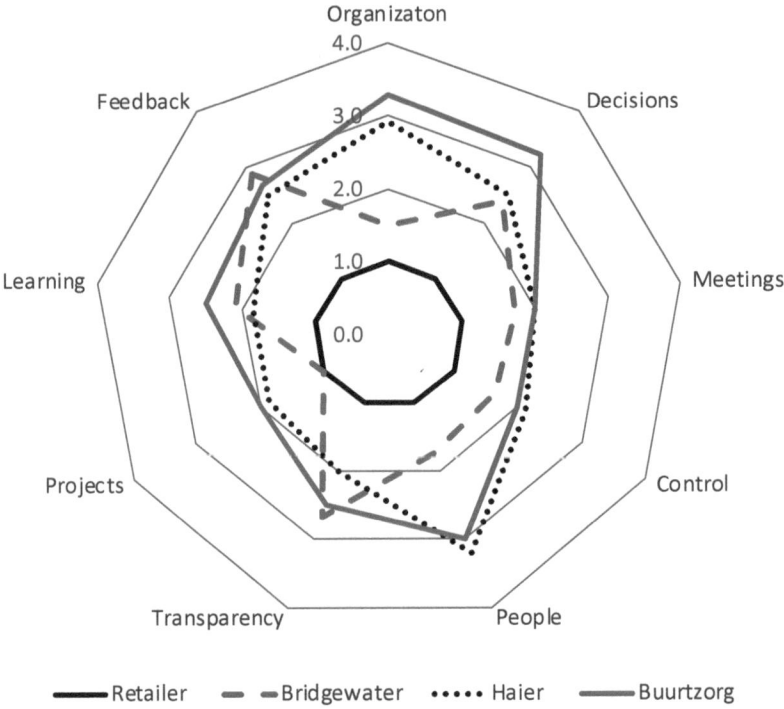

Figure 18 Average Liberation level by category and company

Based on this index, Buurtzorg appears to be the most liberated company of the pack, followed by Haier and Bridgewater. About 40 percent of Bridgewater's practices remain traditional. This shows that Bridgewater has given itself a significant challenge as an empowered company that has maintained the hierarchy but still seeks a high level of liberation ("the self-authoring mind") for its co-workers.

Thesis V: Even highly liberated companies use more traditional work designs

Even self-managed companies include traditional management practices in their work designs, so long as they do their job well and do not cause inconsistencies with the rest of the company's practices. Buurtzorg, for example, relies on traditional managerial wage setting, having no use for more complex reward schemes. This is a simple and efficient practice that does not in any way contradict Buurtzorg's focus on service. There are no bonuses to distract people from looking after their patients and their community. Pay is a hygiene factor and not a motivator, so there is no need for anything more elaborate.

Thesis VI: Higher levels of liberation can be found in small and large companies

The fact that the companies in our sample are all major players in their fields shows that self-management is not a small-scale phenomenon, but a serious way to run global companies, too.

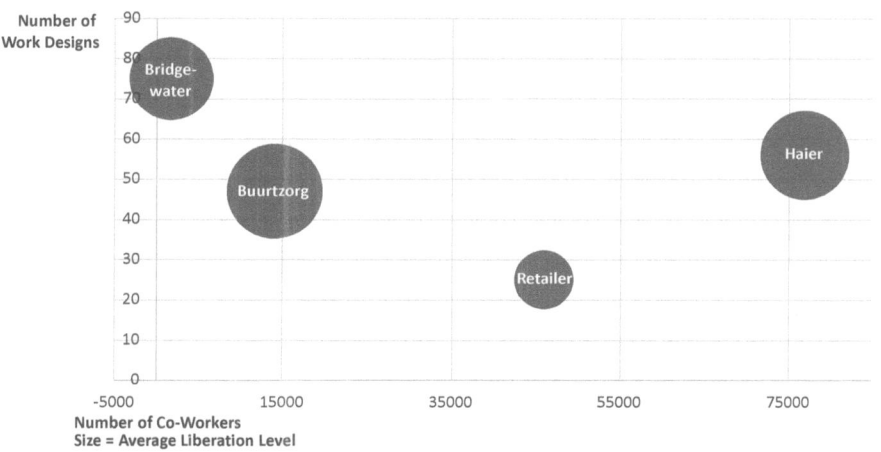

Figure 19 Company size and number of work designs

Not many major companies are fully self-managed; most major companies run self-management only in small pockets of their organization but are solidly hierarchically organized elsewhere. There are many small companies that are more highly liberated than major companies, however. Running a self-managed team or a small company of under 150 co-workers appears to be much easier than running larger organizations in a more liberated way. Speculating further, it may be important to divide operations into some areas where organization via more self-management is crucial and other areas where the hierarchy will do a better job.[142]

---

142 (Moore, 2015)

Thesis VII: The greater the purpose of a company, the more it is self-managed

Given that most self-managed methods originate in the social sphere, this may be a reasonable supposition. Sociocracy, Laloux's Teal organizations, Holacracy, and even the Agile Manifesto have social and humanistic undertones—the former more, the latter less. Even thinkers from a performance-driven perspective, such as Richard Hackman, Jon Katzenbach, Gary Hamel, or Robert Kegan come to the conclusion that purpose is a vital ingredient for the operation of more liberated forms of organization. Let's look at how purpose may have influenced the configuration of work designs in our sample of companies. Figure 20 suggests a relationship between a company's sense of purpose and its liberation level.

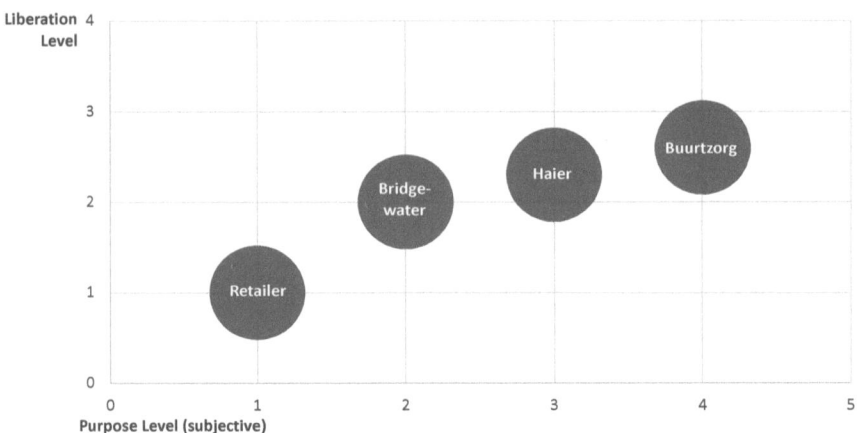

Figure 20 Purpose and Liberation level

The retailer and Bridgewater both follow the creed of shareholder value; as such, their companies' primary purpose is profit. That does not necessarily make them heartless or exploitative organizations, however. Indeed, Bridgewater aspires to be more. Its corporate-level focus may on be high returns for its customers and itself, and it may want its co-workers to become self-authoring (if only as a means to more profits), but working at Bridgewater still means seeking, confronting, and developing one's inner compass, one's purpose in work and life.

In contrast, Haier seeks first to improve the well-being of its clients and believes that economic results, growth, and profit will come as a result. Haier is ruthless in its drive to establish a challenging, entrepreneurial work environment to provide solutions to constantly evolving customer needs. Customer service appears to drive Haier more than hunger for profit. Buurtzorg is a notch higher still on the purpose scale. In addition to the focus on its clients (patients), it adds service to the local social community and the well-being of its workers. It goes beyond the focus on the client without losing sight of it.

So is a more self-managed organization a more purposeful one? I believe this is generally, but not always, true. It is possible to run a highly liberated, self-managed organization without any higher company purpose than to make a profit. However, it will prove harder and harder to do so as people in such an organization are inherently disposed to seek a sense of purpose for their activities and will tend to increasingly ask the nagging question "Why?" Choose self-management and purpose will seep into your company.

Analysis by work design category

More liberated organizations not only use more work designs, but they also tend to favor different category types than more traditional companies.

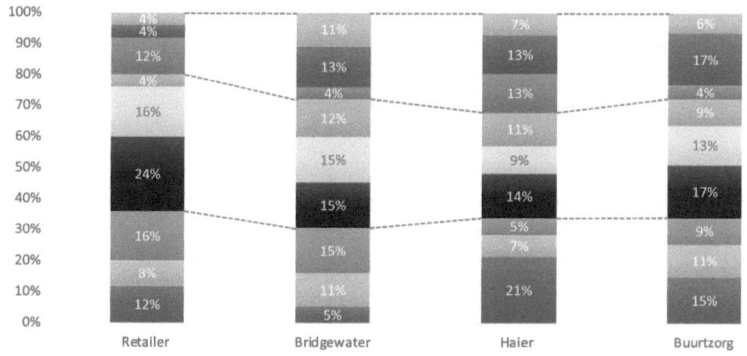

Figure 21 Work designs by category in % of total

Thesis VIII: Development practices are much more important to self-managed companies

Project, learning, and feedback practices are used nearly five times as much in the self-managed company compared to the traditional company (in this sample). In percentages of all work designs, these development practices are still twice as popular.

Thesis IX: Control practices are much more important to hierarchical companies

In the traditional company, nearly one in every two practices is about control (directing, people, transparency) compared to about one in three at a more liberated company like Haier. Haier gives authority to its microenterprises to manage however they deem best and relies on mission command for alignment.

More liberated companies rely much more heavily on transparency instead: transparency practices are about four-to-six times as numerous in the three more-liberated companies, and about two-to-three times as numerous in relative terms (i.e., as a percentage of all work designs).

The differences in the action category (coordination, intelligence, and emotions) appear to be more related to the different focuses of the companies. Bridgewater relies heavily on meetings and decision-making structures. It has no need to focus on organizational practices, as it still uses the hierarchy to coordinate things. By contrast, Haier, with its focus on networked microenterprises, uses far more organizational practices than decision-making or meeting practices.

Thesis X: Digital work designs are central to the more liberated companies in the sample

All three progressive companies rely heavily on work designs that are supported by digital technology. Bridgewater uses apps and cloud systems intensively in its quest for better decisions, and Dalio himself has taken a personal interest in their ongoing development. Haier also relies on a digital core, the Haier platform, to keep microenterprises and individuals communicating and aligned. The existence of companies and the employment of each individual is not defined in legal terms but is defined by being an entity on the Haier system. Everything in Haier's organization is virtual, the hard facts being those that are in the cloud system. The cloud system creates an ecosystem of its own that is much more agile than any legal framework. This way, Haier sets its own rules. It still needs to comply with the legal requirements of the outer world, but it does not let this shape its organization. For example, to create a start-up within Haier, fully equipped with capital, management structures, IT systems, and reward structure, all that is needed is an entry into the Haier system. The start-up's existence on the platform ensures that it will be nourished by the Haier ecosphere. Buurtzorg also invested years in getting its digital platform right and has not stopped extending and improving it since.

Each of the founder/CEOs of these three companies states that without digital technology their companies would not be possible. The role of digital technology in enabling progressive, self-managed organizations is often underappreciated in the literature. There is a lot of lip service paid to IT, but it needs a proper search in IT literature, such as in DevOps handbooks, to find work designs that have real impact. The real challenge is to allow IT practices to break out of their corner and proliferate throughout the business organization.

Our sample is small, and it is based on a non-MECE framework full of assumptions and subjective judgments—which, however plausible it might be, is far from scientific. The analysis does, however, provide some hints for those who are interested in configuring the work design of their organizations.

Let's sum up what we have covered so far: first, we explored a compendium of work designs, brought into some semblance of order in the form of the Liberated Company Map; second, we examined four companies and analyzed their different work design configurations. With these two, we have laid the groundwork to tackle the following question: How can companies be configured for the digital age? The remaining chapters aim to provide a compass for this undertaking.

PART IV:
A COMPASS FOR THE DIGITAL AGE

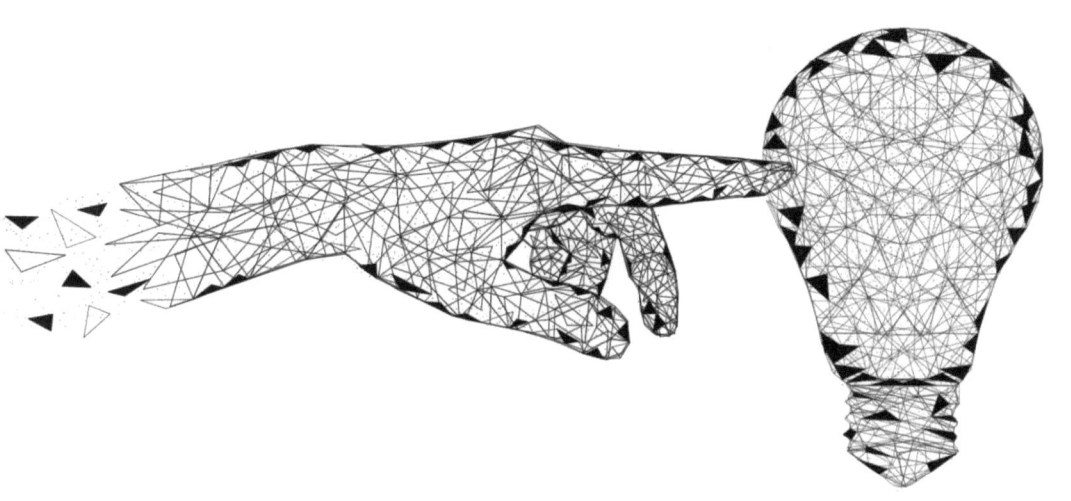

■ Chapter 11: A Compass to Master Complexity

To be on a quest is nothing more or less than to become an asker of questions.
– Sam Keen

A map is much more useful when you also have a compass. Navigating the Liberated Company Map, knowing which work designs to use, and which to change and which to drop also requires a compass. This part of the book provides you with an unusual compass, as it does not offer you true north. In complex systems like businesses, there are no simple answers and there is no single truth. Instead, it offers eleven questions and three ways to answer each of them: "The Eleven Principles of Liberated Companies." These principles represent the epitome of what I have read, experienced, and learned in the last couple of years. There are of course more questions to be asked, and there are certainly other, better ways to answer them. What truly matters is what you do with these questions and answers, and how you and your organization journey forward in the digital age.

The Eleven Principles of Liberated Companies

In a time of rapid change, old truths seem to be less valid than before, while other truths (i.e., those ideas that have been around before) now seem to become more important. And finally, some new truths seem to be emerging. In what seems at times like an ambiguous world, awareness and acceptance of complexity is the only way to cure the blindness that is so common in the workplace.

The first and the second principles—technology and power—have already been discussed (see Chapters 1 and 2). Technology's changing role from a tool to a maker of decisions (and a new co-worker) lies at the root of many changes in business and is driving increasing levels of complexity—in business, in our social fabric, and in our very psychologies. The companies that are likely to prosper are those in which people and technology come together to make the best teams.

The second principle is the question of power. The uneven distribution of power must be addressed. First, because as we have seen, technology favors more equal, networked structures. Second, because the corrosive impacts of a subservient governmentality of powerful and powerless people leads to exploitation. It may be difficult, and in some ways alien, for companies to address questions of power head on, but ignoring this question will undermine all other efforts.

In a more networked age, companies need to become more like typical networks, with less centrality than we are used to. It is not that hierarchy needs to be fully replaced; it is often more about reducing it from a toxic to a healthy dose.[143] You cannot remove the skeleton of a company and expect the body to stay upright. New structures are needed to provide direction and coordination. There are many proven work designs that together, in certain configurations, can provide a strong new skeleton for a company.

The Eleven Principles of Liberated Companies describe what makes up this improved skeleton, or "operating system," of companies in the digital age.[144] They provide answers to the question: "Which truths should we build companies around to be successful in the digital age?" These answers come in the form of directions for building companies towards culture and market, each company at its own pace and according to its own resources. Together with the Liberated Company Map, the Eleven Principles (Figure 22) form a framework to help organizations make choices and experiment with new answers and new configurations.

---

143 There is a similarity between the more liberated governing concepts presented in this book and the concepts described by Nobel Prize laureate Elinor Ostrom: (Ostrom, Governing the Commons, 1990)

144 For early inspiration regarding the principles, I am especially indebted to the work on work environments by Cooperate Rebels, who are at the forefront of organizational design worldwide. See **https://corporate-rebels.com.**

If your answers find their practical impact in work designs, the sum of these answers will make up the trajectory your company or team is taking. Change your answers, change your work designs—and you change the future of your organization.

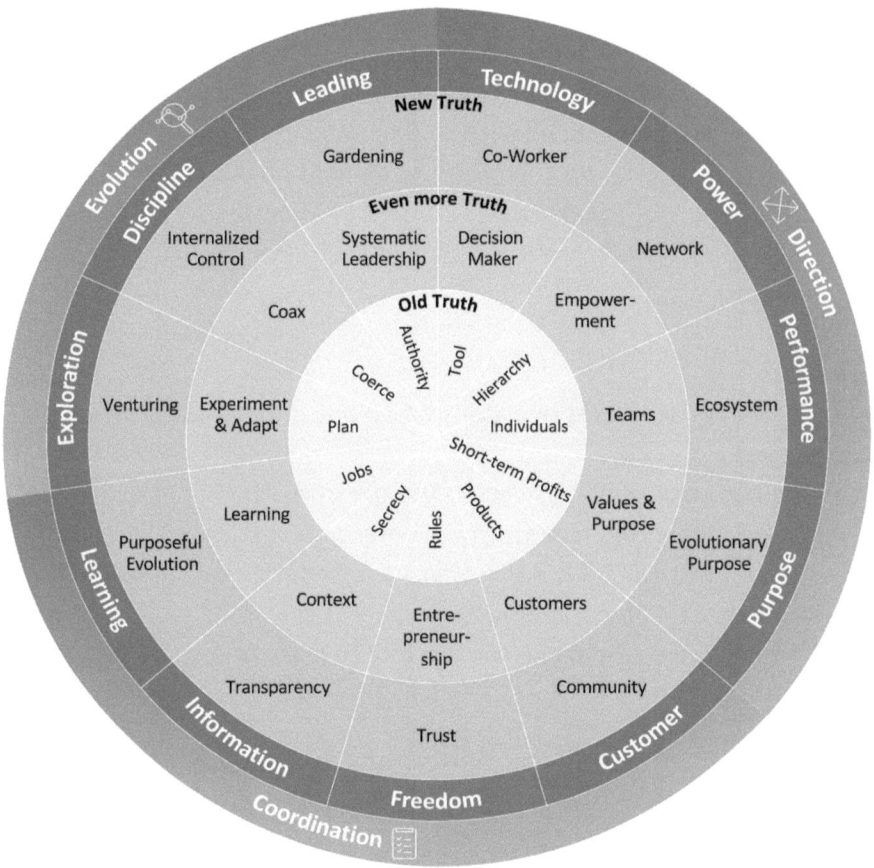

Figure 22 The 11 Principles of Liberated Companies

The principles, listed in the first column, can be understood as questions, such as: What is your idea of technology? What is your idea of power? What is your idea of performance? Answering the first four principles helps a company find its direction. Principles V to VIII are more tactical; they describe the principles that are useful for the coordination of companies. The last three principles are useful for the evolution, development, and improvement of companies. The other three columns show that there are three alternative ways to answer the questions: old truths, truths that are even more true today, and new truths. These answers in combination may give direction to a company's effort to find its way in the digital age.

The first principle, technology, calls on managers and organizers to make their idea of technology explicit so that a company can align with those ideas and put itself on the trajectory of technology (see Chapter 1). Although the second principle, power, has been already discussed in Chapter 2, I'd like to add some important aspects for the understanding of power in the next chapter. The remaining nine principles are elaborated in Chapters 14 to 22, before we arrive at Chapter 23 which offers practical advice for configuring companies with work designs.

Dark Arts
- The digital age raises questions which any organizations needs to answer.
- The nature of one's answers to the old truth, the things even more true and the new truth will determine the trajectory that an organization will take, if these answers find their expression in a configuration of work designs
- The Liberated Company map is a tool to make ones thinking explicit

■ Chapter 12 Power: From Hierarchy to Empowerment and Networks

The "liberation scale"—the choice of running your organization as an authoritarian, empowered, supportive, or self-managed company or team—implies that you are free to aim for any point on the scale. Humans tend towards the mid-points of scales, avoiding extremes. Empowered and supportive organizations seem to be the most reasonable choices—not as exploitative as the hierarchy, yet not as alien as self-management. They are a good compromise, or at least a solid bridge towards the future.

The problem, however, is that the middle ground between hierarchy and self-management is unstable. The stability of the hierarchy, as we have seen, is so great that hierarchy has a strong tendency to re-assert itself as long as arbitrary power resides with some managers. The temptation to use power, with the best of intentions, is immense for those who wield it. With every arbitrary use of power, people will feel less accountable, less like an adult, and more like a child—and if trust is misused, they will feel less trusting and less safe. Organizational psychologist Amy Edmondson writes that "when we set out to create organizations where people can bring their full selves to work, we're swimming upstream against deeply ingrained psychological currents".[145] Empowered organizations have a systematic bias toward more hierarchy. This is even truer in a supportive organization, where people open up much more, display more vulnerability, and are therefore very sensitive to any breach of their autonomous self by the leaders.

---

145 (Edmondson A. C., 2018) Chapter 8.

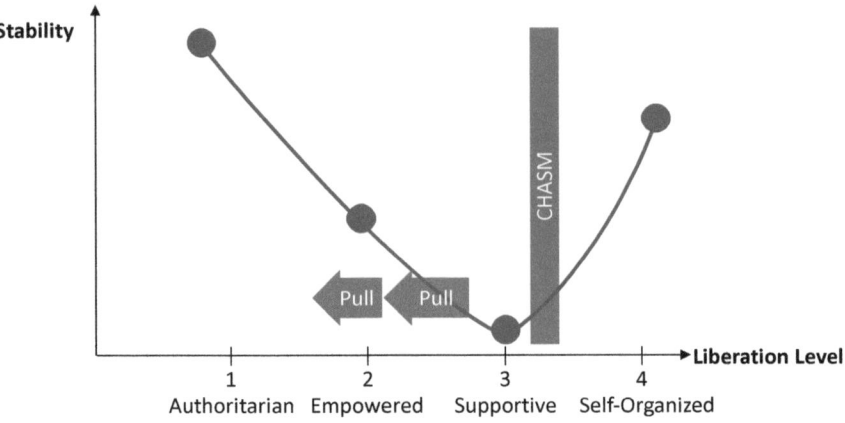

Figure 23 The drift towards hierarchy

However, we shouldn't give up on the empowered or supportive organization. Work designs are excellent ways of regulating empowered and supportive organizations. Appropriately regulated management behavior can hold space for more choices, autonomy, and self-fulfillment for co-workers. The description on a plaque at the entrance to the Harvard Law School describes this neatly: *It is the restraints that make men free.*

The second fallacy in relation to the liberation scale is the belief that a gradual transformation from a hierarchy to a self-managed organization is possible. It is certainly possible to move gradually from an authoritarian to an empowered to a supportive organization, but the step from the supportive to the self-managed organization is highly disruptive. The dissolution of the hierarchy is a revolutionary rather than an evolutionary act. Although a "decider of last resort" may still be available in a self-managed organization,[146] self-management comes as a shock to any co-worker who is used to the hierarchical system. Co-workers will feel the full weight of accountability; managers will either leave the company or join the ranks of their fellow workers; and career seekers will find it hard to adjust to the now missing opportunities for hierarchical promotion. There is a chasm

---

146 As we saw at Buurtzorg, or Gore and AES, two other self-managed companies. See (Laloux, 2014)

between the supportive and the self-managed organization.[147] The reverse process, to turn a self-managed organization into a hierarchical one, is much easier.

This book does not postulate that self-management is always the solution, even for companies operating in complex environments. Often, the best solution for companies facing the digital revolution is to become somewhat less hierarchical, either overall or in a particular part of the organization. The tendency of the hierarchy to establish itself can be countered by conscious work design configuration along the lines of the Eleven Principles—for example, by embracing reflection, transparency, and more distributed decision-making.

However, with the rise of the digital economy with all its complexity, it becomes crucial for all companies to understand where, when, and how to use self-management. Crossing the chasm for the company as a whole might be for a later date. But maybe, given the exponential trajectory of technology, this time might come sooner than expected.

But there is a third fallacy one might fall prey to in using the liberation scale; namely, the cumulative impact of (i) the unstable middle ground between hierarchy and self-management, (ii) the chasm between hierarchy self-management, and (iii) the fact that the space for more self-management can be regulated into existence by using work designs. Looking at these three facts, we are now abler to update our understanding of the liberation level, from a simple scale to a two-dimensional matrix. Let me explain.

---

147 An impressive, radical approach to crossing the chasm employed by Koldo Saratxaga, a veteran of self-managed companies, is described in this post **https://corporate-rebels.com/ner-group/** (retrieved 19 June 2019).

Truly powerful organizations exist in a narrow corridor

The liberation level seems to imply to a transfer of power from managers to the people through more participation, empowerment, more transparency, and devolution of decision-making to individuals and groups. However, power is not a zero-sum game. Just transferring it from managers to people might make coworkers more powerful and ease the weight of oppression from their shoulders, but it might not change anything about the power of the organization.

More self-management is certainly better for the creativity, engagement, learning, experimentation, and growth of people, but it has its own deficiencies, including a tendency toward indecisiveness, political behaviors, lack of strategic behavior of the overall organization, and diffusion of organizational focus.

A simple transfer of power from the hierarchy to the people does not help much. It just trades one set of limitations for another. Granted, there are other limitations that might be helpful for some organizations, like more creativity and willing to sacrifice focus. However, organizations can do better, much better. What if it is possible to increase the power of an organization while simultaneously increasing the power of the people?

Let me explain. The higher the power of an organization, the more it is able to focus all its resources, behaviors, processes, and systems on its targets and re-focus them with lightning speed to market or strategic needs. This is a bit like having a Steven Jobs at the helm, who used Apple's resources with laser focus and strategic foresight. However, a powerful organization is more than about having a powerful leader; it's about having extremely powerful bureaucratic processes at work in all or most parts of the organization: Logistics, HR, Sales, Purchasing, Manufacturing, Finance, etc.

The other, largely independent dimension is the power of the people. The higher it is, the more people are able to express themselves, speak up freely, experiment, and select their work according to their intrinsic drives.

Where most people go wrong is to think that powerful organizations invariably suppress people. While there are despotic organizations, where fear is the dominant feeling inundating the organization, there are other organizations are powerful and at the same time are a place where people can freely flourish in all the many ways they chose to.

Healthy companies only exist in a narrow corridor that allow for both, a powerful organization and powerful coworkers, at any level.[148]

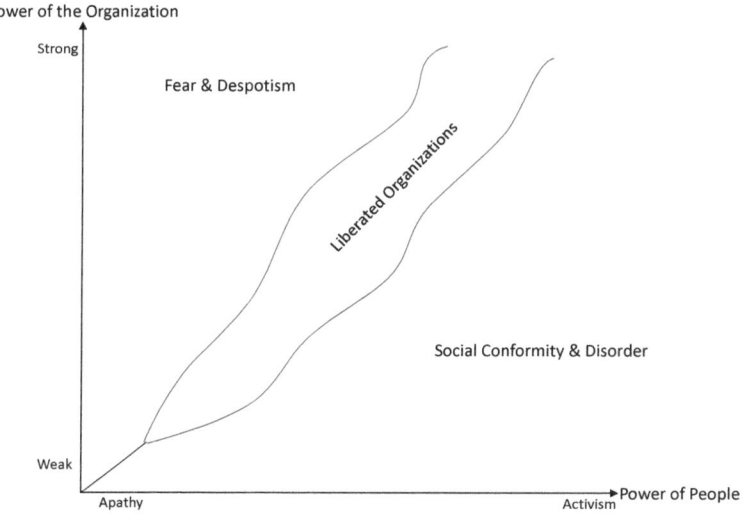

Figure 24 Healthy Companies Exist Only in a Narrow Corridor

Extremely powerful organizations are always struggling to keep in the narrow corridor. If they increase the power of the organization too much—for example, by tolerating despotic managers or overbearing bureaucracies—people will retreat into their inner selves and go into survival mode. Any increase in organizational power needs to be accompanied by an increase in power among the people. Two examples might help unpack this concept.

---

148 The figure is based on Daron Acemoglu and James A. Robinson (2019) *The Narrow Corridor. Acemoglu and Robinson are political scientists and their framework is a political one-. However, I found it valid and useful on organizational level, too. You will find more details on this framework on the* **www.liberated.company** *website.*

Take the introduction of new work processes. It is no secret that work pro-cesses, however brilliantly designed, are likely to fail if people at the work level do not see the need for them. Forcing processes on people will just lead to circumvention. People don't like change.

Or consider a company deciding to pivot to a new strategic direction. Many companies arrange "change programs to roll-out a new strategy to get the buy-in of people." It is a recruiting officer prowling the streets of London to enroll new army recruits in the Victorian Age. Companies engaging with people after all important decisions have been made will likely end up with outward compli-ance and inward apathy or resignation.

The fact is organizations can only be truly powerful if they have both: Pow-erful, bureaucratic institutions delivering great services to customers and employees efficiently AND powerful coworkers who have a real say in the company, are highly motivated to speak up, and communicate their true intentions.

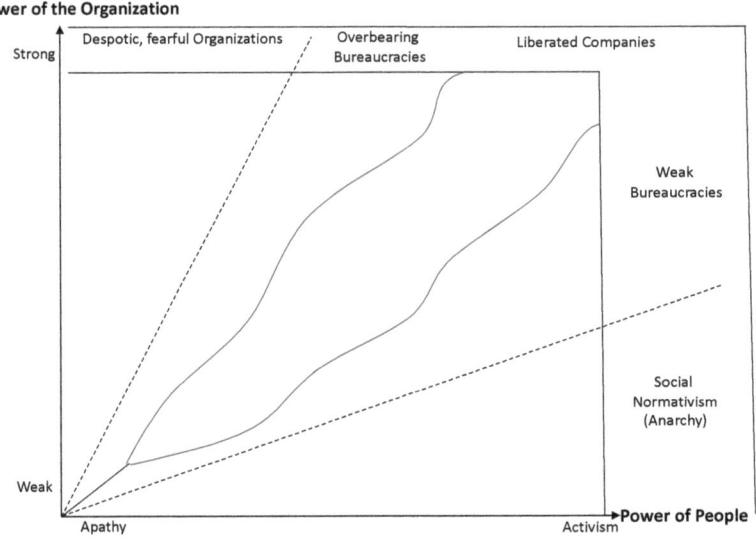

Figure 25 Companies Outside the Corridor are Missing Something

On the other hand, if organizations increase the power of people too much and neglect the focusing capabilities of the organizational bureaucracy, they end up with a social collective of people who engage in all kinds of political behaviors, which are not necessarily helpful for a company's mission.

It is a matter of balance. Liberated Companies manage to turn on the power of their central institutions while allowing people to flourish. The corridor in the middle is where Liberated Companies exist, such as hugely successful companies like Haier, Bridgewater, or Buurtzorg, for example.

Dark Arts
- There is a drift towards authoritarian hierarchy in any organization that can only be overcome by actively investing time and effort in maintaining an organizations configuration of work designs.
- Power is not zero-sum game. Both the organization and the coworkers can and should become more powerful in order for a company and its coworkers to prosper.
- Liberated Companies manage to turn on the power of their central institutions while simultaneously enabling coworkers to flourish.
- It is narrow corridor in which healthy companies exist and it takes sustained balance and effort to stay in that corridor.

Further Reading
- Amy Edmondson (2018) *The Fearless Organization*, Wiley
- Daron Acemoglu and James A. Robinson (2019) *The Narrow Corridor*, Penguin Press

■ Chapter 13 Performance: From Individuals to Teams and Ecosystems

Business is not a question of laws. It's one of designs.
– Kate Raworth[149]

Any organizational theory or management doctrine worth its salt must be based on a theory of performance. Which ways of organizing work well? Under what circumstances? However, most companies and even most business theories are not based on an explicit idea of performance. Asking a manager about their idea of performance generally doesn't produce a conclusive answer. The follow-up question "Why do you believe in this idea of performance?" is even less likely to produce a definitive response.

Yet, to have an explicit idea of performance is incredibly important for a company's work design configurations. This chapter offers a pocket theory of performance that indicates that more liberated companies are often a better choice.

The old truth: The individual

Does individual performance matter much in business? At first, this may seem like a strange question. Of course it does—good people make good business. Surely a business organization must be interested in its constituent parts—each individual employee—performing highly.

Historically, fostering high-performing individuals did not figure in organizational or management theory. The task of the individual was to do the job as defined by a clever manager. Management theory was never meant to optimize an individual's contribution but rather to secure a certain level of performance for the whole organization. Taking account of individual mental abilities and motivations only serves to throw a wrench into the works of a well-thought-out machine.

But individual performance matters much more today. People are not cogs in a machine; it is more essential than ever to understand what makes them productive, what makes them engage, and what motivates them to perform great work. In the digital age, we are finally leaving unskilled labor behind. Blue collar or white collar, everyone is a knowledge worker these days.

The pocket theory of individual performance is a mix of popular belief and academic scholarship largely based on self-determination theory—a refinement of the classical motivational theories of Herzberg or Maslow, paired with sociological studies of individual success.[150]

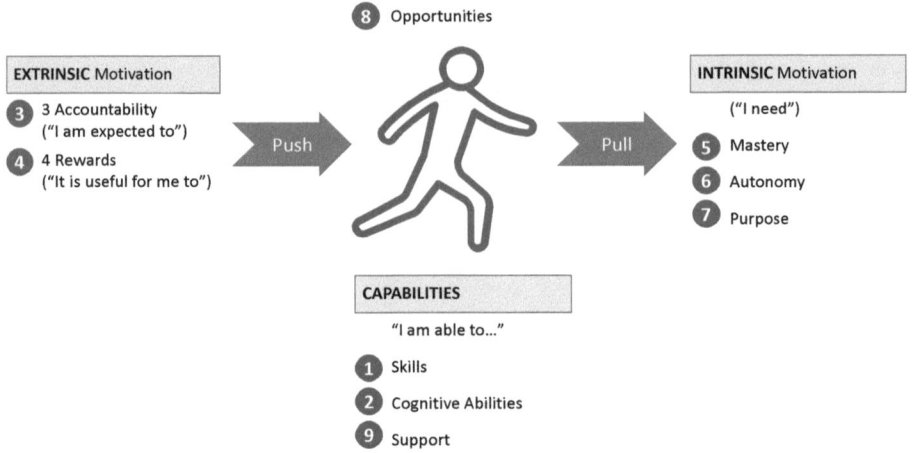

Figure 26 The 9 conditions of individual performance -a pocket theory

According to this theory, nine factors are required in a work environment to foster great performance (see Figure 24). First, there are individual capabilities of people: skills and cognitive abilities (1 and 2). These capabilities are utilized by giving them a job for which they are accountable (3) and rewarded (4). Most traditional companies rely on capabilities and extrinsic motivation.

---

150 Dan Pink has popularized self-determination theory and Malcom Gladwell provides an easy-to-read introduction to the sociology of upward mobility: (Pink, 2011); (Gladwell, 2008)

Fewer companies seek to enhance performance by harnessing people's intrinsic motivation: their drive towards mastery, autonomy, and purpose (5, 6 and 7). Add to that sufficient opportunities, i.e. meaningful choices that people can make (8), and support them when they require it (9), and individual performance will blossom in organizations.

However, most companies do not make much effort beyond factors 1 to 4. Hierarchies find it difficult to utilize intrinsic motivation, as managers and jobs leave people with little scope for autonomous action; in these cases, support is often strongly deficit-oriented. More liberated companies, on the other hand, recognize that people can be developed, that the intrinsic drive of people can be utilized to a greater extent if the company is structured more like a network, that opportunities are richer in networked structures, and that support for people is better delivered by coaching than by managerial oversight.

Even more true: The team

For decades, hymns in praise of the team have been sung all over the business realm. Agile, lean, and nearly all progressive organizations rely on the team as the primary unit of work. More traditional companies, while paying lip service to the "team," utilize workgroups instead, with managers structuring work and assigning tasks to people. In teams, managers leave the structuring and assigning to the team itself and focus on setting the team's directions and work environment.

Teams are tricky to master. They need a whole range of conditions in order to function well. The eleven conditions for effective teams shown in Figure 25 are based largely on Richard Hackman's work on high-performance teams, combined with later studies of team performance.[151]

---

151 (Hackman, 2002); (Edmondson & Schein, Teaming, 2014); (Katzenbach & Smith, 1993)

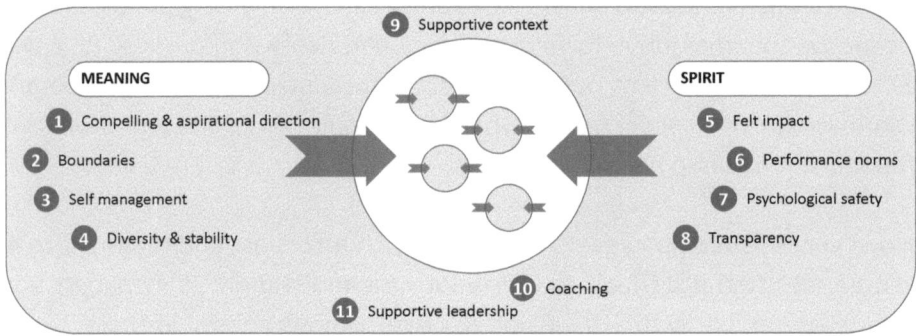

Figure 27 The 11 conditions of effective teams (based on R. Hackman)

First, teams need to have a meaning that is manifest in their direction, their boundaries, their liberties (self-management), and their structure. Second, teams need to imbue their members with the feeling that their work is making an impact, an urge to perform at a high level, and the psychological safety to share their opinions and feelings openly in a transparent work environment. If the company is also supportive of these more "free-wheeling" teams, has leadership that knows how to hold open a space for the team, and refrains from clumsy interventions, teams have a good chance of performing well.

Needless to say, hierarchical companies find it very difficult to provide these eleven conditions, making more liberated companies a much better place for teams. The more complex the business environment becomes, the more teams outperform workgroups. Liberated companies can use high-performance teams at scale.

The new truth: The ecosystem

Great people and great teams sound like a recipe for good company performance, but generally speaking, management has never really believed in the myth of the high-performing individual or team (except the heroic CEO). Overall, the underlying view of people in most organizations is comparable to that of a well-performing cog in a machine.

A popular high-level view of performance that many managers still hold today is the one proposed by business strategist Michel Porter in the 1980s: performance is a function of a good strategy, well-executed in a market susceptible to both the chosen strategy and the way it is executed.[152] Arguably, individuals do not matter much. Only a few people think while the overwhelming majority execute; they are compliant, competent, and reliable—a cog in the machine. Teams do not matter much at all, except for their potential to enhance strategy making or to make execution more efficient on a tactical level. This idea of performance has been overtaken by the digital age. With so much change and unpredictability in the market, it is often impossible to come up with a strategy; likewise, it will be equally impossible to conceive of a state that lasts long enough to be worth pursuing. The most efficient and most clever execution in the world is worthless if the target cannot be pinpointed with reasonable certainty. Some companies adopt a learning strategy that evolves with the market, coupling it with flexible execution, but if it still relies on a tiny elite determining a strategy and hordes of less mindful followers, this logic is only marginally better. A truly dynamic organization eliminates the distinction between strategy and execution: strategy emerges in the course of execution and execution is an integral part of strategy.

Such an arrangement would give everyone the opportunity to engage to the best of their abilities. Such a company would become an ecosystem of people instead of a hardened structure of social differences. In his work on advanced organizations, Frederick Laloux uses three alternative terms to describe sensing, malleable, and purposeful organizations: wholeness, self-management, and evolutionary purpose.[153]

Wholeness

A holistic understanding of the world takes account of more factors to identify the multiple facets of an argument in order to manage dilemmas. Wholeness is the ability to work with a volatile, uncertain, complex, and ambiguous environments; it is the capacity to see things as they are and not take causation lightly.

---

152 (Porter, 1985)
153 (Laloux, 2014)

A company can "produce" wholeness by weaving reflective practices, transparency, and a communication culture of "all there is to know" (where divergent voices are heard) into its DNA. While companies remain primarily about action, wholeness refines their direction and leads to personal growth. Liberated companies that prosper in the digital age can be a strange mixture of careful deliberation and breakneck-speed execution.

Self-management

Self-management is a central enabler of both individual and team performance. Individual performance is enhanced by working in an environment that provides a high level of autonomy. Team performance is very rare without the team self-managing itself. Organizations facing the rapid shifts of the digital revolution therefore need to use more teams instead of just manager-led workgroups.

Evolutionary purpose

In a complex environment where causes and effects are ambiguous, the best way for companies to ensure progress is constant and purposeful evolution of their work designs. We turn to this in the next chapter.

Dark Arts
- Every company and every manager holds a theory of performance.
- Making that theory of performance explicit is a key to improving organizations.
- Traditionally, companies care more about jobs than about people.
- An idea of individual performance may involve nine factors that all need to be present at the same time for people and their performance to prosper. Most companies address capabilities and extrinsic motivation but neglect intrinsic motivation; as a result, they fail to build an environment full of opportunities and support.
- Teams are able to outperform groups of individual actors (workgroups) by several orders of magnitude.
- Teams are difficult to master. They require an organizational environment that supplies eleven factors well.

- Liberated companies enable companies to use high-performance teams at scale.
- In the digital age, a company is more of an ecosystem than a system that can be logically constructed, or "willed into being."
- The ecosystem is likely to rest on wholeness (sensing), self-management (agility), and evolutionary purpose (direction, growth, and improvement).

Further Reading

- On individual performance:
  - ○ Malcom Gladwell (2008) *Outliers* Back Bay Books
  - ○ Daniel Pink (2011) *Drive* Riverhead Books
  - ○ Adam Nicholson (2016), *Seize the Fire* Harper Perennial
- On team performance:
  - ○ J. Richard Hackman, Richard (2002), *Leading Teams* Harvard Business Review Press
  - ○ Jeff Sutherland (2015) *SCRUM* Random House Business
  - ○ Amy Edmundson (2014) *Teaming* Jossey-Bass
- On organizational performance:
  - ○ Renis Likert (1961) *New Patterns of Management* McGraw-Hill
  - ○ Phillip Rosenzweig (2007) *The Halo Effect* Free Press
  - ○ Geoffrey Moore (2015) *Zone to Win* Diversion Books

■ Chapter 14 Purpose: From Short-Term Profits to Values and Evolutionary Purpose

Business has been fully told. There is nothing to get there except money.
– Jan Böhmermann[154]

The old truth: Short-term profits

Most organizations are simply places that earn money where the most important question is "What is the net benefit for the organization?" In the absence of a higher purpose, the short-term profit motive takes over, with the focus shifting to hard, measurable benefits.

Even more true: Values and purpose

In our somewhat secular age, people tend to be led more by individualism and self-fulfillment than ever before.[155] People want to do something at work that makes their time and effort worthwhile beyond the monthly paycheck. Values and purpose can be an invisible hand that guides day-to-day behaviors and decisions, but all too often managers set out to impose a particular purpose or set of values on people in "their" organization.

If there is no systemic way of weaving sense-making into the company's fabric, these corporate exercises are often nothing more than hypocritical gimmickry of no value. The fact is that values and purpose cannot be imposed on people, and the daily grind tends to undermine well thought-out values and purpose. Purpose is a very personal thing which people tend to find in their

154 Jan Böhmermann, a german comedian, in a Tweet from 24 June 2018; https://twitter.com/janboehm/status/1010840153848537091?lang=de retrieved on 14th September 2019). Jan is a German journalist and comedian.
155 (Harari, 2016)

work for themselves, whether it is relationships with others, mastery of some aspect of their work, or even reconfiguring their motivational structure to fit the system over time. A company might even be a "purposeful" place to work despite the absence of an explicit company purpose.

An environment where people are free to seek their purpose autonomously, have plentiful opportunities to do so, and can enlist support when they need to—individual performance conditions 4 to 9 (see Figure 24)—makes this an easy adaptation. There is no need to decouple sense-making from daily work. Given enough space, people will find purpose themselves.

The new truth: Evolutionary purpose

An alternative to enforced top-down or bottom-up visioning is to let purpose and value appear over time without being mandated from above—in other words, to pull it from the organization over time. This view is held by the proponents of learning organizations. A learning organization lets people come up with their own convictions as to the purpose of an organization over time. In order to accomplish this, a company needs a lot of reflective management practices, as well as contemplative exercises where people can speak their mind freely. Embedding them into a company's routine through work designs enables purpose to emerge over time at the grass-roots level.

The right strategy for setting out towards the true north of a company may be a combination of both tactics: imposing purpose on an organization and at the same time pulling it from the organization—i.e. allowing it to emerge from the bottom up. The purpose can be imposed through soul-searching workshops to include all levels of the organization, while simultaneously, the purpose is pulled from the organization as reflective work designs are embedded into the daily work. Leading thinkers such as Robert Kegan, John Kotter, and Henry Mintzberg embrace this hybrid approach to a company's cultural development. It is the only way to shape sustainable corporate cultures.

As always, there are caveats to this hybrid approach of push and pull, vision and learning, and sense-making. First, it requires senior leaders to step back from their ambition to lead. It takes a lot of self-confidence and humility not to mandate a purpose. Second, reflective work designs are a time-consuming investment, in that time is spent talking about work and not directly on the work itself. In most companies today, work takes up 100% of scarce resource and time, while the meta level—reflecting, talking about work, watching other people work, and reframing the perception of one's own work—takes up 0%. Observation of successful, purpose-driven organizations suggests the optimal division is about 95% / 5%—in other words, about two to four hours per week spent on reflection. [156]

Dark Arts

- In the absence of a purpose, the universal rationale for answering the question "why?" becomes: "Short-term profits!"
- Values and purpose exercises are worthless if there is no systemic way of weaving sense-making into the fabric of companies.
- People can find and latch onto their intrinsic motivation more easily if there are ample opportunities and support within a company.
- Purpose is not a one-time deal. It needs to be experienced in order to emerge and evolve organically over time.
- Value-driven and purposeful company cultures can be built best if they are pushed to and pulled from an organization simultaneously by occasional visioning and reflective microstructures that are embedded in daily work.

Further Reading

- Viktor E. Frankl (1984) *Man's Search for Meaning* Beacon Press
- Joel Kurtzman (2010) *Common Purpose* John Wiley & Sons
- John, P. Kotter and James L. Haskett (2011) *Corporate Culture and Performance* Free Press, 2nd edition
- David K. Hurst (2012) *The New Ecology of Leadership* Columbia University Press
- Frederick Laloux (2014) *Reinventing Organizations* Nelson Parker

---

156 (Kegan & Laskow, 2016)

■ Chapter 15 Customer: From Products to Customers and Communities

Throughout history, people have expanded the circle of beings whose interests they are willing to value similarly to their own. The ever-expanding circle of our concern.
– Peter Singer[157]

The old truth: Products

Customer focus seems such an obvious point. It is only natural that companies should focus on customers—after all, it is they who are paying the bills. However, it is often hard to know who the customer really is, especially in bigger businesses. For most people in a company, customers exist more in statistics than in reality. Since customers are using products, improving products must mean happier customers. Products become a proxy for the customer.

The product-centric view was a necessity of the industrial age, when production technology needed to produce large batches to be efficient. Products could not be tailored to individual customers: the cost of too many product variants was prohibitive. Even today, interaction with customers is difficult and costly because there are too many of them and they vary too much. Consequently, the customer exists in statistics more than in reality and the individual customer is largely anonymous.

Even more true: Customers

The product as a proxy for customers is no longer necessary. Today, companies are able to tailor their products and services much more to the needs of a specific customer. Modern technology allows for efficient mass customiza-

---

157 (Singer, 2011)

tion and interaction. Products themselves have increasingly become tracked and intelligent, providing companies with insights into their use. While in the past customer-centricity may have been a hollow appeal to employees or a superficial marketing slogan, modern companies can actually be much more customer-focused.

In a digital world where customer attention is the scarcest and therefore most valuable resource of all, the call for customer-centricity needs to be taken very seriously. Advice on customer-centricity is plentiful. Extreme levels can be observed in the start-up industry, whose mantras are: build a minimal viable product (MVP); test it as early as possible with real customers; vary your offerings to the market again and again; test and learn; vary even your business model; and "pivot" until the product-market fit is found and the second phase of a start-up (scaling) can begin. The challenge is to find a solution to a problem that the customer has—i.e., a job that can be done better with your products than anyone else's. Start-ups are all about customer-centricity.

Management author Peter Block subscribes to the crucial importance of customer-centricity: *"The essence of being customer-focused in the fulfillment of our vision is to allow customers to teach us how to do business."*[158] Yet, this all-out customer focus is hard to maintain in a less-liberated company. Despite all the company's appeals, employees don't work for customers, they work for their boss. Their boss works for another boss. Ultimately the needs of the bosses win over the needs of the customer. Everyone in a hierarchy has their own agenda which only occasionally aligns with the needs of the customer. Customer-centricity is very hard to achieve if nearly all customer contacts fall on people who are the most disenfranchised group inside the whole company—i.e., those at the lowest hierarchical level. True customer-centricity, the type that the digital revolution makes possible, requires a shift of power to the people who are in direct contact with the customer—a strong argument for using circular organization models and self-managed teams, especially at the customer interface.

---

158 (Block, The Empowered Manager, 2016)

Customer-centricity can be overdone, however. It becomes hurtful when it causes people inside a company to take on a reactive stance. A business that only delivers whatever customers say they want will neither be visionary nor economically successful. People are often only able to state what they want as increments to what they have experienced in the past. Ultimately, customer centricity is mandatory for any company as a tactic that must be woven into a company's work designs at micro-level; it cannot replace strategic foresight.

The new truth: Community

In the digital revolution, customer focus is really just the first step towards creating an outward-looking company. If markets keep on changing, and technology offers more and more options that can be exploited, then a company needs to become more and more responsive to all it is connected to. The key in that last sentence is the word "responsive," which means much more than just being "connected." Professor of Management Henry Mintzberg writes: "If you want to understand the difference between a network and a community, ask your Facebook friends to help paint your house: Networks connect. Communities care."[159]

A company is just a part of a value stream that transforms raw materials in a number of work steps to a final product or service. If technology keeps on disrupting value streams, all interfaces of a company to the outside world need to become "sensing," not just the ones that are customer-facing. Companies need to listen to existing and potential suppliers, existing and potential partner companies, existing and potential stakeholders, financiers, and so on. Customer-centricity is just the beginning. What is really important in the long run is to freely interact and to be responsive to the outside world—to become community-centric and caring.

---

159 (Mintzberg, Bedtime Stories for Managers , 2019)

Dark Arts:
- The product has always been an insufficient proxy for the customer.
- Digital technologies support understanding of customers, interacting with customers, and customizing products.
- High levels of customer-centricity can best be achieved through the use of more self-managed teams as they share many characteristics with start-up teams.
- Customer-centricity needs to be an integral part of a company's work designs.
- Companies need to become sensitive to and caring for their surroundings, especially the community they are embedded in.

Further Reading
- Eric Ries (2011) *The Lean Startup* Currency
- David K. Hurst (2016) *The New Ecology of Leadership* Columbia Press
- Henry Mintzberg (2019) *Bedtime Stories for Managers* Berret-Koehler Publishers

■ Chapter 16 Freedom: From Rules to Entrepreneurship and Trust

If you put up fences, you get sheep.
– Brian M. Carney and Isaac Getz[160]

The old truth: Rules

Contrary to its public image, bureaucracy is a great system. Its main principles, listed by Max Weber in 1922,[161] are everywhere to be found in today's public organizations or private businesses:

- Specialized roles
- Recruitment based on merit
- Uniform principles of placement, promotion, and transfer in an administrative system
- Careerism with systematic salary structure
- Hierarchy, responsibility, and accountability
- Subjection of official conduct to strict rules of discipline and control
- Supremacy of abstract rules
- Impersonal authority (office bearer does not bring the office with him)
- Political neutrality

Bureaucracy is today's work environment. It is the way we run things and it has led to the brilliant success of capitalism today. Even Amazon, Netflix, Google, and Apple use bureaucracy to get things done.

---

160 (Carney & Geetz, 2016)
161 (Weber, 2019)

However, many people want to cut down on red tape and unleash initiative and efficiency. They want people to "break the rules" in an entrepreneurial drive that subjugates all means to the end. They focus on "subjection of official conduct to strict rules of discipline and control" and "supremacy of abstract rules." Few people want to abolish specialized roles, merit-based recruitment, or impersonal authority. And even those who are critical about too many rules and too rigid discipline do not want no rules and no discipline; they just want less of them.

In their 2016 book, *Freedom Inc.*, Isaac Getz and Brian Carney argue that most rules and controls are introduced into companies to prevent 3% of co-workers from abusing a company, often in a minor way, and end up punishing the 97% of non-offenders. Other authors claim that management hierarchies have an inbuilt tendency to counter any abuse, however minor, by making up new rules, just to appear in control of the situation.[162] Every failure is addressed with ever-more-restrictive rules, rather than greeted as an opportunity to learn. Staff units are especially prone to proliferating rules in order to prove their worth to an organization.

Still, bureaucracy has proved a useful and inevitable social construct for getting things done in organizations. It simply needs to be more responsive, flexible, risk-taking, and exploratory.

Even more true: Entrepreneurship

Entrepreneurs spot business potential and pursue it. They are risk-taking, focused, committed, and persistent. They subordinate anything and everything to realizing the opportunity they have identified. They get things done. Today's business world is crying out for more entrepreneurs in what appears to be a key response to the digital revolution.

There are three major stumbling blocks that limit the effectiveness of "intra-entrepreneurship": excessive focus on rationality, issues of the hierarchy itself, and regulated accountability. First, the process of innovation does not

---

162 (Alvesson & Spicer, 2016).

lend itself well to rational design and step-by-step process thinking. Innovation is chaotic by nature and human attempts to regulate innovation into existence are usually doomed from the outset. Second, within a hierarchy it is very difficult to take risks. People temper their suggestions and actions in order to not upset the interests of superiors, to not cannibalize existing business, to not reshuffle resources too much, or to not ignore corporate rules. Innovation means change, and change means a reshuffling of resources and accountability, which ultimately upsets established power structures. Some people won't like it. The inherent bias of hierarchies in favor of predictability over results (see Chapter 2) is not helpful in entrepreneurial pursuits.

The third stumbling block is regulated accountability. By defining innovation as a process to be managed, with a series of approvals needed from idea to budget allocation to product design to market launch and finally into operational business, a company ensures that entrepreneurs are exorcised from the system. Suppose a low-level worker came up with a brilliant idea. How likely is the worker to be able to explain the idea to some aloof committee of well-educated people very much removed from the front line? What chance does the worker stand of lobbying the organization without knowing its internal politics? What are the chances that the worker-entrepreneur can recruit capable, driven, and therefore highly valued people? Operational units tend to hold onto their key players, and HR will limit external recruitment attempts. High-powered individuals themselves often prefer to make their careers in the line organization (i.e., where the power is) instead of betting on an uncertain corporate initiative that might be out of favor soon.

"Entrepreneurial behavior" can easily be seen as "open subversion" by someone else. It is in the nature of entrepreneurs to take risks, move fast, and break things. A hierarchy, on the other hand, seeks predictability and conformity. Entrepreneurship and hierarchies therefore don't mix well. In practice, experienced company leaders do not look so much for internal change—they go outside their own companies and invest in start-ups, leading to the dual-mode economy discussed in Chapter 2: The Corrosive Impact of Power Differentials.

New truth: Freedom and trust

A truly entrepreneurial company does two things. It gives people the freedom to act, and it trusts them to handle the resources at their disposal in a responsible manner. Suppose you are a co-worker with an intriguing business idea in a self-managed company:

- If you can realize your idea on your own without the help of anyone, you can go ahead. You do not need to ask anyone's permission.
- If you need any other co-workers to change their way of working, set about convincing them—no permission required.
- If you need significant resources, convince your co-workers of your idea, especially those in an inner circle team. Again, no permission is required.

All that an entrepreneurially minded co-worker needs to do is convince their peers that their idea is worth pursuing. Of course, in a classical hierarchy, any employee able to convince the management hierarchy to follow their lead can do so, but the odds of being heard are stacked heavily against them. Hierarchies want compliance and predictability; they are allergic to risks and change.

An entrepreneurially minded co-worker in a self-managed organization has three advantages. First, everyone is on the same level, so there is more trust between the enterprising co-worker and the workers in charge of releasing resources. Second, no social class barriers need to be crossed. It is not the work-level employee (i.e., a social underling) who advocates a change, but a co-worker appealing to his fellow co-workers. Third, the risk for the co-worker is limited, as they are employed by the company and do not need to fear sanctions if things go awry. If the self-managed company manages to share the benefits of the successful initiative fairly with its enterprising co-workers, nothing much will prevent this company from spawning new businesses again and again.

Working in a more self-managed organization is not so much about taking up a position along the scale of organizations' central dichotomy of autonomy vs.

control; rather, it is more about achieving greater autonomy through different methods of control. A more liberated company can become a hothouse for innovation and entrepreneurship even in its maturity—a constantly changing and reconfiguring network of people, always anticipating market needs, trying new things, and adapting.

Dark Arts

- Despite its bad reputation, bureaucracy is a great system that few people want to abandon: (Digital) Platforms are essentially bureaucracies for the digital age[163].
- Many rules are aimed at the 3% of offenders and end up punishing the 97% of non-offenders.
- There is an inbuilt tendency for the hierarchy to keep coming up with more rules.
- One person's "entrepreneurial behavior" can easily be seen as "open subversion" by somebody else. Entrepreneurs and hierarchies don't mix well.
- Despite all the talk about innovation and entrepreneurship, company leaders are actually looking for entrepreneurs *outside* existing companies, not *inside* them.
- A more self-managed company tends to be a much more entrepreneurial company.

Further Reading:

- Brian M. Carney and Isaac Getz (2016) *Freedom Inc.* Somme Valley House 2nd Edition
- Mats Alvesson and André Spicer (2016) *The Stupidity Paradox* Profile Books

---

163 (Satell, 4 Things you should know about platforms, 2015)

■ Chapter 17 Information: From Secrecy to Context and Transparency

Data is like a Cloud. Clear from a distance, obscure up close.
– Henry Mintzberg[164]

The Old Truth: Secrecy

Limiting access to information is a key feature of organizations that are still anchored in the industrial age. How much information does an employee need? Exactly the amount of information to do the job—in other words, only what they need to know. The worker is not paid for thinking outside their assigned job; there are business-school-educated managers who specialize in that. In such a world, it is simply inefficient to provide more information. The worker gets the amount of information they need to know and not an ounce more.

Today, the dynamics have changed. Information can be made available cheaply; most employees are very well-educated and capable of processing large volumes of complex information. Even so, most organizations do not encourage the free flow of information.

- They restrict access to data by hierarchical level.
- They only want people exposed to information contained in their set of standard reports and discourage questions.
- "Why do you need to know this?" Exploration of data outside a narrowly defined job attracts critical questions from other departments, such as Control or IT, who sense a combination of mischief, mistrust, and inefficiency.

---

164 (Mintzberg, Bedtime Stories for Managers , 2019)

- Data exploration skills, financial literacy, and overall process know-how, is not taught in standard company curricula.

While it might seem like multi-billion investments in IT should trigger an avalanche of data literacy training, this has yet to happen. Companies would derive much greater benefit from all those costly IT systems if their people could make better use of them. Instead, functional specialists tend to be trained only to use this or that system function—just enough to do their narrowly defined job. Less well-informed people are less able to challenge the status quo, ask fewer awkward questions, and are easier to control. Knowledge is power, and lack of knowledge leads to obedience. Restricting information keeps people dependent.

Even more true: Context

To come up with new ways of working, or to find deeper insights, people must be allowed to reach out for information even if it appears to be beyond the scope of their current jobs. They need context to understand their work, and this understanding must lead to action.

The DIKAR model (Data, Information, Knowledge, Action, and Result) describes the way data is processed into action.[165] First, data must be captured and turned into information, whether by systems tracking or by human observation. Just as IT systems track and capture data in databases, people explore, talk to other people, share thoughts and experiences, and capture that data in their memory. Although today's digitalization projects are taking care of the systems side of data capture, the people side—organizational designs that enable people to explore and experience—is often forgotten.

Second, information needs to be turned into knowledge. People need to be able, and motivated, to make sense of the data they have taken in. There are a number of ways an organization can encourage this:

- Providing access to data
- Supplying tools to analyze the data

---

165 See (Venkatraman, 1996)

- Encouraging and teaching analytical expertise and financial literacy
- Encouraging exploration
- Visualizing data
- Using cross-functional teams
- Initiating fact-finding missions
- Encouraging the use of key performance indicators and dashboards

Third, knowledge must lead to action and results. Here, the decision mechanism design is crucial. In a conventional hierarchy, a superior calls the shots and applies whatever decision mechanism they deem best. But as we have seen, the hierarchy isn't the best system when it comes to processing divergent information in a scientific or entrepreneurial manner.

New truth: Transparency

If co-workers are to come up with new insights, they should have the maximum amount of information possible on an "all there is to know" basis. Paradoxically, since the human, not technological, capability to process information is arguably the critical bottleneck determining a company's ability to make sense of its business, companies need to become more human-centric in the digital age.

Humans are bad at systematically processing all the information the physical and virtual worlds have to offer. Until artificial intelligence replaces humans in the workplace, organizations need to become more human-centric to allow humans to do a good job of processing information. As humans are the bottleneck, improving non-bottleneck factors, such as supplying more and more IT systems, is not the answer.[166]

This starts at a very basic level. First, people must have the opportunity to meet and converse with one another independently of organizational units. They need to be able to go out and investigate wherever a problem or their interests may lead them. Alex Pentland, an informatics professor at MIT, argues that innovation in social systems is a function of the opportunity to

166 (Goldratt, 1999)

explore outside your team and the discipline of synthesizing the information in discussions with your team.[167] The word "innovation" makes us think of people like Albert Einstein, Steve Jobs, or Elon Musk. But innovation is happening every day in every company: every problem that is solved creatively is innovation. If firms expect people in the digital world to make good decisions, they need to support free exploration and synthesis by more and more people. They need to sacrifice a bit of short-term efficiency to allow new insights to happen. Efficiency is not worth a jot if the wrong things are done or the right things are done in the wrong way.

The challenge is not so much to allow more free-ranging discussions between people, but rather to tie systematic information processing into the configuration of a company's work design. Professor J. K. Galbraith listed five conditions for better information processing by companies: no blind eyes, allow for slack resources, decentralized decision-making, use of processes, and transparency.[168]

Another powerful reason for providing transparency on an "all there is to know" basis is to build trust towards others and the company. Trust for a company represents what blood is for a body. It underlies every single communication signal that people send, and it is behind all human expressions. Transparency is certainly not enough to build trust in organizations by itself, but it goes a long way.[169]

Dark Arts

- In hierarchies, access to information and literacy is often limited to an "all you need to know basis," which is just enough for people to do their jobs.
- Digitalization thrives on "all there is to know." The two keys to success are the tracking of data and people being able to translate data into action.

---

167 (Pentland, 2014)
168 (Galbraith, Organization Design, 1977)
169 Scholars, including Elinor Ostrom and Adam Grant, show in a series of game theory experiments that transparency itself changes organizational dynamics decisively and for the better.

- Hierarchies are systematically limited in their information-processing capacity, because centrality and exploration do not mix well.
- The true data-processing capacity of a company is determined by the way people and machines are brought together by the organizational design.
- In a world saturated with technology, companies need to become increasingly human-centric. Bottlenecks are created by the human capacity to process information, not IT capacity.
- Transparency helps to create trust and trust is rocket fuel for any organization.

Further Reading
- Nate Silver (2012) *The Signal and the Noise* Penguin
- Adam Grant (2013) *Give and Take* W&N
- Alexander Pentland (2015) *Social Physics* Penguin

■ Chapter 18 Learning: From Jobs to Learning and Purposeful Evolution

Learning is often seen as naive. It is not, but it requires a good deal of sophistication. That makes many simplistic attempts look naïve.
– Henry Mintzberg[170]

Very few companies care about learning. Every company wants to become more productive and efficient, acquire better products—but does the whole company really need to learn for this to happen? Isn't it enough for a few bright people at the top to know what to do and engage experts, like designers, engineers, and marketers? After all, only a few people need to be aware of the really decisive points. For the overwhelming majority of the organization, it is about execution, the daily grind of work. The digital age is often cited as one of the main reasons for turning a company into a learning one. But is this really true? After all, even for digital giants like Amazon, the company is 90% about execution. Do we really need learning companies—or just more clever ways for a limited group of the corporate population to learn?

The old truth: Jobs

What a company really needs from its co-workers is adequate competence. Everyone in an organization is hired to do a certain job as competently as needed. Excess competence is appreciated but not needed; it may lead to boredom and is often too expensive to obtain anyway. Lack of competence is thought to be rectified by providing corrective feedback, functional or soft-skills training, redefining the job, or dismissal. Learning is about gaining adequate competence, nothing more.

---

170 (Mintzberg, Strategy Safari, 2008) p. 240.

Elaborate rituals designed to get a worker to perform at an adequate level of competence include weekly one-on-one meetings to foster a closer relationship between superior and subordinate, and annual appraisals to communicate any performance gaps and calibrate expectations for the next period. Performance is constantly scrutinized by a superior. Managers, after all, are there to oil, adjust, and exchange the cogs in the machine to ensure the smooth functioning of their part of the business.

In a dynamic, complex, and fast-moving work environment, where competence requirements shift rapidly, unpredictably, and significantly, the model of adequate competence breaks down. In a knowledge-intensive environment, the actual level of competence of a co-worker is not as important as their ability to quickly pick up new skills. In knowledge work, it is easier for managers to identify a subordinate's outputs than their inputs. Programmers, for example, are often working on difficult problems where a lot of context is needed to understand the effort that went into a solution. Here, a manager can't identify the effort that went into the task.

Another example is nursing. Nurses are knowledge workers, too, as human health and well-being are incredibly complex. Was it the medication that worked or was it another aspect of the treatment? Is the diagnosis correct? Is the improvement only temporary? No one can easily judge a nurse's efforts, and yet many modern health systems seek to micro-manage the work of a nurse. All the indications are that less micro- and more self-managing would increase the well-being of patients, increase nurses' job satisfaction, and reduce the overall cost to society.[171] Even cleaning jobs can be reimagined as knowledge intensive, as Edalco, a successful Dutch cleaning company, has been demonstrating since 2011.[172]

If a worker consistently fails to produce the requested outputs, a manager can only speculate as to whether adequate competence could be achieved through skills training, more communication, more sensible tasks, a different work environment, or motivation. Where outputs, but not inputs,

---

171 (Gawande, 2009))
172 https://corporate-rebels.com/edalco-services/, retrieved 19 June 2019

can be observed, a manager's efficiency is much diminished. The cogs in the machine can no longer be oiled with precision. The more complex the business environment, the less effective managerial oversight becomes.[173] At some point, it becomes more effective to keep managers out of the learning process and decentralize learning—i.e., to create an environment that allows people to learn whatever they think they need. The software industry has learned this lesson. Micro-managing managers are unlikely to be found in the core operations of Amazon, Spotify, Google, or Facebook. Instead, digital companies are often organized in a number of small, self-managing teams. Managers are usually still around, but they take on a more supportive, coaching role.

Knowledge-intensive work, which according to the OECD is about 30% to 60% of all work in Western societies, is learning-intensive work.[174] Therefore, companies need to become learning companies in their entirety rather than restricting learning to the upper strata of managers and experts. Managing people on the basis of adequate competence is becoming an increasingly inadequate response to the rise of the knowledge worker.

Even more true: Learning

Learning organizations go beyond "adequate competence." They seek to improve people's and organizations' capabilities. Robert Kegan believes learning organizations share certain characteristics:[175]

- They make being a spectator impossible—people need to speak up.
- There are no "campfire moments" when people are asked to do nearimpossible things.
- They encourage vulnerability and allow feelings in.
- They believe that an employee's psyche, imperfection, vulnerability, shame, and unworthiness have a part to play in the organization.
- They treat people as adults, not children.

173 (Drucker, The Effective Executive , 2017)
174 A classic book on this subject is (Davenport, 2005)
175 (Kegan & Laskow, 2016)

- They rely on feedback that penetrates the assumptions and mindsets that lie behind behaviors.
- They develop mental complexity in individuals.
- They are an incubator for development.
- They expect everyone to teach.
- They are constantly stirring things up.
- They rotate people and positions all the time.
- They are not for everyone, as they often offer a stressful but potentially rewarding environment.
- They put development first, in the belief that efficiency follows.

Kegan & Laskow describe empowered and supportive companies that strive towards these ideals, including Bridgewater, which we met before. These companies embrace reflective and learning management practices—and they embrace change. If learning is to be effective, companies need to be malleable and agile. The only risk associated with learning occurs when it is used as an excuse for not acting.[176] Without change, learning is both inconsequential and superfluous.

New truth: Purposeful evolution

A truly learning company is a place where the drive to learn is internalized by co-workers, where everyone is both teacher and pupil, and where people are free to strive for mastery and purpose in any way they like. Peter Senge defines organizational learning in such companies: "Organizational learning is the process of enhancing learners' capacity, individuals and groups, to produce results they truly want to produce."[177]

It is inevitable that purpose will be the crucial role of any learning endeavor. If a company is to utilize people's intrinsic motivations, it must make space for people to find and follow their purpose towards self-fulfillment. It is not difficult to see why there are so few learning organizations. Allowing people to

---

176 (Block, The Right Use of Power, 2002)
177 (Senge, 1990)

find their purpose creates a degree of individuality and diversity that is much harder to control. As a result, it is not easy for a less-liberated company to become a learning company. It requires managers who choose to act consistently against the grain of the hierarchical system; it takes managers who adopt a supportive, non-paternalistic role, coach those who want to be coached, refrain from giving unwanted advice, and allow for failure and experience. Such a manager runs the risk of being seen as weak or indecisive. Efficiency will decline for a time as people sort out their priorities and come to grips with their new freedom. Some subordinates will not care for this freedom and will crave more guidance. Often, the better choice is to remain a hierarch and "to be the best parent one can be."[178]

A learning organization is almost inevitably a more self-managed organization. Only the diversity of the network gives people the space to explore while still aligning their individual path of discovery with the needs of the organization. No other form of human collaboration can do that.

Dark Arts
- Jobs are about adequate competence, not excellence.
- Adequate competence is something that is imposed on employees (cogs in a machine) from the outside.
- Most of today's workers are knowledge workers who find it hard to give their best in paternalistic hierarchies.
- Organizational learning happens only if people learn and if that learning causes a company to change (i.e., to work differently).
- Organizational learning is the process of enhancing the learning capacity of individuals and groups in order to produce the results they truly want to produce.
- A learning company needs a much more sophisticated work design than most hierarchies can deliver; it must center on purposeful evolution of itself and everyone in it.

---

178 (Block, The Empowered Manager, 2016)

Further Reading

- Peter Senge (1990) *The Fifth Discipline* Currency
- Chris Argyris and Donald A. Schön (1999) *Organizational Learning II* FT Press
- Robert Kegan: Lisa Laskow (2016) *An Everyone Culture* Harvard Business Review Press
- Carol Sanford (2017) *The Regenerative Enterprise* Nicolas Brealey Publishing

■ Chapter 19 Exploring: From Plan to Experiment and Venturing

You like the evidence: go get the experience.
– Henry Mintzberg[179]

The old truth: Plan

There are many good things to say about planning. A plan prepares a business for the future, both mentally and physically. It coordinates actions and focuses resources on targets. A plan can be shared and scrutinized. A plan is a document that shows a way of turning an intention into a reality.

Yet planning has been much criticized in recent years.[180] It is often a deterministic exercise, as if future reality can be forecast with certainty. Company plans are often really good at detailing the ordinary, but famously bad at anticipating the seismic shifts in businesses that really matter. [181] Most plans leave neither enough scope for the unexpected nor enough flexibility to react to it. With a plan comes a feeling of security, an insurance policy that says: "we did all the right things."

Medium- and lower-level plans are often infected by these problems, too. Project planners are frequently expected to come up with complex GANTT charts of interrelated tasks that bear little resemblance to reality. Detailed planning and tracking is seen as a badge of honor, showing that you are in control and things are predictable – both highly valued in a hierarchy.

The price of keeping up the pretense of predictability is high. Numbers are routinely fiddled with, creative accounting is rampant, bending facts to fit

---

179 (Mintzberg, Bedtime Stories for Managers, 2019)
180 (Mintzberg, The Rise and Fall of Strategic Planning, 1995); (Bogsnes, 2016)
181 This tendency to focus on the trivial is described entertainingly by (Taleb, 2012)

plans is the norm. Imagine you are a manager in charge of planning in a complex environment. Would you rather say that you will figure it out along the way and come up with a couple of pages to describe your approach, or present an impressively detailed plan with very detailed work-breakdown charts? Most people will choose the latter option, as it makes them look competent, busy, well prepared, and in control. Yet the former is the essence of any agile approach: stop the pretense of control and be prepared for the unexpected.

Senior managers love the feeling of predictability that comes with holding onto a plan. Predictability is what the stock market expects from top-level executives, too. Stock analysts can live with bad numbers, but they abhor surprises. To not make the forecast is a clear sign of management incompetence. Managers and analysts find it much easier to find narratives to explain bad numbers than to explain surprises. Only the incompetent are surprised.

Of course, having no plan is not a good idea. But nor is being held strictly accountable to plans. As long as the ability to "make the numbers" each quarter is the prime route for upward mobility in management, companies will continue to produce risk-averse leaders who are skilled at manipulating the appearance of reality instead of transforming it.

Surprise is an essential component of innovation. Without it, you are doomed to mediocrity.

Even more true: Experiment

Planning is laudable but holding people rigidly accountable to plans is not. The question is: what should people be held accountable for?

The first option is to hold people accountable for results. This is a good option for the medium and long term. Holding people accountable for short-term results is a reasonable strategy, but only if people can really shape results by their actions. However, if the underlying dynamic of a business prevents people from directly translating actions into results, holding people accountable for things like monthly sales or number of software features delivered per month is naive. The customer, the market, and organizational dynamics have a nasty habit of making things complex. Faced with a random distribution of results where one own's actions can control just 20% of the variation, one can deliver the expected results consistently only by under-promising and bending the truth.

In the long run, it is fine to have 20% control of outcomes. But in the short-term business environment, there is no time. Managers and sports coaches alike are quickly replaced if results are not delivered. Again, this is fine, as we are living in a world of imperfect information. No-one knows how much variation in results is controlled by a manager or a coach, but observers are updating their assessment on a manager's or coach's capability with every new result that comes in. With every new failure to live up to expectations the probability that a person is not up to the job increases.[182] It's just Bayes law: At a certain threshold the "fire and replace" trigger is pulled. If once in a while a good manager or coach is a casualty, so be it—probability and imperfect information can cause collateral damage.

The second option is to hold people accountable for their actions. In a perfect world, where it was possible to observe that a person had done all the right things, we would not need to look at results. We would know that people had done their best and chance had intervened. A momentary lack of results could be shrugged off in the certainty that the organization was well prepared for the future.

But this is hugely unrealistic. We have neither the time nor the mental capacity to observe the actions that people do. Ever since human beings have been in business, we have used our limited time and mental capacity to observe and judge the output of human endeavors—the results. The result is a better proxy for measuring human performance than the action.

---

182 Bayes law describes the probability of an event, based on prior knowledge of conditions that might be related to the event. For example, if cancer is related to age, then, using Bayes' theorem, a person's age can be used to more accurately assess the probability that they have cancer this can be done without knowledge of the person's age.

There is, however, a middle course between results/outputs and actions/inputs—a much better way of observing actions without losing sight of the result. It is an alternative to the cowboy mentality of shooting people first and asking questions afterward. It is also probably not only more efficient but meets the ethical need to do right by other people. It is called logical incrementalism.[183]

Logical incrementalism

The idea of logical incrementalism is to allow people to work themselves into a subject, aiming for an overall target cycle by cycle. In contrast to upfront planning, people update their way of working in light of the experience gained and come up with revised and improved plans for the next cycle. Logical incrementalism is a method that allows accountability when causes and effects cannot be clearly distinguished. It is a way of homing in on an overall target, while keeping both target and sequence of work flexible. The target itself may evolve in any of its dimensions in light of changing business needs and the experience gained.

Continually moving the goalposts is no way to hold anyone accountable. The trick is to hold someone accountable without exactly defining what they are accountable for. The crux of the logical incrementalism method is to know what to fix in lieu of the target, as these points demonstrate:

- The overall target and date are fixed—lesser targets and deadlines may change as the work progresses.
- The time period to the deadline is divided into smaller timeframes of equal size, called cycles. The length of these cycles is fixed, providing a drumbeat, a rhythm that increases the intensity and focus of the work.
- People self-commit to a fixed target at the beginning of each cycle, but they are held accountable to that commitment.
- The overall work design remains consistent, including meeting structures, team composition, how work content is prioritized at the beginning of cycles, and how retrospectives are performed at the end of cycles.

---

183 The earliest signs of this thinking can be found in (Quinn, 1980). It has been made popular by SCRUM: (Sutherland, 2015)

Lean startup, agile, SCRUM, continuous improvement, total quality manage-ment, and self-managed work teams are all management approaches that rely heavily on logical incrementalism. A huge number of modern business "buzz words" can be attributed to logical incrementalism, such as *product-market fit, minimal viable product (MVP), ODDA and PDCA cycle, sprint, retrospective, prod-uct backlog*, and *runways*.[184] Other buzz words like *KANBAN, product owner*, and *scrum master* tend to follow those closely. Logical incrementalism is the method of choice for the trail-blazing start-up industry that so many com-panies seek to imitate. Yet most companies find logical incrementalism very hard to use correctly, as it requires managers to give up control, move into a supportive role, and brace themselves for surprises. Logical incrementalism invites the uncertainty of the work, of the market, of reality into the company – with all the surprises and failures that this brings. Less liberated companies are finding it hard to use logical incrementalism as they try to keep surprises and failure out.

Logical incrementalism is a method that is designed to work in complex envi-ronments, not a general-purpose tool to be used for all challenges. Traditional planning remains important, and simpler business environments are better served by rational analysis, a work-breakdown structure, conventional time planning and assigning people to tasks. The key value of planning lies in being prepared for all eventualities and having appropriate tools available to master situations as they occur. "No plan survives the first contact with the enemy", [185] but to have no plan is just lazy unpreparedness, even in complex business settings. It is all about the right level of plan and the right level of adherence to it.[186]

---

184 (Ries, 2011)
185 Commonly attributed to Marshall Erwin Moltke the Elder.
186 A credo of the Beyond Budgeting movement is: fewer targets, more forecasts.

New truth: Venturing

Logical incrementalism is a great way of tinkering your way to success by accumulating improvements. It is most useful if it is paired with revolutionary intent. For example, it seems a crazy idea to invite strangers into your home for sleepovers (Airbnb), to build a business empire on a search algorithm (Google) or to rent out videos or music via the internet (Netflix, Youtube, Spotify). It takes both vision and incremental tinkering to venture to new destinations.

Start-ups are ventures with a vision and the flexibility to let people work in ways they choose, guided by work designs based on logical incrementalism. Self-managed structures are well suited to venturing: questioning old truths without fear of reprisal, changing the organization more easily, and finding and following one's purpose. They provide a system where innovation, learning, and change can prosper without the need to run the gauntlet of the hierarchical power differential or rigid systems of resource allocation.

Venturing can create totally new, unexpected business opportunities that pay off if they are exploited rapidly. German general Erwin Rommel said of the relationship between experimentation and exploitation: "I consciously seek to create complex, uncertain situations – while being fully aware that I have the capabilities at my disposal to master the resulting complexity."[187] It is the ability to experiment while also having the sharply honed tools at one's disposal to execute on a newly revealed business opportunity that makes experimentation worthwhile. More liberated companies have all that is required: an environment that fosters experiments and the agility to exploit insights.

Dark Arts
- Planning is universally useful.
- Planning is susceptible to being hijacked and perverted by the hierarchy's basic need for predictability, for a formula for success that can be broken down into action plans.

---

187 This quote is attributed to Rommel, though I could not identify the source. However, this thinking is clearly visible in his only book: "Infanterie greift an" (Rommel, 1937)

- Have fewer targets and more forecasts: don't hold people accountable for things they can't control but encourage them to look ahead.
- Logical incrementalism is a way of keeping everything as flexible as a complex situation requires, while still keeping accountability alive.
- Experimentation is the journey that connects big aspirations to new realities: evolutionary in action, revolutionary in purpose.
- Venturing is what start-ups and more self-managed companies excel at.

Further Reading
- Henry Mintzberg (2013) *The Rise and Fall of Strategic Planning* Free Press
- Eric Ries (2011), *The Lean Startup* Currency
- Jez Humble, Joanne Molesky, Barry O'Reilly (2015) *Lean Enterprise* O'Reilly and Associates

■ Chapter 20 Discipline: From Coercion to Internalized Control

Working should find us traveling on a personal path of discovery to the company's destination.

The old truth: Coercion

Discipline is key to concerted action. There are two routes to achieving discipline. One is to bend another's will to one's own with rewards and coercion, and this kind of extrinsic motivation is what companies tend to use. The other is to engage people's intrinsic drive for autonomy, mastery, and purpose.

Companies are willing to spend a lot on managerial oversight. On average, 11% of a hierarchical company's workforce are managers. This 11 % coordinates the other 89% of the workforce but consumes about 33% of the total payroll of a typical company, a disproportionate amount. Management thinker Gary Hamel calls this 33% a "management tax."[188] To add insult to injury, hierarchical companies spend all this money intending to discipline people to do their best for the company, but end up spending it on disciplining people to follow their boss's direction—so 33% of personnel costs are spent on non-productive people who then deliver a deficient product. In economic theory, this is known as the principal-agent problem. Asymmetrical information between principal (e.g., a shareholder) and agent (e.g., a manager) is bound to lead to the exploitation of the principal.

Nevertheless, discipline is what every company needs. Achieving discipline by hierarchy has always been costly—maybe too costly to remain competitive in a digital world.

---

188 (Hamel, 2016)

Even more true: Coax

Companies are increasingly opening up some pockets of their organizations to more empowered ways of working that utilize intrinsic motivation. Some managers are experimenting with agile methods and "work hacks" to get work done differently, coaxing and nudging people into new behaviors.[189] While this is laudable, it is quite likely to be just a passing management fad. Many good and useful practices lose their meaning and effectiveness if there are no changes to the underlying system. Agile practices are increasingly being co-opted by the hierarchy as a tool for more control and efficiency instead of more customer value and self-fulfillment. People do not open up because they are told to, nor do they engage their inert drive because of this or that fashionable management practice. To rely on practices alone, while ignoring the underlying question of the power differential, is naïve. As novelist T.S. Eliot wrote: "We had the experience but we missed the meaning."

A good outcome of experiments with new work designs would be for more managers to change their leadership style. To be a better parent (or to be more supportive and delegating) is a good beginning.

The new truth: Internalized control

The alternative to coercion and coaxing is to rely on discipline that comes from within. It is the satisfaction of following their purpose, mastery, and autonomy that turns people into missionaries instead of mercenaries. Not everyone will become a missionary. Some people will love to be able to follow their inner calling, while others enjoy being told what to do. Organizational design is not about turning everyone into missionaries, but about providing an environment that brings out more missionary behavior.

This kind of design can be built by configuring a company with more-liberated work designs (levels 3 and 4). The organizational system can be geared to make it as easy as possible for people to find their inner drive and let their motivations pull them along. In this way, control becomes internalized.

189 (Thaler & Sunstein, 2008)

Internalized control needs to be supported by management practices that are applied deliberately and persistently in a drumbeat rhythm. In a way, these practices regulate internalized control into being. In this kind of organizational environment, co-workers will police themselves and others more. Social control is an important element here. Humans are very aware of their social surroundings; they anticipate the wants and needs of their co-workers and teams and are very good at picking up social signals and reacting to them. Working in a more liberated environment is inevitably about internalized and social control.

Systems based on social control can be quite sinister. In his novel *The Circle* (2013), Dave Eggers describes a system of social control of a fictional Silicon Valley giant from the standpoint of one of its employees. This is a workplace where freedom, autonomy, transparency, and feedback are rampant, but they have turned it into a prison of social control. There are no mind-controlling machines, but there is a social design that provides near-absolute control of workers.

Cybernetics is the academic discipline concerned with the control of complex systems. It is highly theoretical, and its practical application suffers from the unpredictability of its very subject of research, yet it is the science that modern organizational designers often turn to. The holy grail of a cybernetics system designer is a "homeostat"—a device to control a complex system, a "black box" whose inner workings cannot be known. A homeostat is primarily about three things:

- the measurement of input and outputs;
- the ability to regulate the system; and
- the adaptability of the way regulation works.

A homeostat to control companies would operate as follows. First, a company must be measured intensively, because even the smallest signs might become important at some point in time. Modern devices including phones, watches, tablet computers, cameras, and the cloud enable seamless and effortless monitoring. Second, the organizational system can be regulated by co-workers policing themselves. If everyone is an entrepreneur, everyone is in the business of improving themselves and others. If there is enough transparency for people to be able to compare their performance, competition will motivate them. There is little need for a central regulatory authority; people will do that themselves. Third, adaptability can be achieved by absorbing shocks through an autonomous networked structure of co-workers and teams that is all but set up for continuous adaptation. There are—by design—very few interventions by a central authority.

It is not hard to see that such a system is very attractive to Silicon Valley's engineers-turned-start-up-founders-turned-billionaires. Cybernetics is the application of engineering know-how to organizational design. It allows an engineer to design a system that transcends the weaknesses of human cognition and provides a handle on the complexity of the whole company.[190] Cybernetic enthusiasts, far from being dry technocrats, tend to be well-rounded, emotionally sensitive, self-reflecting people. They are often missionaries themselves. The bad thing about having missionaries at the helm of a cybernetic homeostat is that they tend to project their values onto others, using subtle manipulation instead of blunt command and control—automation with a human touch.[191] We are already seeing many cybernetic experiments: Google is a big experiment in elitism; Amazon is a big experiment in high-energy activism; Microsoft is in the midst of an experiment in customer-driven reflection. We are living in exciting times.

Responsible cybernetic design

Still, it remains worthwhile for a company and its employees to reduce the amount of external control and increase the amount of internal control that people have; this gives people's free will more latitude while at the same time recognizing that free will might not be so free after all. There are ways of finding a balance, designing a cybernetic system without becoming an overbearing manipulator. The first is to delegate organizational design to the co-workers of the company itself. In the final chapter of this book, we will explore

---

190 (Schaupp, 2016)
191 As long ago as 1995, Bill Gates forecast the merging of neoliberalism and cybernetics. See (Schaupp, 2016) p. 117.

ways of letting people come up with their own ways of working. Second, the process of organizational design—i.e., which practices a company embraces, discourages, or mandates, and why it does so—should be transparent. Communication, debate, and the solemn consideration of concerns breed trust and understanding. Third, playfulness, humor, and a tolerance of failure are strong antidotes to overbearing cybernetic technocracy. After all, building a perfect homeostat is a contradiction in terms. Organizational designs will work well for some time but will need to be constantly updated. An overly serious, rational, fact-based approach is as inappropriate as an approach based on "firm, unshakeable company values." An ironic, humble, sometimes self-deprecating way of being is a good check against hubris and control mania.

All these methods do not eliminate the potential for manipulation, nor should they. The mission of organizational design is to enable companies to achieve coherent action. Organizing something is always essentially about manipulation, whether by extrinsic or intrinsic psychological methods. One person's manipulation is another's clever nudge. A healthy organizational design should contain checks on mischievous manipulation, achieving conformity of action without conformity of thought. But it is not easy. As Peter Drucker says: "Yes, management is a system of dilemmas. Now get on with it!"

Dark Arts

- Without discipline, there is no company.
- The cost of doing business through the hierarchy is very high. The management tax is typically a third of total personnel costs.
- People are often coaxed into new behaviors through agile, lean, or new work designs or clever HR policies, yet people are likely to recognize charades over time and return to their old ways.
- Internalized control—discipline that comes from within—is a chance for people to grow, but it comes with the threat of manipulation and overbearing social control.
- The dangers of cybernetic control can be mitigated by more participative work designs, transparency, open discussions, and a generally playful attitude to human collaboration.

Further Reading

- Peter Block (2002) *The Right Use of Power* Sounds True (audio book)
- Brian Robertson (2015) *Holacracy* Penguin
- Ray Dalio (2017) *Principles* Simon & Schuster
- Stephen Denning (2018) *The Age of Agile* Amacon

■ Chapter 21 Leadership: From Authority to Systematic Leadership and Gardening

I stopped playing chess and became a gardener.
– Stanley McChrystal[192]

The old truth: Authority

People become leaders because they are appointed to be other people's superior. People become followers because they are subordinated. In a hierarchy, it is as simple as that.

What makes a good leader? Despite the many books that have been written about this, the empirical evidence consistently points towards one thing only: we do not know. There are no specific traits or talents, there is no style, there are no techniques or psychometric tests—there is nothing of predictive value that stands up to academic scrutiny. The lack of any consistent academic evidence for all kinds of fashionable leadership theories has been pointed out by Jeffrey Pfeffer and Phil Rosenzweig, recognized experts in the field of management.[193] Put more positively, leadership coaches, trainers, consultants, and the business press are in the business of selling inspiration, not insights. Simple solutions to complex matters have always been in demand.

Even more true: Systematic leadership

So, what does science have to offer managers? The best advice on leadership I have found, which comes from people who have spent a good part of their

---

192 (McChrystal, Silverman, Tantum, & Chris, 2015)
193 (Pfeffer, 2015); (Rosenzweig, The Halo Effect, 2007)

careers scrutinizing leadership theories, can be summarized in a list of five points that I call Systematic Leadership.[194]

1. *Leadership equals Management.* In *Bedtime Stories for Managers*, Henry Mintzberg says: "The fable that leadership is separate from, and superior to, management has been bad for management and worse for leadership." It does not make much sense to distinguish between them. Management practices are the hardest form of leadership. The words, gestures, and immaterial mindsets of leaders are supportive, but ultimately so tightly combined with management practices that management becomes indistinguishable from leadership.
2. *Management is a craft.* It is a craft that can be learned by most people if they know the tools of management (i.e. management practices) and have the skill to select and apply those tools as the situation requires.
3. *A bias for action and a bias for reflection.* Action paired with critical reflection is what propels a leader towards mastery. With action one exposes oneself to success and failure. With reflection one increases the chance of success and reduces the impact of failures over time.
4. *Which behaviors work is contingent on the environment.* Even an unproven leadership style may work in certain situations. There is some value in learning from the snake-oil peddlers of leadership theories, as they might reframe the management challenge in interesting new ways.
5. *Which leadership/management practices are appropriate is determined to a considerable extent by strategy.* Not only is the situation of a company important, so too is the direction it wants to take. Management is closely intertwined with strategy. The dividing line between strategy and execution is blurred and causality runs in both directions. For example, aiming to become digital for strategic reasons while still retaining traditional "old truth" management practices is a bad idea. A strategy changes which ways of leadership work and which do not.

---

194 (Rosenzweig, The Halo Effect, 2007) (Pfeffer, 2015); (Mintzberg, Simply Managing, 2013); (Senge, 1990); (Malek, 2013)

There are no best styles or traits. Good leadership is simply a result of an honest attempt to lead well, or as Richard W. Scott, a professor of organizational science puts it: "Leading is to attend carefully to the critical importance of mundane administrative systems that preserve precarious organizational values."[195] Systematic Leadership's five points have been compiled from advice given by the world's leading leadership experts, but it is impossible to quantify their impact on an organization's effectiveness, which should be the ultimate measure of any management system.

A group of researchers who have been studying the link between management practices and performance since 2003[196] found a correlation between a company's economic results and the total of all management practices applied in it. Management practices were found to account for about 10% of the variation in a company's results.[197] The other 90% was made up of all other factors, including market positioning, products, customer base, operating model, geography, sector, competition, regulation, supply markets, megatrends, and a large dose of chance. In a complex world, there are no simple recipes. Yet, a 10% direct impact of management practices on company results is really quite good. The indirect impact (good management practices leading to good decisions in other areas such as market positioning, products, productivity, etc.) might be much bigger. Just how much remains a subject of speculation.

Another perspective on good leadership can be found by looking at a person's abilities. According to Philip Rosenzweig and Henry Mintzberg, an ideal leader can be described in six personas. [198]

- A master strategist and tactician who knows how to play the competitive game.
- A professional riverboat gambler who is very well-versed in taking on risks.

---

195 Paraphrased from(Scott, 2014), page 274.
196 World Management Survey, **https://worldmanagementsurvey.org** retrieved on 10th September 2019
197 (Blooom, Dorgan, Dowdy, Rippin, & van Reenen, 2005)
198 Based on (Rosenzweig P. , 2015); (Mintzberg, Simply Managing, 2013)

- A scientist who is skilled in critical thinking, creating hypotheses and learning.
- A good psychologist who knows to shape the outcomes they want and inspire others to pursue those outcomes.
- A craftsman who is skilled in the realms of work design and management.
- An artist who is able to conjure visions in the mind and give expression to them in the real world.

In addition, the ideal leader will need to have the ability to change from one persona to another as the situation demands. Such people are very hard indeed to find. According to Peter Drucker, "No institution can possibly survive if it needs geniuses or supermen to manage it. It must be organized in such a way as to be able to get along under a leadership composed of average human beings."[199]

If superhuman leaders are in short supply, we might wonder about getting an executive team together that combines diverse personalities. The CEO would need good listening skills and the ability to refrain from personal bias and weigh advice fairly. The other members of the leadership team would need incentives to open up and share unbiased, objective advice for the benefit of the company (and not for their own personal agendas).

In theory this could be a good approach, but in practice we can forget it. Senior management teams are the most dysfunctional of all teams.[200] All the members have risen through the ranks of hierarchical systems, all are likely to be skilled at the games of pleasing a superior, all know when to keep up appearances and when to withhold information, and all have their eye on the next step of the career ladder. It is lonely at the top, with each senior manager fighting first and foremost for their own future. Fundamentally, it is the power differential and the principal-agent problem that are rampant in these scenarios. Perhaps it is time to move away from the superhuman, ultra-centralist way of running companies.

---

199 Cited in (Mintzberg, Simply Managing, 2013)
200 (Pfeffer, 2015)

New truth: Gardening

If the complexity and dynamism of the digital age do not lend themselves to the leadership approach we practiced in the industrial revolution, what kind of leadership do we need today? With super-leaders in short supply, do we need to resign ourselves to seeing bad leadership more often and rely on the market to weed out badly led companies over time? A better way to lead companies in the digital age would need to be built on three elements:

- *Holding open the space*: Allowing power to be distributed widely.
- *Gardening*: Taking care of the work design configuration.
- *Emergent and fluid power arrangements*: Allowing people best suited to do so to lead on a particular topic and making leadership appointments less permanent.

Holding the space

In a world of private ownership, where everyone is free to make contracts with everyone, power is by definition asymmetrically distributed. The employer holds all the cards. The employee can walk away from the contract, but he is otherwise quite impotent. Elisabeth Anderson calls the regimes that people are operating in their work life "private government." The distribution of power is hugely one-sided: "To deny employers' authority over workers is like saying Mussolini wasn't a dictator, because Italians could migrate."[201]

Employers can choose to liberate their people or not. This book argues in favor of liberating, as it allows a company and its people to flourish in the digital age. There is a unique overlap between the needs of companies in the digital age and the needs of people. A liberating leader holds open the space for a more liberating way of working. Alternatively, you might call this leader a "servant leader" [202] or a "steward," [203] but I prefer the term "liberated" as it implies direction.

---

201 (Anderson, 2017)
202 A term invented by Robert Greenleaf; see (Sendjaya & Sarros, 2002)
203 (Block, Stewardship, 2003)

Gardening

Being willing to hold open a space for people is one thing, but how best to do it is quite another. The simple answer is to uphold a work design configuration that coincides with your answers to the Eleven Principles of Liberated Companies—in fact, with your ideas.

Rather like a gardener, a leader should tend to the conditions under which great things happen. Tending the garden means configuring and re-configuring an organization so that those within it grow along with the results.

A gardener regards every person and every team of a company as its own entity that must be provided for if it is to blossom. A gardener is constantly assessing what is needed and striving to provide that at all times. A gardener of organizations looks after:

- *Planning the garden*: its mission, its values, its customers, its products, its structures, and its practices.
- *Building the garden*: getting the physical and organizational structures set up so that what is in it can prosper.
- *Planting*: deciding which initiatives to grow, which directions to follow, which teams to seed.
- *Growing*: letting customer value, products, and co-workers blossom.
- *Maintenance*: taking good care of the organization, fertilizing, watering and cutting back when needed.
- *Harvesting*: reaping the benefits of satisfied customers, healthy relationships, and a job well done.

Planning the garden:
It's mission, its values, its customer, its products, its structures and its practices.

Building the garden:
Getting the physical and organizational structures set-up so what's in it can prosper.

Planting:
Decides which initiatives to grow, which directions to follow, which teams to seed.

Growing:
Let's customer value, products, co-workers blossom.

Maintaining:
Taking good care of the organization, fertilizing, watering and cutting back when needed.

Harvesting:
Reaping the benefits of satisfied customers, healthy relationships and of a job well done.

Icons: © Adobe Stock

Figure 28 The Leader: A Gardener

Gardening in organizations means upholding and evolving ever-better configurations of work designs, guided by the Eleven Principles of Liberated Companies. A gardener anticipates changes and will adapt an organization to whatever the future brings: droughts, wind, rain, weeds, vermin. A gardener knows: how to take advantage of opportunities by, for example, replicating environments that caused plants to grow rapidly; that sometimes it is time to cut losses and start anew; that control is indirect; and that all that can be done is to create and maintain the best environment for success. Everything—every structure, every value, every management practice—is an experiment.

Control in a more-liberated organization is far from absolute. A self-managed organization needs to be regarded more like a natural forest ecosystem than a Dutch hothouse. The chances of successful business and social engineering are considerably less than those of biological engineering. Absolute cybernetic control of a company is not possible; people and groups are not predictable. The quest to come up with a homeostat and put it in the hands of an intelligent designer is as futile as it is counter-productive (if pursued too far). A company is a complex system that can and should be tweaked and manipulated for better performance, yet people react to manipulation by gaming the system just as they game the hierarchy.

There are some things that can make manipulation more acceptable. The first is to make one's intentions clear and be transparent about motives. This means, for example, explaining the reasoning behind new work designs. Another is to split the gardener role between people and give the collective a role in governing itself. A useful practice for this is the Company Board, which will be discussed in detail in the next chapter.

We can now complete the definition of the liberating leader: *A systematic leader holds open the space for a more liberating way to work, and who helps shape and maintain a configuration of an organization's work designs but refrains from dominating it.*

All it takes to become a liberating leader are three things: first, to be a systematic leader; second, to refrain from using one's power to the extent of undermining and destroying it by acts of paternalizing power; and third, to have a configuration of work designs in mind that enables groups and people to perform at a higher level.

Emergent and fluid power arrangements

Leadership remains important, even in self-managed companies. Fully egalitarian power structures are impractical and decision-making by collective has its pitfalls. For some jobs, and on certain occasions, it is necessary to provide discretionary powers to some people to ensure that things are done decisively. Clear hierarchical relations of subordination are sometimes advantageous. The advice process, a level 3 management practice, is a great way of combining the advantages of a single decision-maker with its egalitarian surroundings. Another example is the management practice of "roles." Roles are used lavishly and stringently in many self-managed organizations in order to transfer authority to particular people for a time and at the behest of teams. Leadership jobs can be split between people.

Humans have struggled with walking the tightrope between hierarchy and equality for a long time. Over thousands of years of the Roman Republic, dictatorial powers were occasionally granted to single individuals. Today's democracies, with their unique combination of elected representatives, separation of powers, and administrative hierarchy, are nothing but tightrope walks. Everything suggests that in business, too, this combination of hierarchy and more egalitarian forms of rule is possible. More than that, it is needed.

Dark Arts

- People become leaders because they are made the superior of other people.
- Science is unclear about what makes a great leader. However, "systematic leadership" is a useful hypothesis.
- A liberating leader is a systematic leader who holds open the space for a more liberating way of working, and who helps shape and maintain an organization's work design configuration but refrains from dominating it.
- A liberating leader "gardens" organizations, tending them and allowing for emergent and fluid power arrangements.
- Leadership is not a question of style; it is about what a person does with the power they are given.

Further Reading

- Philip Rosenzweig (2007) *The Halo Effect* Free Press
- Henry Mintzberg (2013) *Simply Managing* FT Publishing International
- Peter Block (2013) *Stewardship* Berret-Koehler Publishing
- Jeffrey Pfeffer (2015) *Leadership BS* Harper Business
- Henry Mintzberg (2019) *Bedtime Stories for Managers* Berret-Koehler Publishers

PART V:
HOW TO CONFIGURE COMPANIES

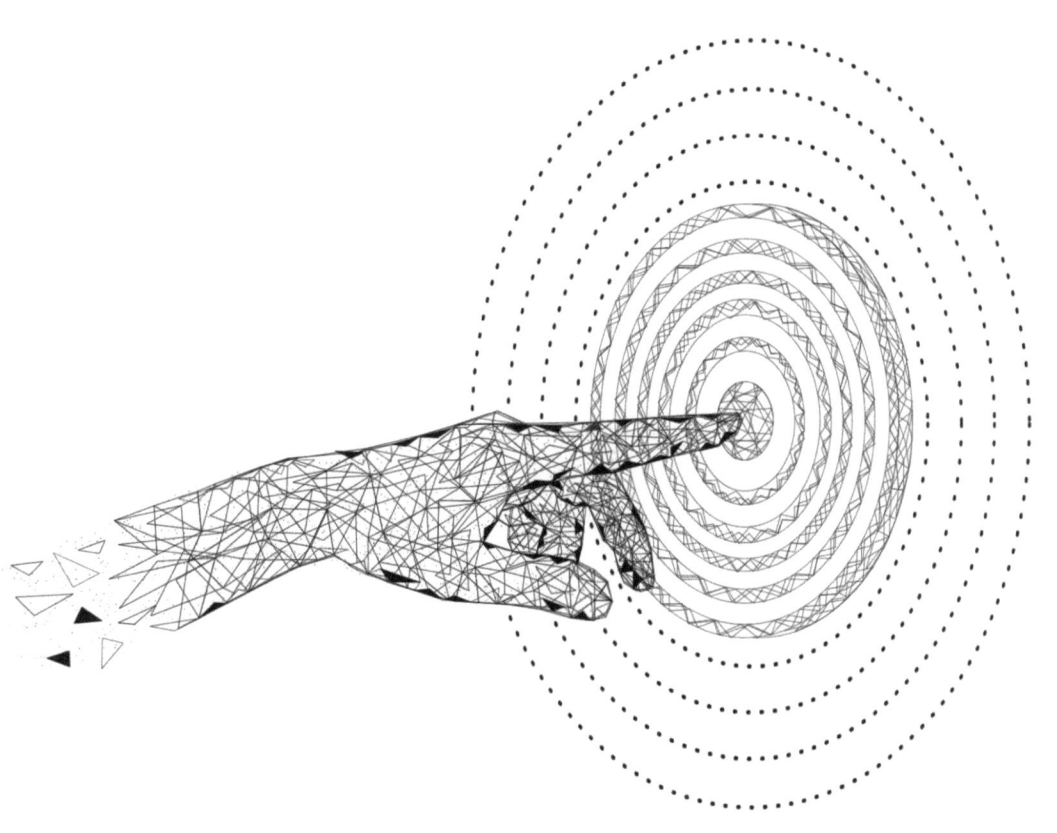

■ Chapter 22: The Journey of Liberation

This book has argued that:

- A company is a complex and purposeful social system.
- Digital technology provides more opportunity for those who know to handle complexity well.
- Companies can become more complexity-capable by becoming more sensing, more purposeful, and more self-managing.

By now, you have a map and a compass for navigating your company through the digital age. I would like to finish by providing you with an itinerary, a backpack, and a pocket travel guide.

The itinerary: Where to start the journey?

Starting the journey towards liberating your company, team, or unit is easy. Anyone at any level can try new work designs and begin the journey. You do not need the support of superiors; all you need from your superiors is their ignorance.[204] To get going is the first priority; lobbying superiors is certainly worthwhile, but it is easier if you can first point to successful experiments with work designs. The decision to liberalize needs has to come from somewhere, so starting up new work designs here and there, demonstrating the benefits, and letting people experience them is helpful.

Don't be afraid to be different. Configurations do not need to be standardized across an organization. The case can even be made that for performance reasons, management practices need to differ in the various parts of an organization (especially if those parts are operating in different environments).

---

204 (Block, Stewardship, 2003)

Amazon's core software engineering operations, for example, are a mixture of liberation level 2 and level 3 operations, while most other employees, especially those working in distribution centers, are working in a traditional hierarchical environment (level 1).

There are six different routes on the journey towards liberation.[205]

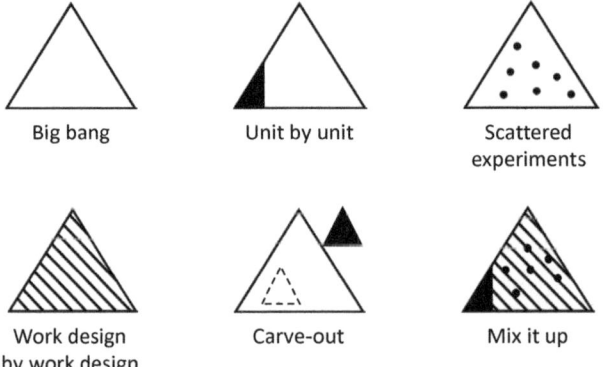

| Big bang | Unit by unit | Scattered experiments |
| Work design by work design | Carve-out | Mix it up |

Figure 29 Six ways to liberate

Big bang

With a steadfast business owner, or a manager who happens to enjoy the full confidence of the business owners, a big bang might be the best option to start liberating a company. Early pioneers of self-management like Brian Robertson and Koldo Saratxaga favor the big bang approach, as it is the only one that radically breaks with the past.

There are a number of prescriptive frameworks for self-managed companies: Holacracy, sociocracy, collegial leadership, or a more project-focused "scaled agile" framework like NEXUS, LeSS, or SafEE. Knowledge of these frameworks is very valuable, as they are not only good configuration templates but excellent quarries from which to extract effective work designs.

---

205 Graphic inspired by a blog article on Corporate Rebels website by **https://corporate-rebels.com/million-dollar-question/** accessed on 10th June 2019

Yet few companies opt to adopt them fully. Holacracy has been adopted by a couple of hundred companies worldwide. Sociocracy mostly applies in the not-for-profit sector, although it has just received an excellent update, making it much more accessible for any company.[206] However, most companies have chosen their own home-made work design configuration. A few companies have even retreated from Holacracy to their own work design configurations.[207]

The experiences on the journey towards liberation appear to be very important. Human, social, and business complexity is endless, and there does not seem to be a single recipe or a work design configuration that is the "best." Just as Bridgewater, Haier, and Buurtzorg did, you have to consciously and continuously work on your configuration to get it "more right" than the last time. The configuration of companies is about betterment, not about optimization.

Unit by unit

Pragmatists like Peter Block suggest starting wherever you are in a hierarchy. Make a deal with higher-level management if you can—i.e., the promise of performance in exchange for the freedom to liberalize a part of the organization—but there is nothing to stop you from initiating small changes. All you need from your superiors is their ignorance. Support is better, but remains optional.

A major aspect of this approach is the need to get the interfaces with the rest of the organization right. More self-managed and more hierarchical organizations do not mix well. Having two different "mental operating systems"—hierarchy and self-management—in one company is challenging, yet it might be a critical qualification for a manager in the digital age.

- The hierarchy wants to identify a single responsible individual, but in a more liberated organization it is often the team that is responsible.
- The hierarchy orders people to do something; the more liberated organization supports people to do what they think is best.

---

206 https://sociocracy30.org. (Bockelbring, 2019)
207 See the enlightening story of Medium: **https://blog.medium.com/management-and-organization-at-medium-2228cc9d93e9** (accessed 26 June 2019).

- The hierarchy controls, rewards, and punishes through a powerful manager—the more liberated organization subtly controls through work design configurations and lets people reward themselves by enabling self-determination.
- The hierarchy seeks predictability and eradication of errors—more liberated organizations seek results by allowing a diversity of approaches, experimentation, failure, and ultimately learning.
- The hierarchy seeks efficiency and reliability—more liberated organizations seek quality in many dimensions, including efficiency. They are more aware and more willing to consider trade-offs.

The list of conflicts between hierarchy and more self-managed ways of working is long, but there are things that can be done to enable their coexistence. The first is to educate and coach managers on the "two operating systems" model and the needs and workings of more liberated, self-managed teams. Second, the links between hierarchical and self-managed units need to be set up with special care. Some useful elements are:

- *Delegates.* Link the more liberated unit to outside entities by sending delegates into meetings with other units. These delegates act like the boss of a self-managed unit in the perception of the outside team.
- *Double linking.* If more intense communication is required, double link your unit with outside units by sending a delegate to their meeting, and let their unit send a delegate to yours.
- *Self-service job titles.* Let people craft their job title to make it easy for their contacts in the organization to understand what they are doing or what their mandate is. Let people be vice presidents to the outside world; the truth in a more liberated company is an egalitarian one.
- *Going native.* Embed some people into the daily work of a more liberated unit for a number of days a week. In highly dynamic teams it is often easier to hunt for issues between two units than to wait and let the people working in the more liberated unit raise those themselves.

Scattered experiments

The next approach—associated with the New Work, agile, and the coaching scene—is to conduct scattered experiments with new work designs here and there. A popular proponent of this approach is Dutch author Jurgen Appelo,[208] who believes enthusiasts at all levels should start trying out small work hacks wherever they are located in the organization. He has even crowdfunded an app that encourages people to experiment with work designs.[209]

This scattergun approach makes starting easy, but the lack of quality control, supporting structures, or coherent design may be frustrating. The danger is that scattered experiments are just another play staged in the corporate theatre of good intentions and will fade just as many other management fads have before them: attractive, but ultimately superficial—or even dishonest.

Practice by practice

A better focus for the liberation effort is to "zoom in" on one work design at a time. It is quite powerful to introduce practices like peer feedback or team-based hiring one at a time; it might be more acceptable to the powers that be, and is easier to quality control. The work designs should, however, be selected with revolutionary intent.

Carve-outs

Some leaders of traditional companies do not lack revolutionary intent. However, they may be blind to the need for an organizational revolution to be able to compete with digital disruptors. These days, almost all major organizations (for e.g., GE, Siemens, Ford, Mercedes, Volkswagen, Porsche, Unilever) have some isolated units inside their organizations that are liberalized. These units

---

208 (Appelo, Management 3.0, 2010) (Appelo, Managing for Happiness, 2016). Check out https://management30.com
209 See https://mindsettlers.com

mostly operate as carve-outs or add-ons to existing organizations. They are often labeled "Innovation Centers" and tend to be focused on product development and IT, though there are self-managed manufacturing operations or plants, too.

Carved-out units are often seen as the seeds for growing this or that new business. The problem with separated units is that their success is very hard to transfer into the core business. Often more liberated carve-outs are an attempt by top management to appear to be doing something while being ultimately unwilling to risk their (and their organization's) fortune by liberating its core. While there is nothing wrong with managing risks, it is wrong to be indecisive in the face of the digital tsunami. Fighting a delaying action is not always helpful. All too often it means squandering attention and resources on symbolism instead of marshaling forces and applying them to the *Schwerpunkt*, the point of decision.

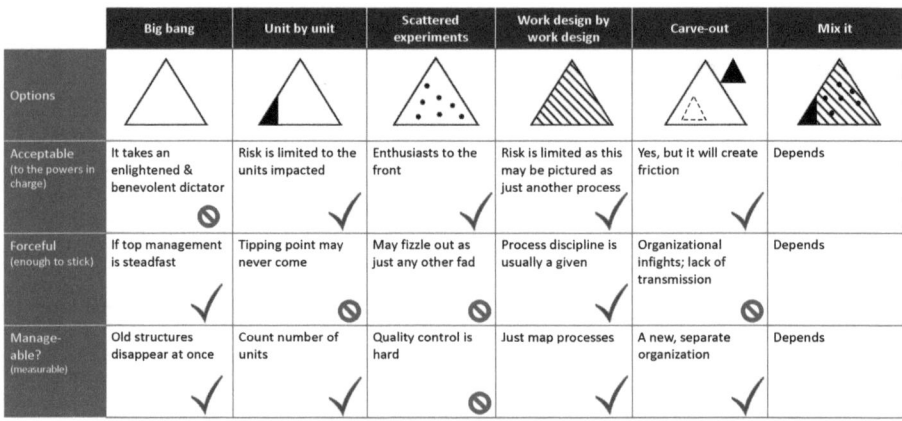

Options	Big bang	Unit by unit	Scattered experiments	Work design by work design	Carve-out	Mix it
Acceptable (to the powers in charge)	It takes an enlightened & benevolent dictator ⊘	Risk is limited to the units impacted ✓	Enthusiasts to the front ✓	Risk is limited as this may be pictured as just another process ✓	Yes, but it will create friction ✓	Depends
Forceful (enough to stick)	If top management is steadfast ✓	Tipping point may never come ⊘	May fizzle out as just any other fad ⊘	Process discipline is usually a given ✓	Organizational infights; lack of transmission ⊘	Depends
Manageable? (measurable)	Old structures disappear at once ✓	Count number of units ✓	Quality control is hard ⊘	Just map processes ✓	A new, separate organization ✓	Depends

Table 19 Six ways to liberate: comparison

Mix it up

The sixth approach is to mix the previous five. For example:

- Pick a unit and reform it, work design by work design.
- Conduct scattered experiments everywhere where enthusiasts can be found but start with one unit in earnest to show how those experiments come to shine if undertaken in a concerted manner.
- Carve out a unit and rotate co-workers between it and the rest of the organization, encouraging them to perform their own experiments or pick a work design to improve the working of their home units.

For the intelligent organizational designer, there are few limits to the creative possibilities.

A backpack: The company board

One great thing about actively configuring and permanently reconfiguring companies with work designs is that the way work is done is constantly questioned and experimented with, which leads to better and better ways of collaborating for everyone in the company. The bad thing is that all the dynamics on the meta-level (i.e., how work is done) may leave people struggling to keep up. To keep the organization aligned, it is important to distinguish between local experiments, global standards, ideas, and discarded work designs.

The company board is helpful for making work design configurations visible.[210] It is a Kanban board that shows work designs on cards in various stages (Figure 28). Potentially beneficial work designs are scrutinized over a number of stages from left to right until they are either actively used or have been found wanting and are discarded.

---

210 The board is inspired by Bernd Österreich, and Claudia Schroeder: (Österreich & Schroeder, 2016) 2016). An English translation under the title *Collegial Leadership* is still pending. Check out **https://kollegiale-fuehrung.de**

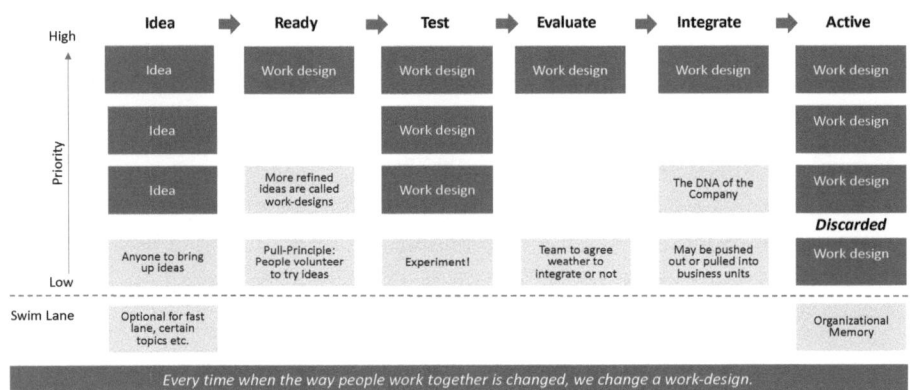

Figure 30 Company Board

Using the board has three major benefits. First, it provides transparency. The company board allows everyone at any time to get a quick overview of what is going on in an organization: ideas that have been raised, experiments that are going on, and which work designs have been tried and discarded. Its right-most column is like an operating manual for an organization, as it explains how the company is run at the work-design level. Second, it is a tool for the continuous improvement of work designs, illustrating the notion that a company's way of working must be actively worked on, just like any other business function. The company board helps to move a company out of a state of sclerosis. It shows that the way we, the co-workers of a company, work together can be changed for the better. It makes people start thinking about how to collaborate better. It shows that how work is done—the status quo—is malleable.

The board can be used at any level—company, unit, or team. In bigger, more diverse companies there can be multiple boards. For companies choosing any approach to liberation other than "big bang" or "practice by practice," there should be multiple boards: at least one for the pioneering unit and one for the rest of the organization.

Every column of the board has a set of rules attached to it. Anyone in the team can bring up a new idea about something that should be done differently and place it in the first column. The only condition is that it must be something to be done, not just an observation or complaint. Often these ideas are proposals for new or adapted work designs, but sometimes they are projects or ideas for analysis. The point of the company board is to capture everything that is important to the way people are working together. It is not necessary to limit the board to work designs, although a limit can be helpful at the company level, where the sheer number of initiatives might be difficult to fit on the board.

Anyone willing to take charge can move a card from the Idea to the Ready column. This "pull" principle increases the chance of successful implementation, although co-workers (or in more hierarchical organizations, a senior leader) may have a right of veto. The name of the person driving the idea should be noted on the card. The card is ready to progress to the Test column once the expected benefits and costs, and how the work design will be tested, have been identified. The card will progress to the Evaluation column once the co-worker in charge of it is ready to discuss the results of the test with the team. If the work design is deemed worth adopting by the team, the card progresses to the Integrate column. Integration of work designs usually involves communication, training, and work on IT systems and might involve the phasing out of obsolescent work designs. The DNA of the organization itself can be found in the Active column.

The way in which the company board is used is critical. It should only be used in a team meeting, because decisions about priorities and transitions from column to column need to be made together. As a rule of thumb, a team maintaining a company board should convene at least every three months for about three hours.

As with all Kanban boards, there are many possible ways of further configuring the board:

- *Priority.* The cards with the highest priority items should be at the top.
- *Definition of done.* As with agile projects, for each column there should be a short "definition of done" (DoD) that describes the gate criteria for when a work design is ready to move to the next stage. The DoD may include such things as documentation, test criteria, approvals, and so on.

- *Work-in-progress (WIP) limits.* Every change needs deliberate, sustained effort in order to succeed. Kanban boards can help to create focus by setting a limit on the maximum number of cards that can be in a column at any one time. It is a good idea to keep the number of work designs in the Test, Evaluate, and Integrate states low in order to ensure that the things to be done receive full attention and actually get done.
- *Swim lanes.* For special topics—for example, high-priority changes or to mark sub-units in a bigger organization—rows may be dedicated to increase transparency or awareness.
- *History of work designs.* Work designs that have been phased out and work designs that have been tested but found wanting should be listed in the box below the active work designs. Keeping an archive of discarded work designs helps to increase the organizational memory of a company. Memos, presentations, and tests describing the discarded work designs should be archived as well. This requires some effort and some companies choose the *Historian* work design to support thorough record-keeping.

The company board is a tool to support both evolutionary improvement and revolutionary transformation. It is a tool to break up the sclerosis of a company and get it moving.[211]

A travel guide: Configuration rules

There are many work designs to choose from. The Eleven Principles of Liberated Companies aim to add high-level direction to a company's liberation effort. There are also some guidelines on a more tactical level, too. A simple pragmatic three-point recipe for choosing work designs is provided by Ari Weinzweig, the founder and CEO of Zingermans, a progressive group of businesses in the US. He names three criteria for an effective work design:[212]

---

211 A useful tool for an initial session with the company board, to prioritize which problems to address with which practices, is a card game described in (Dignan, 2019)
212 (Weinzweig, 2010)

- Work designs should be clear and easy to understand.
- They should be easy to apply so that everybody can do them.
- Leaders should be stubborn enough to stay with them for long enough.

Beyond that simple yet valuable advice, I have compiled a more detailed list, the Twelve Principles of Configuring Companies with Work Designs:[213]

1. *Make the configuration fit your company's purpose.* Every work design configuration needs a theme, be it mental growth for Bridgewater, entrepreneurship for Haier, or caring for Buurtzorg. Every configuration needs a theme, or a vision, that defines the Schwerpunkt of a design. An organizational designer of a company in the digital age needs to answer at least five questions: What is my idea of technology? What is my idea of performance? Of power? Of work? And finally: What is my idea of life? Chapter 9 provides examples of answers given by four other companies.

2. *Look for true north through the compass offered by the Eleven Principles of Liberated Companies.* Which truth do you hold dear for your organization? The more you tend towards the "new truth," the more firmly you should select work designs with high liberation levels for your company's configuration.

3. *No work design stands on its own.* A work design configuration is strong if all the work designs reinforce each other. Liberation level aside, work designs interact with each other in multiple dimensions. For example, new decision processes need new meeting formats and new levels of transparency. Do not force work designs to fit and paint them to match—the goal is coherence, not cherry-picking. A self-reinforcing set of a small number of work designs is immeasurably stronger than a collection of good but independent (or contradictory) ones.

---

213 Inspired by (Sanford, The Regenerative Business , 2017)

4. *Seek simplicity.* Keep the number of work designs low and self-supporting.
5. *Think blast radius.* The severity of the work design hints at the level of care that needs to be taken in adopting that work design. High-severity work designs (such as *self-service remuneration*, *elected superiors*, or *self-directed teams*) have a huge blast radius if things go awry, while low-severity work designs (such as *Kudo cards*, *talking partners*, or *guilds*) may fail without much consequence.
6. *Invest in developmental practices.* Work designs for projects, learning, and feedback are what most distinguish traditional from liberated companies.
7. *Invest in transparency.* Transparency costs nothing and sends a strong signal. At first glance letting go of secrecy might seem easy, but soon discussions about honesty and critique will arise. Transparency makes everyone, especially management, vulnerable. It takes strength to be vulnerable.
8. *Always work on the digital foundation of your work design configuration.* Systems are the glue that hold modern organizations together. They determine ease of communication and transparency and provide opportunities for reflection and learning. I suggest the practice of tool-scaping. It is a crucial part of the job of a liberating leader to get the digital core of companies right. It will be hard to succeed in a digital age without putting digital technology at the center of human work.
9. *The more work designs there are, the more discipline and practice is needed to ensure that they are well applied.* People need time to learn new work designs. They might not find some work designs useful the first-time around, but they must stick with them, listen, modify, and learn. Give it time and make introducing a work design a deliberate effort. Aim to get better every day.
10. *If you keep the hierarchy, you will need a way to ensure consistent behaviors by managers.* It takes an increased number of empowered or self-organized work designs to limit the overreach of superiors. It is a paradox: in order to liberate people, you need to regulate managers more than ever.

11. *Crossing to self-management (level 4) is only possible with a big bang.* We're talking a D-Day operation—a large-scale, consequential, Cortez-like "burn the ships that took you there" leap. The evolutionary, step-by-step method of working your way into new mindsets and work designs will not help you cross this chasm.

12. *In a crisis, a conscious, even disruptive configuration effort might be what is called for.* Evolving work designs is good (and the best option in the long run) but if your company is in dire straits, a revolution might be what is called for. Bold, disruptive initiatives, while supporting the development of the capabilities of people, might help quickly propel a company out of a crisis.

That is a big list of points to consider. Hugh Heclo, a professor of political science, has excellent simplifying advice: "We ought to think through the problem of maintaining ideals amid grubby organizational realities."[214]

Toxic management practices

There are things you should *not* do while liberating your company. Toxic practices that undermine the initiative of people should be reduced or done away with completely. Carol Sanford, a prolific writer on liberated companies, lists work designs that should be used with care:[215]

- *Managerial feedback.* Managerial feedback is very often no more than self-righteous, under-informed projection. It aims at improving people directly instead of improving their self-correcting capability. It is usually a better choice to use peer feedback instead. Not that a peer's feedback lacks bias, but it lacks the power differential that intimidates people into submission, inner resistance, and resignation. Managerial feedback is a great idea in theory, but people tend to overreact to those who have vast power over them.
- *Internal surveys.* These surveys disenfranchise people as they let them complain without taking personal responsibility. They "create the

---

214 (Heclo, 2008) p.296
215 (Sanford, No More Feedback, 2019)

expectation that someone else will take care of me." This undermines the personal agency that liberated companies seek to produce. If you want to know how people are doing, give them opportunities to speak up and provide them with the challenges to let business results speak for themselves.

- *People typologies.* Personality tests like Belbin or Myers-Briggs tend to box people in. They are not aspirational; they encourage people to remain a static version of themselves—"it's just me."
- *Participatory ideation.* Apparently well-meaning participation often only gives the illusion that people are playing a role in decision-making. In fact, those initiatives often only give managers more material to work with. Participation is often too passive, too low-level, and too paternalistic. Instead, try giving people true power and responsibility: the quality of ideas improves if people know they have to deliver on them.
- *"Instant potential" thinking.* Without support, "sink or swim" can result in potential destroyed. Develop potential, don't just utilize it.
- *Bottom-up visioning.* By letting people figure out the purpose, vision, or strategy of a company, you will end up with a compromised pastiche cobbled together around what people are able to agree on. This vision or purpose puts the desires of people in the center, not the entity they serve. It may be a better idea to first discuss what the company seeks and then get people engaged to realize that vision.
- *Institutional ideals.* Statements of the "we are" type box people in. People are different, so allow them to be. Diversity is useful in all forms, even diversity of behaviors. It is better to focus on the company's mission instead. Seek unity in direction, not in ideals or behaviors.
- *Human-centered design.* The suggestion "As long as we keep our people happy, everything else will fall into place" is not true. Until people focus on something beyond themselves, their own and their organization's potential is sure to be wasted.

Consider detoxifying your organization right at the start of your journey. Do not bolt new work designs onto toxic ones.

The case for continuous experimentation with work designs

Do you remember the story of Marc the manager, Eric the employee, and their wood-chopping business (Chapter 4: A Map for Organizing in the Digital Age)? Consciously or not, Marc and Eric adopted new work designs during the brief episode that we were watching. Surely any company, regardless of size and maturity, should seek to consciously improve work designs by:

- Adding new work designs that work better
- Getting rid of those that don't seem to work
- Constantly adapting work designs to changing needs

In a business world that is changing faster than ever, why do we place so much emphasis on the need to act like a daring entrepreneur? Why do idealize the leader who finds ever better problem/solution fits but overwhelmingly fails to engage in experiments with the very ways that we are working together? Instead of seeking to constantly improve our way of collaborating with one another, we focus sharply on business models, productivity figures, financial performance, and the like.

This fixation with ultimate business results is not sensible. Results are important, yes, but they cannot be enforced directly. Rather, they need to be **approached obliquely**, by working better together. Working better together is often interpreted as meaning "being nicer to one another," but ultimately, working better together is more than that. It is striving for something together, with all the conflicts and creative abrasion that come with it. If we can achieve that, results are not guaranteed, but they will come much more easily.

Dark Arts

- You do not need to be in power in order to start experimenting with work designs.
- The most important idea that a company can have is to have an idea about itself, a theme on which it is built.
- Seek simple, self-reinforcing work design configurations.
- Configuration of companies is about betterment, not about optimization.
- The company board is a tool that signals to all that the way work is done is malleable.
- De-toxify work designs. Do not bolt new work designs onto toxic ones.
- Configuration is best done with revolutionary intent (visioning) and evolutionary (company board) action.
- Approach targets obliquely. Aim to do the things you stand for better and better, and financial results are likely to follow.

Further Reading

- Ari Weinzweig (2010) *A Lapsed Anarchist Approach to Building a Great Business* and the other three books of this series: *A Lapsed Anarchists Approach to Being a Better Leader*; *A Lapsed Anarchists Approach to Managing Ourselves*; *A Lapsed Anarchists Guide to the Power of Beliefs*. All published by Zingermans.
- Aaron Dignan (2019) *Brave New Work* Penguin

■ Chapter 23: The Unfinished Business of Liberation

The target must be to anchor our interdependence as well as our joy about one another institutionally and practically.
– Ariadne von Schirach[216]

Society has long suffered from the toxic, detrimental, and exploitative nature of the organizational hierarchy. This has two consequences.

First, the record inequality of wealth and the terminal destruction of many species and the foundations of life on earth tell us that the hugely uneven power differentials in companies have corrupted society. By exploiting others, ourselves, and the earth, we resemble lemmings racing to a cliff. We are blindsided by the things we take for granted, by the necessity to provide for our families, by the fear and shame of falling behind, by the instant gratification that consumption offers. We need to change the system to a more considerate, purposeful, and regenerative one that is better aligned with human, ecological, and technological reality.

Second, there is a better way to live half of our waking hours during our working lives. Wherever we are on the corporate ladder, we just need the courage to start the journey to this place, to start new thinking. Maybe it starts at first in a haphazard fashion, but always with revolutionary intent.

The uneven distribution of power between people—the impotence of the powerless majority—systematically distorts human relationships. People will never truly open up, engage, and be their best in the workplace. You cannot expect agility, creativity, risk-taking, and learning in a kindergarten setting filled with a few "adults" managing numerous "children." Rather than eliminat-

216 (Schirach, 2019)

ing power from the system, however, we should infuse it with more power, allowing emergent and fluid distributions of power. Liberation without solid structures for the distribution and husbanding of power is anarchy.

The call for more self-management is often misunderstood as an anarchic crusade against authority and accountability. People need to be accountable, but there are ways of maintaining accountability and discipline with less hierarchy. By choosing to run most companies today by hierarchy, we are valuing a simple but ultimately limited organizational solution more highly than the complex but potentially much more beneficial solution of more self-managed, liberated companies. No-one can be at their best if everyone is holed up in a system of arbitrary power.

More than ever before, humanity needs flourishing businesses. The quest for better organizations is not optional, either for a company or for society. The climate crisis is unfolding right before our eyes. To continue with exploitative business practices is simply not compatible with our very survival, given the planetary limits we face. The science is clear: we are facing a global extinction crisis.[217] We need two things to safeguard ourselves and our children: technology and political will. We need to aggressively develop and implement new technologies for power generation, agriculture, transportation, and construction. We need to summon up the political will to rally on a global scale, despite all our inequalities.[218] It is unlikely that we will ever leave the industrial age behind and embark on a journey of co-flourishing if we do not rid ourselves of the mindsets and values that come with submitting ourselves to the hierarchy day in, day out.

We need to become more considerate, to enlarge our circle of concern to more than our family and friends. A system that liberates people in business can do much to systematically increase everyone's circle of concern. Utopia is a revolutionary intent, and it can only be built by evolutionary action that builds humanity into the system. No longer should we be seeking to make

217 For a popular account of the extent of the crisis, see (Klein, 2014)
218 An updated view on political theory in the age of climate catastrophe can be found in (Mann & Unwin, 2018)

nature and technology serve us. Now, we need to co-prosper: humanity, nature, and technology together. We need to become more systematic; we need to think in and work on configurations of work designs in a process that is driven by everyone in the organization. Work designs that are arranged in a self-reinforcing configuration offer a way to liberate people, companies, and technology—to everyone's benefit.

Some readers may feel that bringing the climate issue into a business book is inappropriate. They might argue that governments are meant to solve the climate crisis, and businesses should stick to their own concerns and operate within the legal framework that governments provide. But people who spend half the waking hours of their working life in systems of exploitation are mentally geared toward exploitation. This is bound to have a profound impact on the political system and on our private lives. After all, the systems we live in change who we are more profoundly than we will ever be able to change the systems. At a time when survival is at stake, we need to advocate radical change.

A liberated company not only reduces hierarchy but frees itself from exploitation and is able to place itself on the trajectory of technology. There are a number of ways that liberated companies can help humanity reduce climate change or its impacts. First, they are able to explore and make use of the technology much better than any hierarchy could. In our prevailing culture of economic exploitation, more effective companies are all too readily understood as the more profitable ones. Liberated companies can certainly be more profitable, but there are other sides to high performance: agility, resilience, innovation, sustainability, and being true to the mission of any company in our economic system by delivering excellent goods and service to society, instead of extracting the greatest economic value for billionaires. We are so accustomed to egoistical, self-interested actors in business and economic theory that we might be surprised by how handing more and more control of businesses from individuals over to teams can change the way businesses operate in the future. Exit *homo oeconomicus*, enter *homo socialis*.[219]

---

219 (Raworth, 2017)

This does not, however, imply a utopian end to all exploitation. Fights for redistribution of wealth, power, and prestige will remain on the human menu of doing business. However, it was by organizing companies and whole economies on the premise of self-interested actors that we ended up with the exploitative hierarchical corporations of today, with a firmly entrenched shareholder value mindset and with record levels of inequality both globally and nationally. Liberated companies are more egalitarian; they keep an exploitative managerial class from emerging. They can also be more distributive by design if they embrace practices that make ownership or the distribution of profits more equitable. By remaining open to the outside world and a bit closer to the true mission of companies—which is to serve society—liberated companies might achieve more equal and fairer societies. As Naomi Klein says, the goal is to grow the caring economy, and shrink the careless one.

By shedding more of the hierarchy, we can abandon the corrosive power of the hierarchy for the creative power of the collective. It has only been 150 years since the world abandoned slavery. Roughly 100 years ago, the Western world started to liberate half its population by letting women vote. At about the same time, many nations abolished the feudal contract between rich landowners and laborers and replaced it with the bureaucratic contract of the industrial age. About 50 years ago, women in many Western democracies began to be liberated from their bondage to husbands by being allowed to choose their own jobs and the right to divorce. Now might be the time to shed the hierarchical contract and embrace a more democratic contract between people and companies.

Henry Ford introduced the five-day working week in early twentieth-century America, a move considered by many as radical, foolish, and dangerous—not only for his business, but for society. What would the masses do with all that spare time? Many predicted that people would spend their weekends on a diet of violence, sex, and alcohol. Many a leader thinks along similar lines today. It takes guts to give people more of a say in the way they are doing work. Frederick Winslow Taylor, the inventor of today's prevailing style of management, once described one of his best workers, a man named Schmidt, as "stupid as an ox."[220] Schmidt was working in accordance with the detailed work steps laid out by Taylor's management system, seemingly unthinkingly and very effectively. Yet the same "stupid" Schmidt built a house for his family and was an active member of his neighborhood fire brigade.

There is nothing as surprising as people. It is an oddity that many companies do not trust people to buy $1 pencils without management approval, but the same people are allowed by society to buy houses for hundreds of thousands of dollars and take on 25-year loans. As a society we know that people are able to bear huge accountability, but we all but expect them to exploit the company they are working for if we give them the chance to. Wouldn't it be better to let people buy those pencils with company money without any approval while at the same time ensuring that breaches of trust will be noticed and acted upon? If we start from a position of mistrust, we will only reap mistrust and benefit-seeking.

I agree completely with the idea that the competent need to rule the less competent. However, what is important is that people should be allowed to come up through the ranks and be leaders at those times when their competence is demanded by the situation, and be allowed to be followers at those times when other people are more competent. Leadership does not have to be a fixed position in a hierarchy. If we really want to embrace the digital revolution and achieve a true meritocracy, we can dare to use a more agile distribution of power.[221]

No one can foretell the speed and the extent of the replacement of hierarchies with more liberated companies. There is even some doubt that this will ever happen. Maybe humans are just biologically primed to live in hierarchies. Nevertheless, history shows us that the spell of unchecked autocracy and monarchy can be and has been broken before. Representative democracy and the rule of the collective, though under threat today, have proven their worth. At the dawn of the digital revolution, it may be necessary to go a step

---

220 (Kanigel, 1997)
221 For further reading on the broader issues of a new eco-social system, see (Bregman, 2018) or Jamie Susskinds account of the digital-political challenges: (Susskind, 2018)

further and democratize businesses from places of subordination to individuals to places of individual self-determination bounded by the sense of shared responsibility that comes with striving together. A more liberated company "enhances the lives of all who work within it and enriches the lives of all those who are touched by it."[222] They co-prosper, and they flourish together with their surroundings.

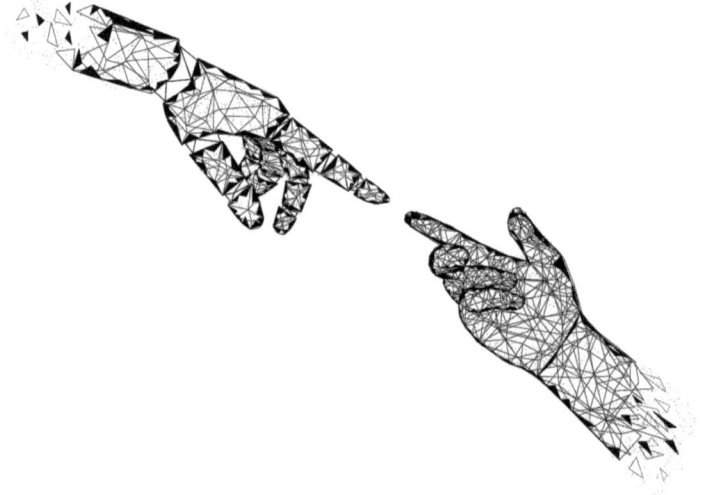

---

222 (Hawken, 1988)

Acknowledgement

I like to thank...

- Professor Jürgen Hauschildt (1936-2008) for lightening up the fire for organizational research inside me in the early 1990's
- Thomas Dressen, Frank Pupkes and Ronald A. Koch for being great sparring partners
- Keith Povey and Nancy Richardson, Cornwall, UK, for their ruthless crusade against my verbose writing
- Keith Gordon, Santa Cruz, US, for editing like a pro
- Stephanie Héno, info@lustianodesign.de, Frankfurt, Germany for the graphical design of figures, tables, slides, and infographics
- David Moldawer, New York, US, for navigating me through the publishing jungle
- Ivana Mijalkovic, miaiva@gmail.com, Belgrade, Serbia, for the cover and interior design
- My wife Andrea for her unwavering support

***

Further Info's can be found on www.liberated.company
- **Printable A0 Model Overview:** https://liberated.company/resources/the-liberated-company-model/
- **Figures and Tables for Download:** https://liberated.company/resources/
- **A Compendium of Management Practices:** https://liberated.company/resources/the-compendium-of-management-practices/
- **A Genealogy of concepts beneath Liberated Companies**: https://liberated.company/references/

If you like this book, consider writing a few nice words on a platform like Amazon. Every rating and review helps!

***

Tables

Figures

Index

D

E

M

S

Bibliography

Österreich, B., & Schroeder, C. (2016). *Das Kollegial Geführte Unternehmen*. Vahlen.

Adorno, T. W. (2003). Reflexionen zur Klassenthese. *Sozilogische Schriften I*.

Agyris, C., & Schön, D. A. (1999). *Organizational Learning II*. FT Press.

Alvesson, M., & Spicer, A. (2016). *The Stupidity Paradox*. Profile Books.

Anderson, E. (2017). *Private Government*. Princeton University Press.

Andresen, M. (20. August 2011). Why Software is Eating the World in Wall Street Journal. *Wallstreet Journal*.

Appelo, J. (2010). *Management 3.0*. Addison Wesley Professional.

Appelo, J. (2016). *Managing for Happiness*. Wiley.

Arendt, H. (1951). *The Origins of Totalitarianism*. Schocken Books.

Birkinshaw, J. (2012). *Reinventing Management* . Wiley John + Sons.

Block, P. (2002). *The Right Use of Power*. Sounds True.

Block, P. (2003). *Stewardship*. Berret-Koehler Publishing.

Block, P. (2016). *The Empowered Manager*. Wiley.

Bloom, N., van Reemen, J., Genakos, C., & Sadun, R. (February 2012). Management Practices across Firms and Countries. *Academy of Management Perspectives, 26*(1), 31. https://www.nber.org/papers/w17850.pdf.

Blooom, N., Dorgan, S., Dowdy, J., Rippin, T., & van Reenen, J. (2005). Management Practices: the impact on company performance. *Centerpiece, 10*(2), 2-6.

Bock, L. (2016). *Work Rules!* John Murray.

Bockelbring, J. (September 2019). *Sociocracy 3.0*. https://sociocracy30.org.

Bogsnes, B. (2016). *Implementing Beyond Budgeting*. Wiley.

Bregman, R. (2018). *Utopia for Realists* . Bloomsbury Publishing.

Brown, B. (2016). *Daring Greatly*. Penguin.

Brynjolfson, E., & McAfee, A. (2014). *The Second Machine Age*. Norton & Company.

Bungay-Stainer, M. (2016). *The Coaching Habit*. Box of Crayons PR.

Burke, J. (1978). *Connections*. Little, Brown and Company.

Cao, Y. (2018). *The Haier Model*. LID Publishing.

Carney, B., & Geetz, I. (2016). *Freedom Inc.* Somme Valley House.

Coase, R. H. (1937). The Nature of the Firm. *Economica, 4*(16), 386-388.

Cohen, M., March, J., & Olsen, J. P. (1972). The garbage can model of organizational choice. *Administrative Science Quarterly, 17*(1), 1-25.

Collins, J. (2001). *From Good to Great.* Random House Business.

Conway, M. (5. April 1968). How Do Committees Invent? *Datamation, 5*(14), 28-31.

Dalio, R. (2018). *Principles.* Simon & Schuster.

Davenport, T. (2005). *Thinking for a Living.* Harvard Business Review Press.

Deming, W. E. (2000). *Out of the Crisis.* The MIT Press.

Deming, W. E. (2012). *The Essential Deming.* McGraw-Hill Education.

Denning, S. (2018). *The Age of Agile.* Amacom.

Dignan, A. (2019). *Brave New Work.* Portfolio.

Downs, A. (1964). Inside Bureaucracy. *CA: Rand Corporation.*

Drucker, P. (2012). *Managing for Results.* Routledge.

Drucker, P. (2017). *The Effective Executive* . Harper Business.

Dunbar, R. (June 1992). Neocortex size as a constraint on group size in primates. *Journal of Human Evolution, 22*(6), 469-493.

Edmondson, A. C. (1999). Psychological Safety and Learning Behavior in Work Teams. *Administrative Science Quarterly, 44*(2), 350-383.

Edmondson, A. C. (2018). *The Fearless Organization: Creating Psychological Safety in the Workplace for Learning, Innovation, and Growth.* Wiley.

Edmondson, A. C., & Schein, E. (2014). *Teaming.* Jossey-Bass.

Emery, F., & Trist, E. L. (1969). *Systems Thinking.* Penguin.

Fairlough, G. (2007). *The Three Ways of Getting Things Done.* Triarchy Press.

Fayol, H. (1917). *Administration industrielle et générale; prévoyance, organisation, commandement, coordination, contrôle.* Paris: H. Dunod et E. Pinat.

Ferguson, N. (2018). *The Square and the Tower* . Penguin.

Foucault, M. (2008). *The Birth of Biopolitics: Lectures at the Collège de France* . Palgrave Macmillan.

Frankl, V. E. (1984). *Man's Search for Meaning.* Beacon Press.

Fried, J., & Heinemeier, D. (2018). *It does not have to be crazy at work.* Harper Business.

Galbraith, J. R. (1973). *Designing Complex Organizations* . Addison-Wesley.

Galbraith, J. R. (1977). *Organization Design.* Addison Wesley.

Galbraith, J. R. (2008). *Designing Matrix Organizations That Actually Work* . John Wiley & Sons.

Gallner, L., Harrington, B., & Grant, A. (January 2018). Why People Really Quit Their Jobs. *Harvard Business Review.*

Gallup. (20. August 2019). *State of the Global Workplace.* Gallup.com: https://www.gallup.de/183833/state-the-global-workplace.aspx

Gawande, A. (2009). *The Checklist Manifesto.* Macmillan USA.

Gino, F. (2013). *Sidetracked.* Harvard Business Review Press.

Gladwell, M. (2008). *Outliers.* Back Bay Books.

Goldratt, E. (1999). *Theory of Constraints.* North River Press.

Goldsworthy, A. (2000). *Roman Warfare.* Basic Books.

Goleman, D. (1995). *Emotional Intelligence.* Bantam.

Grant, A. (2013). *Give and Take.* W&N.

Greif, A. (2006). *Institutions and the path to the Modern Economy* . Cambridge University Press.

Habermas, J. (1990). Discourse Ethics: Notes on a Program of Philosophical Justification. *Moral Conciousness and Communicative Action*, 43-115.

Hackman, J. R. (2002). *Leading Teams.* Harvard Business Review Press.

Hamel, G. (2016). *What Matters Now.* Jossey-Bass.

Harari, Y. (2016). *Homo Deus: A Brief History of Tomorrow.* Vintage.

Hawken, P. (1988). *Growing a Business* . Simon & Schuster.

Heclo, H. (2008). *On Thinking Institutionally* . Oxford University Press.

Hollister, R., & Watkins, M. (September 2018). Too Many Projects. *Harvard Business Review*, 64-69.

Horstman, M. (2016). *The Effective Manager.* Wiley.

Humble, J., Mollesky, J., & O'Reilly, B. (2015). *Lean Enterprise.* O'Reilly and Associates.

Hurst, D. K. (2012). *The New Ecology of Leadership.* Columbia University Press.

Ismael, S. (2014). *Exponential Organizations.* Diversion Publishing.

Kahn, W. A. (1990). Psychological Conditions of Personal Engagement. *Academy of Management Journal*, 708.

Kahnemann, D. (2011). *Thinking Fast and Slow*. Penguin.

Kanigel, R. (1997). *One Best Way*. Little, Brown and Company.

Katzenbach, J. R., & Smith, D. K. (1993). *Wisdom of Teams*. Harvard Business Review Press.

Kegan, R., & Laskow, L. (2016). *An Everyone Culture*. Harvard Business Review Press.

Keith, E. (2018). *Where The Action Is*. Second Rise.

Kelly, K. (2011). *What Technology Wants*. Penguin.

Kent Beck, W. C. (2001). *Manifesto for Agile Software Development*. AgileManifesto.org: http://agilemanifesto.org

Klein, N. (2014). *This Changes Everything* . Simon & Schuster.

Kotter, J. P. (2014). *Accelerate*. Harvard Business Review Press.

Kotter, J. P., & Haskett, J. L. (2011). *Corporate Culture and Performance*. Free Press.

Kurtzman, J. (2010). *Common Purpose*. John Wiley & Sons.

Kurzweil, R. (2006). *The Singularity is Near*. Penguin.

Laloux, F. (2014). *Reinventing Organizations*. Nelson Parker.

Lencioni, P. (2007). *Death By Meeting*. Jossey-Bass.

Likert, R. (1961). *New Patterns of Management* . McGraw-Hill.

Lipmanowicz, H., & McCandles, K. (2014). *Liberating Structures*. Liberating Structures Press.

Maggio, P. J., & Powell, W. W. (2012). *The New Institutionalism in Organizational Analysis*. University of Chicago Press.

Malek, F. (2013). *Strategy: Navigating the Complexity of the New World* . Campus Verlag.

Mann, G., & Unwin, J. (2018). *Climate Leviathan*. Verso.

Marquet, D. L. (27. May 2015). 6 Myths about Empowering Employees. *Harvard Business Review*. Hard Business Review.

Marquet, D. L. (2016). *Turn That Ship Around*. Penguin.

Martin, P. K. (2015). *Matrix Management Reinvented*. Matrix Management Institute.

McChrystal, S., Silverman, D., Tantum, C., & Chris, F. (2015). *Teams of Teams*. Penguin.

Meadows, D. H. (2001). Dancing with Systems. *Whole Earth*(106), 58.

Mintzberg, H. (1995). *The Rise and Fall of Strategic Planning*. Free Press.

Mintzberg, H. (2008). *Strategy Safari*. Pearson Education Canada.

Mintzberg, H. (2013). *Simply Managing*. FT Publishing International.

Mintzberg, H. (2019). *Bedtime Stories for Managers*.
Berret-Koehler Publishers.

Moore, G. (2015). *Zone to Win*. Diversion Books.

Nandram, S. S. (2015). *Organizational Innovation by Integrating Simplification*. Springer.

Nicholson, A. (2016). *Seize the Fire*. Harper Perennial.

Nietzche, F. (1974). *Thus Spoke Zarathustra*. (R. J. Hollingdale, Hrsg.)
Penguin Books.

Nohira, N., & Joyce, W. (2003). *What Really Works*. Harper Business.

Ohno, T. (1988). *Workplace Management*. Mc Graw-Hill Education.

Ostrom, E. (1990). *Governing the Commons*. Cambridge University Press.

Ostrom, E. (2005). *Understanding Institutional Diversity*.
Princeton Paperbacks.

Pentland, A. (2014). *Social Physics*. Penguin.

Peter, L. J., & Hull, R. (1969). *The Peter Principle*. Harper Business.

Peters, T. (1992). *Liberation Management*. Knopf.

Peters, T., & Waterman, R. H. (1982). *In Search of Excellence*.
Profile Books.

Pfeffer, J. (2015). *Leadership BS*. Harper Business.

Pflaeging, N. (2014). *Organize for Complexity*. Beta Codex Publishing.

Pink, D. (2011). *Drive*. Riverhead Books.

Porter, M. E. (1985). *Competitive Strategy*. Free Press.

Quinn, J. B. (1980). *Strategies for Change*. R.D. Irwin.

Raworth, K. (2017). *Doughnut Economics* . Random House Business.

Ries, E. (2011). *The Lean Startup*. Currency.

Roberston, B. (2015). *Holacracy*. Penguin.

Rommel, E. (1937). *Infanterie Greift An*. Voggenreiter.

Rosenzweig, P. (2007). *The Halo Effect*. Free Press.

Rosenzweig, P. (12 2010). Robert S. McNamara and the Evolution of Modern Management. *Harvard Business Review*.

Rosenzweig, P. (2015). *Left Brain, Right Stuff*. Public Affairs.

Rosling, H. (2018). *Factfulness*. Flatiron Books.

Sanford, C. (2017). *The Regenerative Business* . Nicolas Brealey Publishing.

Sanford, C. (2019). *No More Feedback*. Interoctave.

Satell, G. (17. May 2015). 4 Things you should know about platforms. *Forbes*.

Satell, G. (June 2015). *What makes an Organization Networked*. Abgerufen am June 2019 von Havard Business Review: https://hbr.org/2015/06/what-makes-an-organization-networked

Schaupp, S. (2016). *Digitale Selbstüberwachung* . Grasswurzelrevolution e.V.

Schirach, A. v. (2019). *Die psychotische Gesellschaft: Wie wir Angst und Ohnmacht überwinden*. Tropen.

Scott, W. R. (2014). *Institutions and Organizations* . Sage Publications.

Sendjaya, S., & Sarros, J. C. (2002). Servant Leadership: Its Origin, Development, and Application in Organizations. *Journal of Leadership and Organizational Studies, 9*(2), 57-64.

Senge, P. (1990). *The Fifth Discipline*. Currency.

Shorris, E. (1983). *The Oppressed Middle* . Anchor Press/Double Day.

Silver, N. (2012). *The Signal and the Noise*. Penguin.

Singer, P. (2011). *The Expanding Circle* . Princeton University Press.

Spears, S. (2010). *The High Velocity Edge* . McGraw-Hill Education.

Susskind, J. (2018). *Future Politics*. Oxford University Press.

Sutherland, J. (2015). *Scrum*. Random House Business.

Taleb, N. (2012). *Antifragile*. Penguin.

Taylor, F. W. (1911). *Principles of Scientific Management*. Harper and Brothers.

Tetlock, P. (2016). *Superforecasting*. Random House Books.

Thaler, R. H., & Sunstein, C. R. (2008). *Nudge*. Yale University Press.

Tolstoy, L. (1894). *The Kingdom of God is Within You*. Casell Publishing Company.

Venkatraman, N. (1996). Managing IT Resources as a Value Center. *IS Executive Seminar Series*.

Weber, M. (2019). *Economy and Society* . Harvard University Press.

Weinzweig, A. (2010). *A Lapsed Anarchist Approach to Building a Great Business*. Zingermans.

Weinzweig, A. (2012). *A Lapsed Anarchists Approach to Being a Better Leader*. Zingermans.

Weinzweig, A. (2013). *A Lapsed Anarchist's Approach to Managing Ourselves*. Zingermans.

Weinzweig, A. (2016). *A Lapsed Anarchists Guide to the Power of Beliefs*. Zingermans.

Westrum, R. (2004). A Typology of Organizational Cultures. *Qual Saf Health Care, 13*(2), 22-27.

Wood, C., Lauret, A., Sandoval, K., & Bill , D. (2016). *The API Economy*. Nordic APIs AB.

Zucker, L. (1983). Organizations as Institutions. *Research in the Sociology of Organizations, 2*, 1-42.

About the Author

Frank Thun has helped organizations around the globe to digitalize their operations as a project manager, CIO, COO, and coach. He studied Economics at the Universities of Kiel, Germany, and Glasgow, Scotland, and holds a Master of Economics. He worked for start-ups and prominent companies like Daimler, Volkswagen, Capgemini Ernst & Young, General Electrics, Nokia Networks, Bayer, Philips, Schneider Electric and Invensys.

Frank is married, blessed with three daughters and lives near Hamburg, Germany.

To learn more visit:
www.liberated.company
or find me at:
www.linkedin.com/in/frankthun.